Slaves to Faith

A Therapist Looks Inside the Fundamentalist Mind

CALVIN MERCER

Foreword by Martin E. Marty

PRAEGER

Westport, Connecticut
London

Library of Congress Cataloging-in-Publication Data

Mercer, Calvin R.

Slaves to faith : a therapist looks inside the fundamentalist mind / Calvin Mercer ; foreword by Martin E. Marty.

p. cm.

Includes bibliographical references (p.) and index.

ISBN 978–0–313–36496–9 (alk. paper)

1. Fundamentalism—Psychology. 2. Psychology, Religious. I. Title.

BT82.2.M56 2009

270.8′2—dc22 2008047575

British Library Cataloguing in Publication Data is available.

Library of Congress Catalog Card Number: 2008047575
ISBN: 978–0–313–36496–9

First published in 2009

Praeger Publishers, 88 Post Road West, Westport, CT 06881
An imprint of Greenwood Publishing Group, Inc.
www.praeger.com

Printed in the United States of America

The paper used in this book complies with the Permanent Paper Standard issued by the National Information Standards Organization (Z39.48–1984).

10 9 8 7 6 5 4 3 2 1

Slaves to Faith

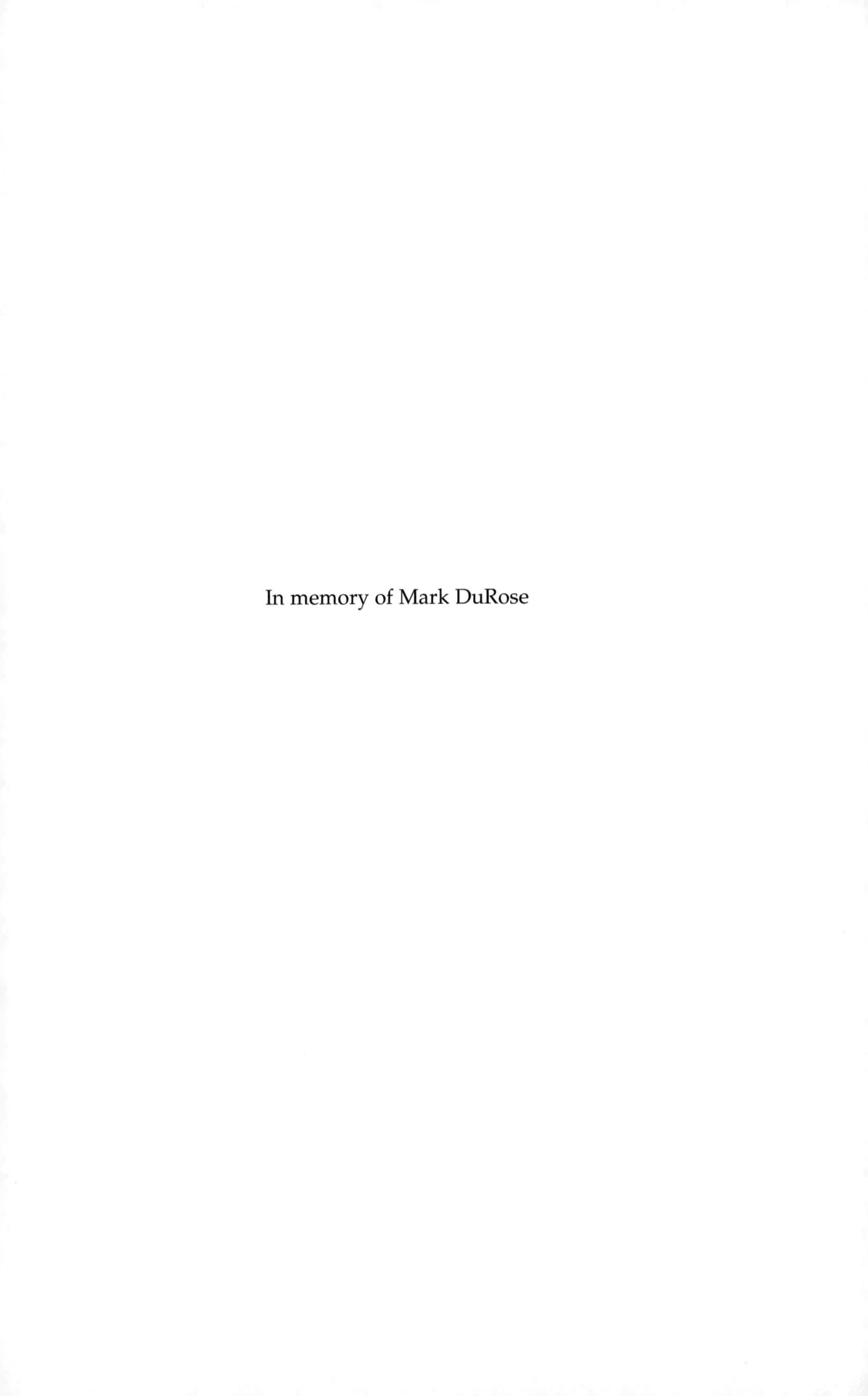

In memory of Mark DuRose

Contents

Foreword

In 1988 the American Academy of Arts and Sciences asked me to lead a six-to-ten-year, five-volume, ten-conference, 100-scholars' study of modern religious fundamentalisms. This I did, with Professor R. Scott Appleby, in what became *The Fundamentalism Project*. If you are an Olympic-level weight lifter, you can hoist all 3,750 pages that the *Project* published in those five volumes and still have energy left to open them and start reading. Now, for the most haunting thing about the *Project* as context: in its books you will learn about 23 movements within the major religions. You will learn the history, sociology, anthropology, political science, and other aspects of the subject. What you won't find there is the discipline Calvin Mercer represents and from which he imparts knowledge and insight: psychology.

No psychology in a study of fundamentalism? If you, dear reader, are a fundamentalist, you'd be astounded to find psychology underrepresented in our *Project*. This book is a contribution to bringing balance. Your enemies—and you'll have some—will "psychologize" your analysis of the fundamentalist version of the faith. They might decide that you chose it in an Oedipal rage because your father was too secular. Or, if you are an ex- or anti-fundamentalist, you are likely to be doing a pop-psychoanalytic job on your enemy, or your friend in fundamentalism. You'll try to find what in her ego, libido, id, or dreams led her to take refuge in such a religious abode. Still others will decide on psychological grounds that if you are fundamentalist, you are because (a) you are so scared that you take refuge in fundamentalism or (b) you are so arrogant that you will use fundamentalism as an arsenal from which to fire away at weak-kneed believers or the beliefless masses.

Those who read much in this field may be tempted to do a psychological exercise on author Mercer: Why was he a fundamentalist? What in his innards, his conscience or consciousness, led him to rebel and find his own new spiritual home away from fundamentalism? I'll confess that for a moment when I started reading the section "My Journey Out of Fundamentalism," I wanted to be alert to find out what was going on in his mind when the journey began and what is there now. The world is full of ex-Catholics, ex-fundamentalists, ex-liberals, ex-conservatives, and ex-Mormons, and you will find all kinds of journeys represented by them. Some make their move quietly, gliding from one commitment to another. Some do it in rage, making noise about their past enslavement, or in ecstasy, sounding off loudly about their new liberty. Philosopher Max Scheler says that one who leaves a faith community, an apostate, "spends his whole subsequent career taking revenge on his own spiritual past."

There is no question that Mercer's own journey colors his outlook, and he does not try to be a cold-fish "objective" teacher and writer, but he does try to be fair. There is no spirit of revenge, only the spirit of the teacher. As a bonus, the reader gets chapters that provide a short history of North American fundamentalism. As a side issue, readers will also get some informed if nontechnical theological musings. Yet it is the mind-set of the fundamentalist that beckons on these pages.

Knowing that psychologists can be just as sectarian as church members can be, we have to learn not what "sect" but which school of psychology gives shape to author Mercer's journey right down into its current stages. I guess that's the third bonus: a short course in "cognitive therapy," the approach in Mercer's clinical practice and this book.

Back to *The Fundamentalism Project:* why did it not accent psychological approaches? One reason is that "cognitive therapists" and their colleagues had not done so much on fundamentalism by 1988. Mercer's book shows how far clinicians and theoretical psychologists have come in two decades. We would now have a richer talent pool of experts on whom to draw.

The bigger reason was this: our hosts, the American Academy of Arts and Sciences and, we might say, the American academy as it characteristically treats human subjects, tends to be steadfastly secular. We wanted to stress fundamentalism's religious dimensions, which were slighted in the mass media, in clinics, and on campus. And the psychology we read at the time tended to be reductionist. It used the words "nothing but" so often that some scholars call it "nothing buttery." In that approach, this or that religion is "nothing but . . . " something else. Everything is reduced to psychological processes.

By now the religious point has been made and we can more blithely and yet more ardently use the promising instruments of psychology with less fear of reductionism. Mercer takes the reader aside and discusses his methods and techniques, so readers can appraise him. It is hard to picture anyone among his students or readers who would not find issues to raise, questions to bring up, and counterarguments and testimony. Our professor-therapist-author gives every evidence that he would welcome that—just as he shows that he hopes the reader will be open to questioning, learning, and changing.

Only a person with a fundamentalist mind-set, whether in support of fundamentalist *or* hard-line liberal outlooks, would oppose Mercer's methods. Let the questioning, learning, and changing begin.

Martin E. Marty
Emeritus, The University of Chicago

Preface: My Longest Email

This book is, in a sense, a long email to my good friend and colleague Dr. Derek Maher.

Derek came to our university's Religious Studies Program as a Buddhist Studies specialist. After teaching for about a year, Derek queried me one Friday, via email, with a question that seemed simple enough. Knowing that my specialty was Christian Studies, with particular expertise in the Bible, and that I had taught at our southern university for many years, he asked if I could provide guidance that would help him understand and work with fundamentalist Christian students. Derek is a good scholar, master teacher, and compassionate soul. This combination of qualities almost always results in quality teaching, regardless of the student's psychological profile or intellectual ability. But Derek is also Canadian and Buddhist. He didn't have a chance with fundamentalist students. He needed to understand Christian fundamentalists in order to enhance his interactions with and teaching of these students.

So, on Saturday morning I sat down to compose what I thought would be a short email response, giving a bit of advice, drawing upon my years of teaching fundamentalists. Before the weekend was over, the email turned into 18 single-spaced pages. I found myself drawing on my clinical experience as a therapist much more than I would have anticipated. Over the next few months the pages continued to grow, finally issuing in this book.

Along the way to writing this book, I delivered the substance of my psychological understanding of the typical fundamentalist (Part Three) to a group of religion scholars at the annual meeting of the American

Academy of Religion. Professional society meetings of scholars consist, in large part, of academics giving reports of their research to a handful of other scholars on the various narrow, sometimes arcane, subjects of their research. To give some examples, on the particular time slot that I made my presentation, other scholars were giving lectures that included the following titles: "A Journey Behind the Canvas: Bringing Tillich into an Interpretation of the Paintings of Kandinsky," "Biography and Historical Context: Life Narratives of *dGe lugs pa* Textbook Authors," "Kant's Conflicted Divinity: Contradictory Thrusts in Kant's Philosophy of Religion," and "Intimacy and Union in Early Female Sufi Discourse."

I mention my presentation to other religion scholars, a little step on the way to the present book, because the reception I received when I presented my ideas was quite interesting and atypical, at least in my experience. At these meetings, one can readily tell if the handful of scholars gathered for your particular presentation is "with you" or, rather, the attendees are fumbling through the program guide to determine where to go next, even as you are speaking in front of the group. In all my years of making presentations at these scholarly meetings, I have never spoken to an audience exhibiting such rapt attention. In all fairness, I must add that I do not think the professors gathered to hear me were enamored by my charisma. I am certain that what brought them to my presentation, and had them hanging on every word, was the subject matter of my talk. In the program booklet my presentation was entitled "'But the Bible Says . . .' Teaching Fundamentalist Christian Students." My intuition during the presentation, confirmed by subsequent conversations with some of those in attendance, was that many of these professors had one or more fundamentalist students in their classes and, like Derek, were absolutely perplexed as to how to deal with them. The professors attended my presentation to hear something specific that would help them communicate with the fundamentalist Christian students in their offices and classrooms back home.

When I give presentations about fundamentalism to laypersons—both Christian and non-Christian—at conferences, retreats, and public lectures, I find the same level of interest. Many people, especially those who have not lived close to or worked with fundamentalists, are puzzled by Christians of this theological and ideological persuasion. People who have occasion to interact with fundamentalists on religious, political, or social issues are often frustrated in these conversations because non-fundamentalists often do not understand the language and orientation of the fundamentalist.

I have worked all of my professional life in contexts where I have had close interaction with fundamentalists. I admit that, occasionally, I have felt that I had all of fundamentalism I could take. Sometimes I have wanted to throw up my hands and walk away. So, in addition to offering the scholarly community a new psychological model for understanding this religious group, the book is also a personal effort to understand fundamentalists and their ideology and clarify for myself how to be a more effective teacher, neighbor, and citizen.

So, Derek, here I offer this now 260-page "email." I hope it is useful to you. In addition to the academic community, to whom I offer this thesis for debate, perhaps the book will also be of some value to legions of Americans (and Canadians)—teachers, policy makers, reporters, citizens, even religious leaders—who are perplexed by the mind and world of fundamentalist and evangelical Christians.

Acknowledgments

Two people gave a very careful reading of the manuscript and provided detailed, line-by-line feedback. Dr. Derek Maher, my colleague in Religious Studies at East Carolina University, brought an "outsider" reading. His feedback, both in content and style, was substantial. Derek believed in this project from the beginning. I appreciate the time he took from his own research projects to contribute to this book. I took 99 percent of his suggestions. Dr. Susan Vickery-Mercer, my wife, herself raised a fundamentalist, gave the "insider" reading, and did it during one of our vacation weeks. It was not the kind of leisurely vacation reading she would have preferred, but the book is much better for her generosity. She is an excellent editor and the book has a gentler tone as a result of Susan's input.

The heart of my psychological analysis of fundamentalism draws on the cognitive therapy model. Dr. E. Thomas Dowd, President of the American Academy of Cognitive and Behavioral Psychology, international editor of the *Journal of Cognitive Psychotherapy,* and Professor of Psychology at Kent State University, read a draft of Part Three. He offered a number of helpful suggestions. Dr. Aaron Beck, father of cognitive therapy, generously responded to me, clarifying a question I had about his model.

Several members of my family read drafts of the manuscript and their feedback was helpful. My mom, Edna Ruth Mercer, agreed to read a draft. She is a conservative Christian; I worried that she would feel hurt and disappointed. She felt neither and only asked that I not think of all fundamentalists as being the same. My mom and I disagree on many things theological, but I will always deeply appreciate her willingness to discuss anything with me without it interfering with our love and respect for each other. My sister, Willa Wood, helped me see how my frustration with fundamentalists was getting in the way of stating clearly what I wanted to say in a number of places. My sister-in-law, Dr. Vicki Stemmons Mercer, and my brother, Rex Mercer, helped me formulate a logical arrangement of the chapters and clear up ambiguous sections of the manuscript.

At East Carolina University, my colleagues in history, Dr. Carl Swanson and Dr. Michael Palmer, offered feedback on the short section in Chapter 9 entitled "Right-Wing Politics." The East Carolina Interlibrary Loan staff laid the world of scholarship at my fingertips. Susan Adams, in my front office, and my research assistants, Nabeel H. Arastu, F. Harmon Driscoll, Chris Flora, and Nicole Frambach, provided valuable assistance in tracking down sources and confirming factual information. Susan Adams also placed the final draft in proper style, with the assistance of Jamie Lynn Maniscaleo, and did much of the work on the index.

Anthony Chiffolo has been a superb editor, and I appreciate his guidance throughout this project.

Part of the material in Chapter 5 is from Calvin Mercer, "Contemporary Language and New Translations of the Bible: The Impact of Feminism," *Religion & Public Education* 17 (Winter 1990): 89–98 and is reprinted with permission. Part of the material in Chapter 9 is from Calvin Mercer, "Sexual Violence and the Male Warrior God," *Lexington Theological Quarterly* 41 (Spring 2006): 23–37 and is reprinted with permission.

Introduction

FUNDAMENTALISTS AND EVANGELICALS

There is an interesting story about one of the early religion teachers at the public university where I serve. I hope the story is apocryphal, but it could be true. Even if not historically accurate, it makes my point.

As the story goes, the religion teacher, in each of his Bible courses, always walked into class on the first day with the Bible in hand. Before doing or saying anything else, he slammed the Bible on the floor, stomped on it several times, and proclaimed, "This is what I think about the Bible. Now, if you have a problem with what I think, I recommend you drop this course." This kind of action is an extreme response to what many teachers view as the irritatingly narrow-minded stubbornness of fundamentalist Christian students. The irony, of course, is that in this case the professor is illustrating the opposite narrow-mindedness. Both sorts of narrow-mindedness obstruct mutual understanding and communication between those who are and are not Christian fundamentalists.

My goal is twofold. First and foremost, I want to provide some theoretical orientation with regard to the theological, and especially the psychological, world of fundamentalist and evangelical Christianity. In short, I want to help you understand the fundamentalist Christian. Understanding fundamentalists will help you also understand other conservative Christians, like evangelicals. This is not a specialized clinical text. However, based on my clinical training and experience, I do offer a novel psychological understanding of the fundamentalist mind. While understanding will be rewarding in itself, it will also serve as the basis for a secondary goal, which is to enable you as a non-fundamentalist to communicate more effectively with fundamentalist and evangelical Christians, *should you wish to do so.* I am well aware that many people have not the slightest interest in talking to a fundamentalist. However, understanding how to do so will help you understand the fundamentalist, regardless of whether or not you ever talk to one.

Some people would like to engage in dialogue with fundamentalists. Like the professors who heard my talk at the scholarly meeting, many people become frustrated and stymied when they attempt to converse with fundamentalists and evangelicals about religion, politics, social policy, and other substantive matters. Of course, quality dialogue between people with radically different worldviews is always a challenge, but I believe the barriers can be overcome in this case. I hope to pave the way for healing conversations. I believe that the general discourse in American life can be enhanced by promoting greater mutual understanding between fundamentalists and those who are puzzled by them. Non-Christians should understand that those puzzled by fundamentalists include many Christians. While my main interest is to help the reader bridge the gap in understanding the fundamentalists, I do not deny that I think many fundamentalist ideas are psychologically unhealthy, theologically questionable, and politically dangerous. I would be quite pleased if this book indirectly contributed to fundamentalists rethinking some of their positions.

While I have written for the non-fundamentalist, I know that a few fundamentalists may stumble onto this book. If so, my word to you is that I believe (along with you and the Bible) in the biblical saying that "the truth will set you free." One of my seminary professors once told me, "The truth will set you free, but first it will piss you off." If you read this book as a fundamentalist, my hope is that you can move through any irritation that might arise and absorb the factual information about the Bible and your religion that might be helpful, understand your fundamentalism in a larger historical context, and allow new truths to surface for yourself. All of us, fundamentalists and non-fundamentalists, need to always be open to allowing greater growth and freedom. I do believe that the truth, in the end, will set us free.

FUNDAMENTALISM AS A "HABIT OF MIND"

Following this introduction, which will include an account of my personal exit from fundamentalism, I will begin telling the "stories" of fundamentalism, beginning with the historical and cultural story. Living in some regions of the world, especially in the southern United States, it is easy for Christians and non-Christians to conclude that fundamentalism is what Christianity looks like worldwide and throughout history. That is, of course, far from accurate. Fundamentalist Christianity is a movement in Christianity that has an identifiable origin and development story, as I will show in Part One on the history of fundamentalist Christianity. Interestingly, most fundamentalist Christians will recognize some of the names and movements in that history, but will not really understand their movement in its larger historical and cultural context. Next, I will devote Part Two to the various, sometimes strange, points of the fundamentalist theological system. With the historical/cultural and theological contexts in place, I will provide in Part Three my psychological analysis of the fundamentalist mind, drawing upon the respected cognitive model of Aaron Beck. In some ways this is the heart of my contribution to understanding fundamentalist Christians, but that story is best told within the well-considered historical and theological contexts. Finally, in the last part I turn to strategies for dialogue with fundamentalists.

Before moving too far into the subject, it will be useful to give some attention to terminology. One of the more thoughtful discussions of the term "fundamentalism" comes in the excellent and extensive *Fundamentalism Project,* a series of scholarly monographs edited by Martin E. Marty and R. Scott Appleby.

> Religious fundamentalism has appeared in the twentieth century as a tendency, a habit of mind, found within religious communities and paradigmatically embodied in certain representative individuals and movements. It manifests itself as a strategy, or set of strategies, by which beleaguered believers attempt to preserve their distinctive identity as a people or group. Feeling this identity to be at risk in the contemporary era, these believers fortify it by a selective retrieval of doctrines, beliefs, and practices from a sacred past. These retrieved "fundamentals" are refined, modified, and sanctioned in a spirit of pragmatism: they are to serve as a bulwark against the encroachment of outsiders who threaten to draw the believers into a syncretistic, areligious, or irreligious cultural milieu. Moreover, fundamentalists present the retrieved fundamentals alongside unprecedented claims and doctrinal innovations. These innovations and supporting doctrines lend the retrieved and updated fundamentals an urgency and charismatic intensity reminiscent of the religious experiences that originally forged communal identity.[1]

I consider this an excellent start in understanding the typical fundamentalist. There are several elements in this description that will be important in the course of this book. It is central to my understanding that at the psychological level, fundamentalism is primarily a reaction to the perceived sense of a loss of identity. When fundamentalists address this threat, it leads them to strategies that mix traditional notions and novel ideas into "fundamentals" of the faith that are used to defend against the threat. The operative term used by empirical researchers for what

Marty and Appleby describe is "restorative." Fundamentalism is a "restorative sect," in that it "attempts to maintain or restore beliefs and practices that oppose changed values in the dominant culture."[2] An example of such changed values that fundamentalists oppose is women's rights. The Marty and Appleby *Fundamentalism Project* is mainly oriented toward understanding fundamentalism as a movement or group in various societies. My psychological focus, in Part Three, is on understanding the mind and world of the typical individual fundamentalist.

As Marty and Appleby explain, fundamentalism is a modern phenomenon found across religions. The term "fundamentalism" was invented in the United States in the 1920s to refer to an extremely conservative and reactionary movement in Christianity. I will explore the origins of this term in Part One. In the last 30 years the term was applied first to certain movements in Islam and now to movements in other religions as well. While my focus is on fundamentalist Protestant Christians, what I say can be useful in understanding fundamentalist Catholics, fundamentalist Muslims, and fundamentalists of other religions. Although it would probably make many fundamentalist Christians quite angry to hear this, I am convinced that if the particularized Christian terminology were eliminated from much of contemporary Christian fundamentalist rhetoric, what remains is a framework that would be familiar to fundamentalists from other religions. Fundamentalism in its Christian form is a particular theology, but the structure of the worldview, and, indeed, the psychology, is similar across religions.

One of the most valuable facets of the *Fundamentalism Project* is that it brings under one cover scholarly analyses and critiques of various fundamentalist movements and groups from around the world. In the first volume, there are excellent essays on Jewish Haredim, Sunni fundamentalism in Egypt and the Sudan, activist Shi'ism in Iran and Iraq, Sikh fundamentalism, Theravada Buddhist fundamentalism, and other groups and movements. By casting the net widely, synthetic attempts can be made to understand fundamentalism as spanning the globe, rather than as some isolated phenomenon peculiar to a particular country or region. Marty and Appleby suggest a number of typical impulses that run though many of the fundamentalist and fundamentalist-like movements and groups in today's world. Fundamentalists form dramatic eschatologies; name, dramatize, and mythologize the enemy; engage in missionary work with zeal; exhibit a crisis of identity; replace inherited structures with their comprehensive ideological system; and seek out charismatic and authoritarian male leaders.[3] My analysis will show that Christian fundamentalism exhibits all these typical impulses.

While all fundamentalists share many common characteristics, it is helpful to distinguish religious fundamentalists from syncretic movements.[4] Syncretic fundamentalists are motivated less by religion than by ethnocultural or ethnonational considerations. To address social or political concerns, syncretic fundamentalists turn to the relevant religious base for legitimacy, organization, and "troops." Examples of syncretic fundamentalism include the Ulster Protestants, Hindu RSS, Sinhala Buddhists, and the Kach movement in Israel. The fundamentalist Christian movement in America is religious fundamentalism and, in the reverse process of syncretic movements, is drawn into politics and cultural wars because of religious beliefs.

ANGRY EVANGELICALS

I should point out that while I use "fundamentalist" in my title, I am also discussing Christians who might more properly be labeled "evangelical" or "conservative." Fundamentalism is one form of evangelical Protestantism. All fundamentalists are evangelical, but most evangelicals are not fundamentalist, so goes the formula. Fundamentalism itself is a vast movement with clear cut meaning for many who accept its tenets, but with a more nuanced meaning for others. In places I am going to generalize about fundamentalism in ways that identify overarching trends, core features of identity, and other central elements. So what I say about fundamentalism, while likely more relevant for this extreme version of Christianity, can also be applied more or less to other versions of conservative Christianity, like evangelicalism.

Both fundamentalists and evangelicals are Protestant Christians who stress the good news (the word "evangelical" is derived from the New Testament Greek word *euaggelion,* literally "good news") of personal salvation in a conversion experience through faith in Jesus Christ, the authority of the Bible as the ultimate religious scripture, evangelistic attempts to convert others, and personal morality. The term evangelical refers to a larger, less conservative, and less militant group than the term fundamentalist. Evangelicals are more likely to obtain degrees from prestigious institutions, participate in mainstream scholarly organizations and debates, and exhibit openness to ecumenical dialogue. Further distinctions between fundamentalism and evangelicalism can be quite important in some contexts, but for this book, I can gloss over many of the differences between the two because my main interest is in the common psychology that drives both types of conservative Protestant Christians. I will use the term fundamentalism as my main focus and terminology, with the understanding that much of what I say will apply to many, perhaps most, evangelical Christians. The distinction between the two will become clearer in Part One on the historical and cultural story, where I chart the origin, development, and various splits of the fundamentalist movement in America.

George Marsden, a leading authority on fundamentalism, observed, "A fundamentalist is an evangelical who is angry about something."[5] A number of scholars (for example, Harriet A. Harris and James Barr) contend that evangelicals reflect to one degree or another a fundamentalist mentality. All fundamentalists and many, perhaps most, evangelicals as well reject scientific and historical consensus where it is perceived to contradict a literal reading of the Bible, and are resistant to critical thinking about religion. This oppositional stance, manifesting in extreme form as anger, may mask an underlying anxiety, the details and dynamics of which I will later discuss in psychological terms. Many interpreters have noted the extreme hostility fundamentalists have towards modern ideas, religious and other.[6] Marty and Appleby's work makes this hostility clear, as is implied in the extended quotation above. Marty and Appleby note that it is no insult to fundamentalists to describe them as "fighting back," because fundamentalists see themselves as militant.[7] Fundamentalists fight to defend traditional evangelical beliefs against modern secular and theological trends.

In the last century, conservative Christianity, in the form of fundamentalism or evangelicalism or some other version, has clearly eclipsed moderate and liberal forms of Christianity as the dominant perspective in the United States. Many observers of fundamentalism see it as an integral part of modernity in that it is a sharp reaction to contemporary society informed by the scientific worldview and other concurrent secular ideologies. Scholars differ on what cluster of factors are to be taken into account in the origin and persistence of fundamentalism, but it is generally agreed that reacting to modernity is at least one important factor. In Part One, we will see how Protestant fundamentalists in America emerged in opposition to intellectual and social developments that were changing the face of the young nation. For now, the primary point to keep in mind is that if, indeed, fundamentalism is an integral part of modernity, then fundamentalism is here to stay, and may even increase in appeal and strength.

While fundamentalists are different from all other Christians, understanding fundamentalists will give the reader insight in understanding all Christians who consider themselves conservative and traditional.

MY JOURNEY OUT OF FUNDAMENTALISM

While I take a scholarly approach to understanding fundamentalists, I do not write this book solely from the ivory tower, surrounded by the monographs and technical journal articles of other scholars. My own story informs this book and perhaps it would be appropriate to get the short version of that story on the table.

I grew up in a fundamentalist Christian family and church in the rural South. Original Free Will Baptist was the Protestant denomination that nurtured and shaped me as a kid growing up in the 1960s and 1970s. The most well-known Baptists in America are the Southern Baptists. There are some differences between Free Will and Southern Baptists. Theologically, the Free Will denomination emphasizes human "free will" over the idea of God's predestination, although few American denominations now stress predestination. Free Will Baptists also practice "feet washing," which can be a quite meaningful humility ritual and is performed in the context of "communion" (what Roman Catholics call the Eucharist). Setting aside relatively minor differences like these, I grew up in the tradition most Americans think of as "Baptist."

As I will explain later in my discussion of the anti-intellectualism of fundamentalism, there is a suspicion and aversion to the secular educational system within "hard-core" fundamentalist circles. Fortunately, my parents believed in a good education for secular career paths. After high school graduation, I went off to college to study accounting at the University of North Carolina at Chapel Hill.

In my home state of North Carolina, UNC-Chapel Hill had the reputation of being the hotbed of liberalism. Indeed, it was embroiled in the thick of things in the McCarthy era. A few years ago UNC-Chapel Hill received bad (or good, depending on one's point of view) press for requiring freshmen to read Michael Sells's *Approaching the Qur'an: The Early Revelations.* While the requirement to read this book may have been controversial at other schools, the degree of controversy in the state of North Carolina was probably due to the lingering perception among the state's conservatives that UNC-Chapel Hill is still where all the liberals congregate to promote their humanistic ideas and hatch their secular programs.

My personal mission at UNC-Chapel Hill was to maintain my Christian fundamentalism while being trained as an accountant. A macroeconomics course began the process of eroding what turned out to be a quite superficial love for accounting. Microeconomics and Accounting 1 finished off what illusions were left that I could find fulfillment in that profession.

As for my Christian fundamentalism, it proved to be more resilient. Somehow, miraculously, I was able to maintain it through four years at the university. The particular vehicle that enabled me to resist the "secular humanism" of Chapel Hill was an evangelical organization called Campus Crusade for Christ, the brainchild of an innovative and visionary evangelical leader named Bill Bright. Later, I will place this and other fundamentalist and evangelical organizations in a historical and theological context. For now, it is sufficient to simply note that the Campus Crusade group helped keep me true to the fundamentalist faith. Campus Crusade and similar organizations continue to serve this same purpose for hundreds of thousands of American college students.

Nonetheless, at least one fertile seed was planted during my four years at UNC-Chapel Hill. While I was not a religion major, I did take a couple of religion courses as electives from the very popular professor of the Bible, Dr. Bernard Boyd. Dr. Boyd's classes were held in huge lecture halls in order to accommodate the hundreds of students scrambling to gain entrance into his courses. Unfortunately, too often the scramble to register for certain college courses is because those courses have reputations as an "easy A." That was certainly not the case with Dr. Boyd's Bible classes. I recently ran across notes showing the grade distribution for one of his tests. Forty-three percent of the class made an unacceptable grade of "D" or "F." Dr. Boyd was a popular professor because he was a master teacher who knew how to enroll his students into his passion for the material he taught.

In Dr. Boyd's classes, for the first time in my life, I was introduced to someone who took a rigorous scholarly, or critical, approach to the Bible. At the same time, he obviously respected and loved the text. The word "critical" can be misleading, in that the ordinary use of the word sometimes connotes finding fault (for example, "he was critical of the way the game was coached"). Always, in this book, I use the word critical as a synonym for scholarly and basically I mean using one's rational faculties to analyze evidence and draw conclusions. While the issue of bias is a tricky one, the scholarly reading of the Bible, at least in theory, attempts a reading unbiased by devotional agenda. In the critical study of the Bible or anything else, there is no connotation of tearing down or finding fault.

The preachers and Sunday School teachers of my childhood, and the Campus Crusade leaders of my college years, had not introduced me to a scholarly reading of the Bible. My fundamentalist teachers had sometimes built a straw man in order to ridicule or destroy some scholarly position. In these enterprises, they presented their "evidence" in a scholarly guise, but I now see the inaccuracy of their arguments. So, before Dr. Boyd, I did not have the skills to read the Bible with an open and critical mind. While I consciously and fervently resisted the general approach and conclusions of Dr. Boyd, at a deeper level I suppose Dr. Boyd's intelligent and rigorous study, along with his passion for the text of the Bible, planted a seed that simply had to grow, even though the sprouting would come years later.

Upon graduation from the university, I attended graduate school at Southeastern Seminary, a Southern Baptist seminary in Wake Forest, North Carolina, which, at that time, was an institution that gave voice to moderate Christianity. Many Southern Baptists, especially in their colleges and seminaries, actually embraced moderate elements of the Christian religion. As part of the general political turn to the right in the 1980s, fundamentalist elements in the Southern Baptist denomination took over the denomination's institutions. The seminary I attended is now a fundamentalist training school; all of my professors have fled or been forced out. In fact, when I was there as a student, some fundamentalist students brought tape recorders to class in order to catch the "liberal professor" in some heretical statement. So, when I attended, the seminary, while very Baptist and very Christian, was still introducing its students to the tools of critical study and to the range of theological options. Even though I was then a committed fundamentalist, I attended this moderate Baptist seminary because of geographical and family considerations. At least that was what was operating at the conscious level in my mind. I was a fundamentalist and was determined to remain one.

When I entered seminary, intending to become a minister, I held firmly to a number of fundamentalist beliefs, three of which are relevant for my story. First, the Bible is completely without any kind of error. Second, the truth of the universe is contained within the pages of the 66 books of the Old and New Testaments of the Protestant Bible. Third, anyone who does not accept Jesus Christ as their personal savior will burn for eternity in a literal hell.

Until now, I have not told many people the next segment of this story, but it seems relevant because in Part Three I will attempt to explain the workings of the fundamentalist mind. There I was, a fundamentalist Christian, about to begin my first day of classes at a moderate, therefore non-fundamentalist, seminary. I remember, as clear as if it occurred this morning, going about an hour early to campus. I sat down in one of the empty classrooms. The classroom felt cold and damp. I prayed something very close to the following prayer:

> Dear Lord God. I am anxious, as I am about to begin classes here at this liberal seminary. I am not anxious about the academic difficulty, but I am very anxious about the bad doctrine that I know is taught here by some professors. I want to obtain my degree so I can go out and serve you. As I attend classes at this liberal seminary, I pray that you will keep me from being influenced by the professors here and what they teach. I believe the Bible is your inspired word, without any error whatsoever, and that it contains the truth of the universe. I trust and pray that you will keep my beliefs pure and unchanged, so that my soul may be saved. In the name of Jesus Christ I pray, Amen.

From where I sit today, the prayer is a very strange one. I was about to embark on three years of rigorous graduate education, and I prayed that I would not be influenced or changed by that education. In that sense, I suppose I exhibited the worst attitude that any student can bring to their studies.

The prayer is as revealing as it is strange. As I recall the prayer, I vividly remember the words and I also remember the feeling of anxiety. I felt that if I were not strong enough to resist the heretical influence, my soul was in danger. The prayer also reveals the absolutely crucial role in my thinking of a fundamentalist view of the Bible. By the way, within a year or two I became, and have remained since, deeply and eternally grateful to God that my prayer request was *not* answered.

I have always been a bit obsessive about things. My thinking about the number two belief above—the Bible contains the truth of the universe—was that if, indeed, the truth of the universe was in the pages of this book, then it was appropriate for me to become an expert on this book. I figured that even a liberal seminary could teach me the grammar and syntax in which the inspired scriptures were written. So, in seminary I plunged into Hebrew, the language of the Old Testament, and Greek, the language of the New Testament. In addition to reading the Bible in the original languages, I also began to learn about the long, complicated, and messy historical process that finally gave us the various books of the Christian Bible. Actually, the process is also quite interesting and delightful, and to this day I am still fascinated by the twists and turns of this story and I love to study, research, and teach the Bible. However, at the time, what I was learning about the history of the Bible was extremely disturbing to me. It flew in the face of my fundamentalist theology and began to eat away at the identity I had constructed for myself around my core fundamentalist values.

For fundamentalists, the temptation and strong tendency are to resist any new notions, however rational, that present a theological or psychological challenge to an identity built on the fundamentalist system. I will ever be grateful that my reasoning ability won out over the dogma and absolutism of my fundamentalist orientation. I was learning things—factual data, not just theories—that simply would not allow me to maintain some of my fundamentalist beliefs about the Bible. I had to either deny my intellect or revise my theology.

Fortunately, at the same time that I was taking courses in biblical languages and history, I was also taking courses on the history and theology of Christianity. I began to see my parochial version of Christianity in a larger historical context. That, along with the theology courses, gave me, for the first time in my life, a critical perspective on my Christianity, and it gave me legitimate alternative theological options to consider. I saw that I did not have to choose between my brain and my religion. My theological perspective shifted to a more moderate version, which was actually more in line with classical Christianity.

Like Dr. Boyd, I fell madly in love with the world of the Bible that was opened for me by honest inquiry and critical study. I stayed at the seminary for a second graduate degree. Finally, I moved on to complete a doctorate in biblical studies at another school, and new chapters opened up in my personal and religious journey. I will stop the story at this point, because it is the seminary days, and the evolution out of the fundamentalist camp, that are most relevant for this study.

I have ventured into this autobiographical account because I want the reader to understand that I was a fundamentalist for a long time, and I took this religious path very seriously. I do not write this book as an outside critic with no empathetic appreciation of the fundamentalist mind. I should also say that I consider it a high privilege to work as an educator with fundamentalist students. Unlike my (hopefully mythical) predecessor who stormed into class, threw the Bible on the classroom floor, and stomped on it, I almost always enjoy conversations with fundamentalists, especially when the conversations are open and forthright.

My graduate education at the doctorate level, and my primary profession, is in the academic study of religion, with a focus on biblical studies and the history of hermeneutics (the science of interpretation, in this case, interpreting the Bible). While I do not think religious behavior can always be reduced to psychology, I do think this young discipline can be extremely useful in understanding human religiosity. In addition to my education in religion, I have a graduate degree in clinical psychology, specifically in psychometric assessment and psychotherapy. I practiced professionally part-time for about a decade. My psychotherapy experience was, first, with students in a university mental health service. Then, for many years, I was a clinician in a psychiatric private practice, working with a team of psychiatrists and other mental health workers. Through this experience, I came to realize that my understanding of mental health could shine a new light on the nature of fundamentalism because of the delicate emotional issues involved. Before delving into the fascinating psychology of the fundamentalist mind, I need to lay the groundwork by providing the historical and theological stories.

PART ONE

The Birth of Fundamentalism

CHAPTER 1

Who Are the Christians?

EMERGENCE OF CHRISTIANITY

As is the case with most ideologies and movements, many ideas and historical currents contributed to the emergence of fundamentalism. While I use psychology, as well as other disciplines, to interpret religious behavior, I am primarily a historian. Even as a therapist, I found that when doing the "intake" of a new client, spending a session or two reconstructing the story (that is, history) of the client and his or her issues was usually an essential ingredient in giving an accurate diagnosis and formulating an effective treatment plan. It is most unfortunate, and dangerous, when individuals, religions, and societies are ignorant of their past. To live in the present without an awareness of history is to lose a vital perspective on the present and future.

My intention in this part of the book is to place fundamentalism in the context of the historical Christian religion and to show how it relates to modern developments in religion and culture. Many, perhaps most, Christians today are woefully ignorant of even the most basic elements of their religious history. Most fundamentalists naïvely think their form of Christianity was lifted intact from Jesus of the first century. I will show that fundamentalism is actually a rather modern development, although in the sense of being in battle with modern and secular culture. While I may have a novel twist or two, this interpretation is certainly not new with me; presenting it here will provide an important context for understanding the psychological interpretation provided in Part Three.

I will start at the beginning. In the first century of the common era, Christianity emerged out of the old and venerable religion of Judaism. Jesus and the early disciples were Jews. In fact, some of my students do a double take when they hear me say that Jesus was not a Christian. It is a true statement. Jesus was a Jew. Paul and the other disciples started the Christian church after Jesus. Jesus, Paul, and the other disciples were not fundamentalists either. I know many of today's fundamentalist Christians like to think they are direct theological descendents of Jesus, Peter, and Paul, but they are not, and I will demonstrate this.

In any case, the Christian church began as a small, sectarian, and heretical movement within Judaism. This general pattern is common in the history of religion. Many religions began as small, heretical—we could even say "cult"—movements within a larger and established religion. Buddhism began this way in the larger context of Hinduism, to take an example from the east. The process of early Christianity, over several decades, distinguishing itself from its parent religion is a complex and fascinating story that will not concern us here in detail. The point is that under Paul and those who associated with his more radical theology, Christianity evolved as a separate religious identity, and eventually as a full-blown religion on its own.

One of the more remarkable stories in the history of religions is the phenomenal growth of Christianity in the first four centuries. I could speculate on the reasons, but whatever they were, people in the Greco-Roman world were captivated by and drawn to the message of Christ. To make a long and complex story short, by 312 CE, the year of the supposed conversion of the Roman Emperor Constantine, the tiny, sometimes persecuted, Jewish heretical movement of Christians had become the dominant religion of the great Roman Empire. Emperor Constantine, perhaps for political purposes, proclaimed Christianity as the official religion of the empire.

While this development into the official and major religion of the culture may have seemed like a striking success, it brought the new religion a host of troubles. Increasingly, Christianity sold out for money and political power. The parallel to later periods in Christian history are remarkable. As I will explain later, since the 1980s certain important strands of fundamentalism have become increasingly aligned with a particular, namely right-wing, political orientation. In my opinion, Christianity has compromised its integrity whenever it has formed these kinds of political alignments. In the ancient period, some Christians felt that Christianity had lost its soul because of its political and fiscal obsessions. This feeling, in the fourth and fifth centuries, led thousands of Christians to flee to the desert to pray, fast, and recapture the true spirit of simple Jesus who had nowhere to lay his head. So many of these early desert dwellers fled to the deserts in Syria, Egypt, and Palestine that they began to bump into one another and meet for prayer and worship. This was the beginning of the monastic movement in Christianity. My own Monastic Project, mentioned in Part Three, is an attempt to recapture the spirit, and to some degree, the actual practices of such monastic movements.

In the next part of the book, I will detail the various aspects of the fundamentalist theological system with respect to doctrines of the Bible, Jesus Christ, salvation, and the end of time. In the case of each doctrine, I will point out the origin and development of the doctrine. Suffice it to say here that in these early centuries of Christianity, none of the distinctive fundamentalist doctrines were in place as the official doctrine of the religion. Elements of what became the fundamentalist doctrinal system can be identified in these early centuries, but it is simply a gross misreading of history to think of Christianity in the New Testament and in the early centuries as reflecting any sort of viewpoint like that found in modern fundamentalism.

Rather than presenting a coherent and agreed upon theological system, the early centuries of the religion are characterized by many intense debates about the correct response to a host of theological questions. "Patristics" is from the Latin word meaning "father" and refers to a subspecialty among scholars of the Christian religion; these scholars study developments in the early centuries of the religion. Patristic scholars find that Christians in these early centuries, embroiled in these theological disputes, wrote many books and held numerous church councils in an attempt to sort out correct doctrine from heresy. There was no general agreement on most of the theological questions to which many fundamentalists naïvely and confidently assert their "inspired" answers with respect to the Bible, Jesus, and the end of time. In Part Two, I will discuss the fundamentalist view of these topics. A quick glance at some of the more important events and at the work of some of the more important Christian leaders during these early centuries indicates just how fluid the Christian belief system was. The books and records of the church councils from this period reveal seemingly endless debates about the trinity, the nature of Christ, the relationship of the Holy Spirit to God, the books that have scriptural status, and a host of other issues.

It is not easy for most fundamentalist Christians to acknowledge, but heresy can be understood as the theological position of the losers in a doctrinal debate. I can illustrate this by reaching back into first century Christianity. We have evidence from the New Testament of an important and intense debate that erupted among the earliest Christians. As mentioned previously, early Christianity emerged out of Judaism and the earliest Christians were Jews. Eventually Christianity began to appeal to non-Jews, to Gentiles from the larger Greco-Roman world. When this happened, some early Christians—we can call them Jewish Christians—advocated the position that Gentile converts should come into Christianity the same way the Jewish Christians had, that is, via Judaism. The Jewish Christians had followed God all their life, working hard, for example, to keep kosher in their Jewish religion. These Jewish Christians did not think it was fair for "pagans" from the Greco-Roman world to become

Christians simply by affirming faith in Jesus Christ. So, the conservative Jewish Christians required Gentiles to do two things, in addition to having faith in Jesus Christ. They required Gentiles to keep the Jewish kosher laws and to practice circumcision for the men. Both of these practices were central to Judaism.

James and Peter and others apparently stood on the side of the conservative Jewish Christians in this debate. They were opposed by the great apostle Paul, who argued that the only thing required for becoming a Christian was faith in Jesus Christ. The controversy on this issue became so great that the leaders of the early movement came to Jerusalem in a meeting designed to address the problem. We have record of this Jerusalem conference in the book of Acts, chapter 15. Paul gives his account of the meeting in Galatians, chapter 2.

Paul won the debate and new Gentile Christians from the Greco-Roman world were not required to practice circumcision or keep kosher. The orthodox position came to be that faith in Jesus Christ was sufficient to gain salvation. Requiring new converts to practice circumcision and keep kosher became a heretical view. But what if Paul had lost the debate with the conservative Jewish Christians? Then, his view would have been considered the heretical position and that of the conservative Jewish Christians would have become the orthodox position. If this outcome had occurred, I think it would have altered the course of Christianity. In fact, thinking of this early debate and its possible outcome purely as a historian, if Paul had lost, there would be no Christian religion today. It was the position of Paul and like-minded persons that distinguished Christianity from Judaism. If the conservative Jewish Christian position had won out, then Christianity conceivably would have remained under the umbrella of Judaism. I speculate that Christianity, rather than developing into a separate religion, would have remained a branch of Judaism and today we would have the branches of Judaism now in existence (Orthodox, Reform, Conservative, Reconstructionist) along with a fifth branch of Judaism—Christian Judaism.

Of course, my suggestion about how things would have developed if Paul had lost the theological debate cannot be proven. However, I have indulged in a bit of speculation to make my point that what is judged to be an orthodox doctrine in a theological debate is in effect the position of the winners. The position of the losers in a theological debate is judged to be heresy. Another related aspect of this issue is that the majority position (and usually the politically stronger position) becomes orthodoxy and the minority position becomes heresy. Looking at theological debates in this way certainly undermines the notion that there is a single correct theological position that is revealed by God to people. Of course, one can maintain that what is eventually judged to be orthodox doctrine is the "true" doctrine and God is divinely guiding the church as it locates this truth. While this is an acceptable theological position, it cannot be proven. What we as historians can uncover is the complicated—we could even say messy—process by which Christianity has arrived at its orthodoxy. Even if as a Christian one affirms an orthodox theology, having an appreciation of the historical process behind that theology gives the believer a measure of intellectual honesty and humility. Most fundamentalists, as far as I can tell, are almost totally unaware of the historical background and processes that led to the development of Christian doctrine.

It has been suggested that the theological confusion of Christianity gave impetus to the new religion Islam in the sixth century. It is simplistic to suggest that Islam arose for any single reason. However, I do think that one of the attractive features of Islam was that it offered a clear and simple message. In the midst of a Christianity that was embroiled in tedious questions about the trinity—there is one God but in three persons—Islam shouts out "There is no God but Allah," an uncompromising monotheism without any debate or question. On this point Islam stood with Judaism in questioning what appeared to be Christianity's compromise on the monotheistic principle.

Christianity was bogged down in debate about the nature of Jesus Christ—divine, human, or both. Contrast that with Islam that proclaims "Muhammad is God's prophet," an uncompromising assertion that Muhammad is a human being, not divine, because there is only one God. Islam is built around five pillars and the first one is the confession, "There is no God but Allah, and Muhammad is his prophet." Every good Muslim utters this confession daily. I have had Muslims tell me that the mere utterance of this confession is what makes someone a Muslim. While that may be an extreme view, it illustrates the centrality for Muslims of this confession and the theology it contains. These clear, straightforward, uncompromising theological assertions are in stark contrast to the centuries of seemingly endless debates about particular points of Christian doctrine. When compared to the subtle teachings of some of the other major religions like Christianity, Buddhism, and Hinduism, Islam has a more streamlined theology, easy to grasp and proclaim.

It is true that some of the theological questions that occupied the early Christians were eventually settled. However, many aspects of Christianity's troubled theological journey continued through the early centuries, through the Middle Ages, and into the sixteenth century Protestant Reformation. While politics certainly played its role in the emergence of that movement, the theological disputes also continued to be divisive. There are today three main branches of Christianity: Orthodox, Roman Catholic, and Protestant. The church split into two factions in the eleventh century. The Orthodox branch thrived in the eastern part of the Roman empire. "Orthodox" is capitalized here to refer to a major branch of Christianity, not to be confused with "orthodox" in the sense of correct doctrine. Today,

Orthodox Christianity has major centers in Constantinople, Alexandria, Antioch, Jerusalem, Armenia, Russia, Romania, Bulgaria, Serbia, and Soviet Georgia. There are also many Orthodox Churches in Greece, Cyprus, Poland, Czechoslovakia, and Finland. The Roman Catholic Church evolved in western Europe and today is found predominantly there and in the Americas, Japan, and Australia. While there were theological issues behind the split between Roman Catholic and Orthodox Christianity, the causes of the split were enough political and geographical that these fascinating episodes will not occupy us here. Also, the roots of today's Christian fundamentalist movement are located not in the Orthodox branch of the Christian religion, but rather in the Protestant branch. However, it helps to put Protestant fundamentalism in this larger perspective of Christianity worldwide, because fundamentalists in general are unaware of the historical and global diversity of the religion.

PROTESTANT REFORMATION

Protestantism by nature entails a spirit of "protest." The Protestant Reformation did not result in a single homogeneous expression of Christianity. Rather, the "protest" and "reform" tendencies resulted in a wide array of movements, many of them evolving into the hundreds of Protestant denominations and subgroups in existence today. Protestants are still an unsettled bunch. To this day they continue to fight theological battles among themselves; battles that result in increasing numbers of official denominations. The *Yellow Pages* of any southern city of any size will reveal, for example, a wide array of Protestant denominations. Looking only under the category of Baptists, one may find Southern Baptists, Missionary Baptists, Original Free Will Baptists, National Free Will Baptists, Pentecostal Free Will Baptists, and perhaps a few other brands. According to the current census, there are over 900 Protestant denominations in the United States. Fundamentalism, of course, is not limited to specific denominations or organizations. It is a theological system, and I think a psychological orientation, that cuts across many denominations and organizations in American religious history.

This next major chapter in Christian history is central to the historical story of fundamentalism. In the sixteenth century, Christianity experienced a major upheaval that altered the landscape of the religion forever. The Protestant Reformation is sometimes thought of in purely theological terms. It certainly did involve theology and I will discuss that aspect. However, the Protestant Reformation was also a political, economic, social, and cultural event. It illustrates well the contention that religion both influences and is influenced by broader environments.

The Roman Catholic Church in the sixteenth century was beset by corruption. That may sound like an anti-Catholic statement, but I think

Roman Catholic scholars of their own history will agree that the church of this period had problems that cried out for reform. Simony and the selling of indulgences are but two examples of the corruption of the church in this period. Simony refers to the selling of church offices for money. An indulgence is a remission of anticipated punishment due to sin.

In the full story of Protestantism, there are many persons who deserve credit as precursors to and leaders in the Reformation. For our purposes, we can mention just the most well-known name, Martin Luther. Luther was a Roman Catholic monk who became concerned about the selling of indulgences and, eventually, about a number of other issues. What began as a reform impulse with Luther and others took on a life all its own and evolved into a major branch of the religion. The theological roots of fundamentalism can be traced back to several emphases of Luther and other Protestant Reformers.

Because of the tension between the Roman Catholic Church and the Protestant Reformers, some of the Protestant doctrines can be seen as forged, in part, in contradistinction to Roman Catholic doctrines. The Protestants, contrary to Roman Catholicism, insisted on *sola scriptura,* the teaching that one is guided in faith and belief by scripture only. The Protestants were not fundamentalists on this point, but the Protestant emphasis on scripture certainly provided the theological context for the development of the extreme fundamentalist doctrine of scripture.

It is common to hear fundamentalists say that Catholics "add to" the word of God. A typical comment is, "They worship Mary and do all sorts of other things that are not in the Bible." This is not true and reflects ignorance of the Catholic tradition. This issue and many of the other differences between Protestants and Roman Catholics can be explained by gaining clarity about the way the two traditions understand the doctrine of revelation. By "revelation," I do not mean the book of Revelation in the New Testament, but rather the doctrine of revelation. The doctrine of revelation is the doctrine of how God has revealed truth to human beings. It is the theological equivalence to the philosophical notion of epistemology, the study of the limits and nature of knowledge. How do you know what you know? If a Christian says, "Jesus is divine," then how do they know this? To say it another way, how does God reveal truth to human beings? Catholics and Protestants answer this question in a very different way.

For Protestants, the basic way God reveals truth to human beings is through the Bible. This was one of the central concepts of the Protestant Reformation—*sola scriptura.* The Bible, as defined by Protestants, consists of 66 books of the Old and New Testaments. So in the Protestant scheme of things, God revealed truth to the Hebrew prophets, Jesus, Peter, and Paul and then terminated the revelatory process. For fundamentalist Protestants, the Bible is the only source of authority and truth. A Roman

Catholic cannot get his or her mind around this concept, that God would stop revealing truth to the church. For Catholics, Peter and Paul stand at the beginning of the church tradition, but that tradition continues through the ages, and includes Jerome, Augustine, St. Thomas Aquinas, and other Catholic saints and teachers. Doctrines that come after the biblical period in the history of the church must be consistent with the Bible, but God can and does reveal "new" truth through the church, and specifically through the pope when he speaks *Ex Cathedra* (literally "from the chair"), that is, with revelatory authority on certain kinds of doctrinal issues. Roman Catholics cannot understand why Protestants believe that God stopped revealing truth to the church at the end of the first-century biblical period. For Protestants, using anything beyond the New Testament is "adding" to the Bible. For Catholics, the Protestants are simply not listening to what God is continuing to reveal to the church.

Most of the beliefs and practices that some Protestants, and especially fundamentalists, find distasteful (for example, veneration of Mary and the saints) arose in the second century and following. Roman Catholics believe that any new revelation will be consistent with the Bible, but certainly God can continue to provide new truths to the church. So when Protestants accuse Catholics of adding to the Bible, the Catholic response, understandably, is yes and what is the problem with that.

There has been much misunderstanding of and antipathy toward Roman Catholicism, particularly among fundamentalist Protestants. The fundamentalist aversion to things Roman Catholic goes back to the origins of the fundamentalist movement in an America that was opening its arms to immigrants, many of whom were Catholic.

The bad blood between Catholics and fundamentalist Protestants, of course, has a much deeper history in the sixteenth-century Protestant Reformation. Many Catholics will today admit that the church had serious problems in the sixteenth century. The Protestant Reformation, led by men like Martin Luther and John Calvin, was initially an attempt to reform the church. The reform rather quickly turned into one of the great divides in the Christian religion. The Roman Catholic Church reacted strongly to the Protestants and dug their heels in at the Council of Trent, emphasizing Catholic distinctions in the face of Protestant resistance.

The bad blood between Catholics and Protestants in general lasted, unfortunately, until the last century. In the 1960s the Roman Catholic Church held the important Second Vatican Council, a formal meeting of bishops and other high church officials in Roman Catholicism. There is a telling story about Pope John XXIII who opened the Council. I have never determined if the story is historical or apocryphal, but, regardless, it is revealing. The story is that the pope, as he was about to begin the proceedings, made a comment that it was stuffy in the room. He walked over to a window and opened it and then proceeded to begin the Vatican II

Council. While the reforms of Vatican II did not totally break down the walls between Catholic and Protestant, it certainly brought in a breath of fresh air. The reforms of Vatican II included more lay involvement in the church, presenting mass in the language of the people, and greater emphasis on lay reading of the Bible. Another result of Vatican II was an openness to dialogue with Protestants. The long, cold war was over for mainstream Protestants. It was the new attitudes stemming from Vatican II that prompted many Protestants to learn about and dialogue with their Catholic brothers and sisters. My own extensive visits to Roman Catholic Trappist monasteries have occurred in the larger context of the thawing of relations between Catholics and Protestants.

Unfortunately, some Protestants, especially fundamentalists, operate as if Vatican II never occurred. They continue to see Catholics as having strange and perverse practices that are anti-Christian. The differences between Catholics and Protestants are significant, and I do not mean to minimize them. However, the differences are understandable and when understood in historical and theological context, fundamentalists have no more sure footing in God and the Bible than the Catholics.

THE AMERICAN RELIGIOUS REVIVALS

Several capable scholars have examined the historical origin and development of fundamentalism. In the following sketch, I draw upon the fine work of a number of historians, and especially that of George M. Marsden, Ernest R. Sandeen, Nancy Ammerman, Mark A. Noll, and George W. Dollar. Noll is an evangelical and Dollar is a fundamentalist; both provide informative and sympathetic treatments of their subjects.

Not all scholars of the origins of fundamentalism make as much of the religious revivals tradition in American history as I do. In my mind, the nature of fundamentalism owes very much to the revival tradition in American Christianity. In this context, revival refers to mass evangelism where people are urged to make an immediate decision to convert to Christianity. Several periods of revival have shaped the Christian landscape. The First Great Awakening, from about 1740–50, is associated with the preaching of British evangelist George Whitefield and the learned sermons of Jonathan Edwards. In Edwards's sermons we see elements that became central to fundamentalist revival preaching; I have in mind, for example, his sermon on "Sinners in the Hands of an Angry God." His sermons were simple and pressed for a decision. While this first period of revival made an impact on the emerging nation, it was the second period of revival that really molded the subsequent development of fundamentalism.

The Second Great Awakening, sometimes called the Great Revival, swept across the states from about 1790 to the 1840s and exhibited characteristics that can be traced to present-day fundamentalists' attitudes and practices. During this period, revivals were held in eastern cities and on the frontier. In our nation's history, it was a time of invention, experimentation, and adventure. The frontier revivals took place during a time when several new states were added to the union. Life on the frontier was also hard and rough. The pioneers by necessity expended much of their time and energy providing food, clothing, shelter, and safety for their families. There was little time and opportunity for recreation.

The frontier revivals were periodic events that brought to a largely uneducated community the opportunity for respite from the hard labors of the farm. The revivals were held in large "camp meetings." I suppose these revivals were so designated because some of the people came from such a distance, and usually stayed for days, that they had to "camp" in their wagons or tents. In these early revival days, the preachers rode into town and had a discrete period of time—perhaps a few days—for the revival, before they rode on to the next town. The frontier context, and the parameters within which the revival preachers worked, dictated the nature of the religion that resulted. The revival preacher needed to get conversions fast and with evidence. His sermons were laced with vivid depictions of the fires and torment of hell, the uncertainty of life, the evils of drinking (and a host of other sins), and the need for immediate conversion. Because the revival lasted only a few days or so, there was no opportunity for the revival preacher to see evidence of a changed life over the seasons of a life. The evidence of conversion existed in the various and immediate physical and emotional expressions of the converted. Fast conversions, accompanied with vivid evidence, led to an emotionally charged form of religiosity with almost no intellectual or deep theological content. I like Winthrop Hudson's description that the frontier convert was "like Augustus Longstreet's 'honest Georgian' who preferred his whiskey straight and his politics and religion red hot."[1]

The flavor of this great revival can be seen in the ministry of Peter Cartwright who, fortunately, has left us a description of these revivals. According to his account, Cartwright preached over 14,000 sermons and baptized 12,000 persons. Here are some selections from his 1857 autobiography that help us see the rank emotionalism of these camp meetings.

> It is true we could not, many of us, conjugate a verb or parse a sentence, and murdered the king's English almost every lick. But there was a Divine unction attended the word preached, and thousands fell under the mighty power of God.[2]

Speaking of the important Cane Ridge, Kentucky, camp meeting, he says:

> The meeting was protracted for weeks. Ministers of almost all denominations flocked in from far and near. The meeting was kept up night and day. Thousands

heard of the mighty work, and came on foot, on horseback, in carriages and wagons. It was supposed that there were in attendance at times during the meeting from twelve to twenty-five thousand people. Hundreds fell prostrate under the mighty power of God, as men slain in battle. Stands were erected in the woods from which preachers of different Churches proclaimed repentance toward God and faith in our Lord Jesus Christ, and it was supposed, by eye and ear witnesses, that between one and two thousand souls were happily and powerfully converted to God during the meeting. It was not unusual for one, two, three, and four to seven preachers to be addressing the listening thousands at the same time from the different stands erected for the purpose. The heavenly fire spread in almost every direction. It was said, by truthful witnesses, that at times more than one thousand persons broke out into loud shouting all at once, and that the shouts could be heard for miles around.[3]

And, in another account, he reports:

Ten, twenty, and sometimes thirty ministers, of different denominations, would come together and preach night and day, four or five days together; and, indeed, I have known these camp-meetings to last three or four weeks, and great good resulted from them. I have seen more than a hundred sinners fall like dead men under one powerful sermon, and I have seen and heard more than five hundred Christians all shouting aloud the high praises of God at once; and I will venture to assert that many happy thousands were awakened and converted to God at these camp-meetings. Some sinners mocked, some of the old dry professors opposed, some of the old starched Presbyterian preachers preached against these exercises, but still the work went on and spread almost in every direction, gathering additional force, until our country seemed all coming home to God.[4]

The "exercises" he refers to are examples of the evidence of conversion I mentioned earlier. Here is a vivid description of the jerking exercise.

A new exercise broke out among us, called the *jerks,* which was overwhelming in its effects upon the bodies and minds of the people. No matter whether they were saints or sinners, they would be taken under a warm song or sermon, and seized with a convulsive jerking all over, which they could not by any possibility avoid, and the more they resisted the more they jerked. If they would not strive against it and pray in good earnest, the jerking would usually abate. I have seen more than five hundred persons jerking at one time in my large congregations. Most usually persons taken with the jerks, to obtain relief, as they said, would rise up and dance. Some would run, but could not get away. Some would resist; on such the jerks were generally very severe.[5] There were many other strange and wild exercises into which the subjects of this revival fell; such, for instance, as what was called the running, jumping, barking exercise. . . . They professed to fall into trances and see visions; they would fall at meetings and sometimes at home, and lay apparently powerless and motionless for days, sometimes for a week at a time, without food or drink; and when they came to, they professed to have seen heaven and hell, to have seen God, angels, the devil and the damned; they would prophesy, and, under the pretense of Divine inspiration, predict the time of the end of the world, and the ushering in of the great millennium.[6]

The "millennium" refers to the wild speculations about the end of the world that became a feature of fundamentalism. I will discuss it in much more detail in Part Two of the book. During the revival, such millennial speculation served to heighten the emotional intensity of the revival experience.

These frontier camp meetings and the religion they offered up clearly met some widespread longing, or at least promised to. Red River, Kentucky, and surrounding counties, was the scene for an early series of meetings in 1800. The religion of the camp meeting spread like wildfire and, as we have seen, estimates are that between 12,000 and 25,000 people attended the revival the next year at Cane Ridge, Kentucky. The largest community in Kentucky at the time, Lexington, had barely 2,000 citizens.[7]

By the middle of the nineteenth century, most revival efforts were held indoors in local churches. These later "protracted meetings" took the place of the camp meetings held outdoors or in temporary shelters. As the protracted meeting form developed, the revivals lasted a week to ten days, although local enthusiasm and results could prompt the revivalist to continue the meeting for a month or so. With law clerk-turned-evangelist Charles G. Finney (1792–1875), the revival moved from the rough rural frontier to the "new" frontier of urban America. In campaigns in Philadelphia, New York, and Boston, Finney experimented with a variety of approaches that brought planning and organization to the effort. Such measures were perfected by Dwight L. Moody (1837–1899), a shoe salesman turned preacher who brought then cutting edge business practices to the gospel effort—planning, publicity, big budgets. Moody's simplified sermons packaged the message as the "three R's": ruined by sin, redeemed by Christ, and regenerated by the Holy Ghost. In 1886 Moody founded the Moody Bible Institute which became an important fundamentalist training center.

If one thinks the lawyerly Finney and the businessman Moody portend a shift away from the rough, intellectually empty content of the frontier revivalist, Billy Sunday (1863–1935) brought the tradition back to its roots. In Pittsburgh, Philadelphia, Los Angeles, Boston, and Washington, this converted professional baseball player dished out gospel drama in strong doses. Rolling up his sleeves, he demolished chairs, slid across the stage to mimic a sinner trying to reach heaven as only a seasoned base runner can, and jumped on the bandwagon to fight "booze, tobacco, and dancing." The height of his popularity was during World War I and, in a tone that sounds familiar to our contemporary ears, he preached that Christianity and patriotism are one and the same.[8] A nightmarish image I cannot get out of my head is the ex-baseball player turned evangelist ending his sermons by jumping onto the Christian pulpit and waving an American flag.[9] Billy Graham's well-run mass crusades throughout the last half of the twentieth century reflect the maturation of the techniques of urban evangelists like Finney and Moody. While the structure and organization had advanced with the urban revivalists, the message was pretty much the same old story: repent from your sinful behavior, give your heart to Jesus.

It is tempting to call "revival theology" an oxymoron, but in retrospect the Second Great Awakening did bring about some shifts in theology in America. Traditionally, in Christianity the sovereignty of God is given heavy weight. A well-known, and perhaps extreme, example of this is the Calvinistic emphasis on election. John Calvin, the Protestant reformer, promoted an idea that has been called "double-edged predestination," the idea that God has elected some to salvation and some to damnation, and there is nothing that the human being can do about it. While Calvin's formulation of the doctrine is probably unusual in its severity, in light of the long Christian tradition, it does serve to illustrate the centrality of the sovereignty of God in traditional Christianity. Arminianism, traced back to Jacob Arminius (1559–1609), emphasized the role of human beings in their salvation. The debate over predestination and free will is an old one, going at least as far back as Augustine (354–430 CE), who stressed God's sovereignty, and Pelagius (ca. 415 CE), who stressed free will. The point is that in the Second Great Awakening there was a sharp turn to Arminianism. Salvation was granted to those who sincerely seek God, and seeking God with conviction is accompanied by intense emotionalism.

Once saved, the convert must live a holy life, full of good works. This point bumps us into another theological controversy. Traditionally, the Christian teaching has been that salvation is a once and for all event, often captured in the phrase "once saved, always saved." However, the Arminian traditions argue that a Christian can lose his or her salvation. How this can occur and on what basis is debated in Arminian circles. The important point, for our purposes, is that the Arminian theology was made to order for a revival mentality that made strong appeal to the emotions, urged quick and evident conversions, and stressed personal morality.

The revival converts were as anti-institutional as they were anti-intellectual and anti-theological. They did not need the stuffy old traditions of institutionalized religion. They had Christ in their heart and the good book in their hand. I have devoted my working life—thus far—toward the practice of my chosen profession in institutional contexts. No one has to persuade me of the uselessness, even danger, of much (not all, fortunately) of the bureaucratic mentality of institutions. I am reminded here of the words of the itinerate preacher and civil rights worker—and definitely not fundamentalist—Will Campbell, whom I had the privilege of spending a day with a few years back. In his disarmingly plain way of putting things, Campbell pierces to the heart of the matter in his memoir, *Forty Acres and a Goat:*

> It was a sad and disillusioning lesson to learn. Why wasn't he told that in the first grade? Or the first day at the university? That *all* institutions, every last one of them—no matter the claim, no matter the purpose, no matter the stated goals—exist sooner or later for their own selves, are self-loving, self-concerned, self-regarding, self-preserving, and are lusting for the soul of all who come near them.[10]

One of the small points I would like to make is that moderates and liberals should listen to fundamentalists in the same manner that moderates and liberals want fundamentalists to listen to them, because sometimes fundamentalists can offer a perspective that society needs to hear. I think that is the case here. The irony is that the anti-institutionalism of the early revivals has been abandoned by many fundamentalists. We see this abandonment in the pioneers of conservative social activism in the 1980s, such as the Moral Majority, as well as the more recent politically astute Christians successfully backing conservative administrative and legislative candidates in the first decade of the twenty-first century.

Visits to fundamentalist churches today reveal many practices that can be traced to the early revival periods. In fact, many fundamentalist churches annually still have "revival" weeks. An outside evangelist is called in to preach the revival, or in local parlance, "hold revival," and emphasis is placed on "winning lost souls to Christ." Traditionally, at the end of each revival sermon, an "altar call" is made, inviting sinners to "walk the aisle" and "give their hearts to Christ." Walking the aisle, often with great emotion as God's Holy Spirit convicts the sinner, is a carryover from the old revival emphasis on physical manifestations as evidence of conversion. In the frontier revivals, the sinners were urged to walk the aisle to an area in front of the pulpit where those "under conviction" were urged to come. Often, those responding would sit on a designated "mourner's bench" or "anxious bench." Popular television evangelists often use the word "revival" to market their meetings and shows. In the second quarter of the twentieth century, Charles E. Fuller, a pioneer in the use of radio for religious purposes, called his program the "Old-Fashioned Revival Hour." Rev. Jimmy Swaggart has used the "camp meeting" term to designate his revival services.

The contemporary accounts of these revivals by Cartwright and others help us gain a feel for the flavor and impact of these religious events. However, nothing can take the place of visiting churches where many of these practices are alive and well. I will give one example from my experience to illustrate.

Some years ago I took a friend to a Pentecostal fundamentalist church service that I knew continued some of the practices of the old revival camp meetings. Consistent with some of the old styles of revival preaching, the evangelist preached loudly, in a sing-song style, repeating phrases, calling for conviction, and with great emotion. Gradually, the standing congregation of about 200 began to sway their bodies, raise their hands to heaven, and pray, sometimes in shouts and sometimes quietly as if speaking to God in private. After about 20 minutes, some people began to step outside the church pews, dancing in the aisle, crying, and waving their arms. Several members of the congregation made their way to the front and the evangelist, having come down from the pulpit, prayed with and over them at the altar, usually holding their head in his hands. Suddenly, after being touched and prayed over by the evangelist, one of the more excited members screamed and fell to the floor and lay motionless. My friend, who was not familiar with these modern-day fundamentalist services that utilized old-fashioned revival practices, was concerned that the lady who had fallen on the floor had suffered a heart attack, fainting spell, or other emergency medical condition. She insisted to me that someone should check on the fallen parishioner. While a medical emergency was theoretically possible, I insisted that we remain in our pew, because the lady had simply been "slain in the Spirit," one of the exercises that is common in this form of religiosity. Sure enough, about 20 minutes later, the lady slowly pulled herself up and, gaining composure, joyfully shouted praises to God with her hands raised to heaven.

While a number of practices in today's fundamentalist churches can be traced back to the early revival periods, it is the theology (primitive though it is) inherited from the revivals that may be more significant. As explained earlier, the frontier revivals, perhaps by necessity, degenerated into highly emotional expressions of religiosity. Preaching the gospel, and responding to it, required little education or knowledge. To be an effective evangelist, the crucial tools were a strong voice, a charismatic personality, a few simple biblical phrases, a vivid description of hell, and a Bible to pound on. With this legacy, and in light of the psychological profile I will detail in Part Three, it is easy to see why the typical fundamentalist Christian today frowns on scholarly inquiry and resorts to the defense mechanism of prooftexting when confronted with questions that might challenge the tight fundamentalist system. Prooftexting, which I discuss in more detail in Chapter 11, means quoting the Bible to prove a point, even when the text quoted does not, in any reasonable interpretation, support the point. In my opinion, the impact of the old revivals on the development of fundamentalism is enormous.

CHAPTER 2

The Fighting Fundamentalists

FUNDAMENTALISTS EMERGE

Every religious movement in every age is influenced to one degree or another by the surrounding culture. As our narration of history moves closer to fundamentalism *per se,* we need to consider carefully the larger cultural context that gave birth to this movement. Fundamentalists would strongly disagree, but a case can be made that fundamentalism is actually a "modern" development in religion. It is modern in that it is largely a sharp reaction against modern developments in science and other intellectual domains. It is also modern in that it adopts some modern strategies and techniques (for example, television). For our purposes, the most important and interesting point is that fundamentalism represents a backlash against modernity.

The last quarter of the nineteenth century saw profound changes sweep through the American religious, social, and intellectual landscape. Immigration from Europe brought an influx of Roman Catholics, Jews, and Eastern Orthodox Christians who moved in worlds quite different from that created by traditional American Protestantism. Charles Darwin's *On the Origin of Species by Means of Natural Selection* was published in 1859. Perhaps because of the more explicit title, his *The Descent of Man* in 1871 stirred up even more opposition. Darwin's theories of natural selection and survival of the fittest challenged traditional notions about the origin of human beings. While Darwin's theories were the flashpoint, they were part of a general rise of scientific inquiry and a corresponding decline of reliance on biblical stories for understanding the world in the nineteenth century. This broad intellectual movement included new academic disciplines like sociology and psychology, both of which yielded theorists who gave explanation to religious behavior.

In 1860, the year after Darwin's *Origin of Species* was published, a group of Anglican clergymen published *Essays and Reviews*, a collection that made available to lay people the results of the scholarly investigation of the Bible that had been developing since the late eighteenth century. This scholarship, largely German in origin, included arguments that the first five books of the Bible were not written by Moses, the book of Isaiah had at least two different sources, King David did not write all the Psalms, and miracle stories in the Bible are not to be taken literally. The direct study of the Bible by critics guided by a rational examination of evidence was too much to bear for the revival-inspired and revival-informed religion of American Christians who ended up in the fundamentalist camp.

Most Protestants were persuaded by the new ideas, but the few who resisted generated what has come to be the powerful fundamentalist Christian movement in American history. In this larger view of movements and trends, fundamentalism is a reaction to the marginalization of religion. My particular interest, of course, is how these larger social forces get expressed in the mind of the individual fundamentalist Christian.

If there was an intellectual center in the earliest years of the fundamentalist movement, it was Princeton Seminary in Princeton, New Jersey. Founded in 1812, it was the home of professors who reflect what has been called the "Princeton theology." Charles Hodge (1797–1878), his son A. A. Hodge (1823–1886), and Benjamin B. Warfield (1851–1921) were leading proponents. For our purposes it is not necessary to chart all of the details. The Princeton theologians aspired to scholarly excellence while defending doctrines, some of which—especially the inspiration and authority of the Bible—became central to fundamentalist theology. For the sake of accuracy, I should point out that some of these early "academic fundamentalists" held some views that would be considered too liberal for today's extreme fundamentalist theological program. The struggle against marginalization in the face of modern developments can be seen in Charles Hodge's *What is Darwinism?* (1874), the first systematic Christian attack on evolution. Here Hodge says that "Religion has to fight for its life against a large class of scientific men."[1]

A majority of Protestants and most academics were persuaded by the new intellectual and scientific ideas, but a vocal minority fought back hard. In 1886 Dwight Moody, one of the revivalist preachers of the Second Great Awakening, founded the Moody Bible Institute. This Chicago school became an important training center for Christian leaders who wanted to combat what today is called "secular humanism" and win the world for Christ. In these early years the most publicized (as an example, front page of the *New York Times*) skirmish was the 1891 heresy trial of Charles Briggs, a liberal Presbyterian, whose denomination suspended him from the ministry for his defense of the new scholarly ideas about the Bible. The battle raged in the first quarter of the twentieth century and increasing numbers were won over to the resistance. In the 1920s the nationwide conflict was fierce in this first major wave of political activism from Christians who were to become known as fundamentalists. Preachers denounced "liberalism" and "modernism" from their pulpits. Some of these leaders, holding tightly to their version of Christianity, mobilized to combat modernism in the schools and churches. The central debate issues were evolution (science), alcohol (morality), and Catholicism (theology).

A group of conservative Protestant Christians published, from 1910 through 1915, a series of 12 booklets called *The Fundamentals: A Testimony to Truth.* I have heard about these books for years and recently tracked down an original copy. As I write I have on my desk the first of three thick volumes, containing the 12 booklets that made an important impact on the direction of religion in America. The foreword reads:

> This book is the first of a series which will be published and sent to every pastor, evangelist, missionary, theological professor, theological student, Sunday school superintendent, Y.M.C.A. and Y.W.C.A. secretary in the English speaking world, so far as the addresses of all these can be obtained. Two intelligent, consecrated Christian laymen bear the expense, because they believe that the time has come when a new statement of the fundamentals of Christianity should be made.[2]

The idea for the pamphlet series came from Lyman Stewart, a millionaire from California who made his fortune in oil investments. He controlled the Union Oil Company. Lyman Stewart was the primary theological and organizing force behind the project, although his brother, Milton, helped with the funding. In a letter to his brother Milton, Lyman Stewart made an interesting comment that the American Tobacco Company was spending millions on free cigarettes in order to give potential consumers a taste, and that Christians should do the same with the gospel. Scholars have noted the interesting coincidence (if, indeed, it was a coincidence) that Stewart was prompted to start the pamphlet project due, in part, to a sermon he heard about "something that one of those infidel professors in Chicago University has published." Chicago University was founded by John D. Rockefeller, Stewart's competitor in the oil industry.

Stewart was also involved in funding and promoting various other publications important in the early stages of the fundamentalist movement. For example, he supported important publications on the end-time, such as C. I. Scofield's *Scofield Reference Bible* and W. E. Blackstone's *Jesus is Coming.* I will discuss the fundamentalist doctrine of the end-time, or premillennial dispensationalism, in Part Two.

The 12-volume pamphlet series contained articles written by recognized fundamentalist ministers and teachers, some of whom were authentic academics, including Benjamin B. Warfield, James Orr, Charles R. Erdman, and E. Y. Mullins. Interestingly, most of the 41 American authors were from northeastern cities; only five were southerners and five from west of the Mississippi. The project cost approximately $200,000, which funded distribution of about three million copies. Many churches used this document as a statement of faith. About a third of the 90 articles are devoted to a defense of biblical inspiration and authority and about a third are expositions on central fundamentalist doctrines, like bodily resurrection of Jesus, personal salvation, and evangelism. The rest consists of personal testimonies and various appeals. The volumes contain occasional attacks on Mormonism, Christian Science, Roman Catholicism, Darwinism, and communism. Although the extent of their impact is debated, certainly these booklets, at the very least, reflect concerns growing in a substantial segment of the religious community and contributed in some significant degree to the development of fundamentalism at that critical juncture in American history. They became a "symbolic point of reference" for the fundamentalist opposition to modernism.[3]

Before leaving this subject, I should note that interpreters have suggested that *The Fundamentals* pamphlets are not as "fundamentalist" as the movement that eventually adopted their name as its own. For example, the authors of *The Fundamentals* do not emphasize premillennial dispensationalism, the peculiar doctrine of the end-time that is an obsession of most fundamentalists today.

While it is easy to suggest that the fundamentalist movement received its name from the title given to the 12 volumes, some credit should also be given to use of the term by Curtis Lee Laws, a Baptist editor who in 1920 used the term to refer to his conservative party in a battle that was unfolding in the Northern Baptist Convention. Foreshadowing the militant character of fundamentalism, Laws asserted that he and his party were ready "to do battle royal for the Fundamentals."[4]

The Fundamentals booklet series, and the fighting fundamentalists who promoted this ideology, reflected and further fueled a conflict that was sometimes characterized by open, angry debate. Nearly every major Protestant denomination saw at least one heresy trial, usually of a liberal seminary professor. The fundamentalists lost, outnumbered by moderate Christians who maintained control of the major denominations, but the personal and institutional wounds were deep on both sides.

Fundamentalists and non-fundamentalists fought on many fronts at the local church and denominational levels. One of the more severe and important of the battlefronts was in the area of education. The larger issue in this particular combat is the role of intellectual inquiry. Mark A. Noll is a careful, thoughtful, and respected evangelical scholar and scholar of evangelicalism. In *The Scandal of the Evangelical Mind,* he bemoans the evangelical community's lack of intellectual inquiry that has substance and integrity, and calls for rectifying this deficit. Whatever critique he makes about the evangelical community can be multiplied if one considers this issue in the fundamentalist movement. Noll does not mince words. The first sentence of his book makes the claim that "The scandal of the evangelical mind is that there is not much of an evangelical mind."[5] Surely his characterization of fundamentalism would be at least equally harsh.

Noll unpacks his thesis by a careful review of the history of the "scandal." For the anti-intellectual fundamentalist, it is ironic that the history of Christianity has drawn its share of highly intelligent and informed people. From the apostle Paul, knowledgeable of the intellectual currents of his day; through Jerome, Augustine, and Aquinas, likewise giants in their day; to Luther, Calvin, and a host of modern thinkers, we find learned individuals who are the primary shapers of the Christian tradition. The fundamentalist forefathers include Luther and Calvin, important Protestant Reformers who were staunch advocates of higher education and opponents of anti-intellectual movements. Calvin, in particular, advocated the study of astronomy, geography, and biology and Calvinists of the Reformation period were often good scientists. Why, then, has evangelical, and especially fundamentalist, Christianity exhibited such an anti-intellectual streak?

Noll and others suggest that the revivalist origins, especially that of the Second Great Awakening, are among the primary forces shaping the anti-intellectualism of evangelicalism and especially fundamentalism. I agree fully. As I described earlier, religion in the revival mode is reduced to a very simple and emotional formula. The revival preacher did not need to be educated, and in fact education could very well be seen as the work of the devil. What is required is a *King James Bible,* loud voice, and the repetition of "prooftexts" spiced with gut-wrenching accounts of one's own conversion and, of course, vivid descriptions of heaven and hell. The tired frontier family, on "vacation" from the hard manual work of the farm and during the revival sleeping on the ground or in their wagon, had no particular interest in or use for theological subtleties or for education in general. They wanted exactly what the revival preacher dished up.

Noll cites the separation of church and state as a second and related factor in the anti-intellectualism of fundamentalism. Separation of church and state, in my opinion, has resulted in enormous good for our country and for Christianity in America. Noll agrees, but he points out that separation propelled churches into competition for converts, rather than their being assigned by the government segments of the population in the European pattern. So, individual churches and denominations as a whole had to appeal directly to individuals and the revival service was the major method. As Noll puts it, revivalism and separation of church and state combined to produce a utilitarian strategy that emphasized numerical results, and that left no time or room in the churches for thoughtful and reasoned theology.[6] Quantity over quality. It is an American doctrine not limited to the fundamentalist camp.

FIGHTING ABOUT EVOLUTION

Unfortunately, Christianity's conservative elements have often resisted new insights and information from the scientific world. Perhaps the most famous example is Galileo who was condemned by the Catholic Church for asserting scientific findings. Galileo Galilei (1564–1642) drew upon the work of Nicolaus Copernicus (1473–1543), the Polish astronomer who a hundred years earlier hypothesized that certain mathematical difficulties could be explained by the view that the earth moved around the sun, rather than vice versa. Galileo perfected the telescope that he used to empirically test Copernicus's hypothesis. Galileo's contention that the earth and other planets were rapidly moving around the sun contradicted what the Catholic Church taught, as well as a literal reading of such passages as Psalm 93:1, where the psalmist says to God, "He has established the world [meaning, earth]; it shall never be moved." Galileo was called before the Inquisition, the agency of the Roman Catholic Church charged with rooting out and suppressing heresy. Under pressure, Galileo recanted and spent the last years of his life under house arrest, because he dared suggest that the earth moved, thereby questioning the official religious teachings.

The literalist fundamentalist approach has always insisted that everything, including human beings, was created in seven 24-hour days. The term "creationism" or "creation science" is the term used by current fundamentalists who continue this old battle about evolution. Shrewdly, many fundamentalists today present their traditional belief in the guise of scientific discourse and hence the term "creation science." A recent nonscientific theory propounded by religious conservatives is that of "intelligent design," the idea that even if evolution occurred at all, the natural selection process expounded by Darwin and evolutionary scientists cannot explain the outcome. Only by positing an omniscient creator, an intelligent Designer in the complexity of nature, can one explain how things turned out. Intelligent design makes a higher power, rather than evolution, responsible for the universe and life. Fundamentalist Christians use the "intelligent design" terminology as their latest way of couching the traditional creationist position in the acceptable language of science. A Seattle think tank called "Discovery Institute" provides support for current efforts to carve out the intelligent design argument.[7]

Creationism of whatever form provides a literal and exact account of the beginnings of the world, yielding symmetry with premillennial dispensationalism's exact account of the end of time. Noll gives revealing quotations from fundamentalist creation scientists and dispensationalists that show authors connecting creation with end-time scenarios, and wrapping it all up in true worship of the God who began it all and will end it all.

Historians of fundamentalism have pointed out that the early proponents were not nearly as extreme in their assessments of the science of evolution as fundamentalists of the last few decades. Most conservative Protestants, before the heyday of fundamentalism in the 1930s, saw no problem interpreting the "days" of Genesis, chapter 1, as long geological ages, or that a gap of undefined length existed between God's first creative act (Genesis 1:1) and subsequent acts of creation (Genesis 1:2 ff). In this view, it was during this lengthy gap, between the times depicted in the first two verses of the Bible, that fossils formed in the earth.

These sober conservative positions were overturned by the work of George McCready Price, a lay geologist with little formal training. In 1923 he published *The New Geology,* arguing for a literal reading of Genesis. His calculations required that creation of the world occurred 6,000–8,000 years ago. The great flood was the method God used to rearrange the features of the earth and set the geological past that scientists discover.

Within a few years of the publication of Price's book, the anti-intellectualism of fundamentalism received wide public exposure via enormous press coverage of the famous 1925 Scopes Monkey Trial in Dayton, Tennessee. In this debate about what was to be taught in the public schools, the "victory" for the fundamentalists and their attorney William Jennings Bryan was transformed into defeat for the fundamentalists because of the way the anti-evolutionists were depicted. At the trial, both Clarence Darrow, who made the legal case for evolution, and the national media covering the story, depicted the fundamentalists as ignorant, intolerant, uneducated, and reactionary.

While the debate on origins is usually depicted in stark terms between naturalistic evolutionists and supernaturalistic creationists, theistic evolutionists, often from a Christian perspective, believe that God has created the world and human beings using evolution as the means. Members of the evangelical American Scientific Affiliation (ASA) often reflect this view. The ASA, founded in 1941 by evangelical scientists, was viewed by creationist flood geologists as the forum that would propel their ideas into respectability. The ASA, however, for the most part, held to the older conservative and less radical "day-age" and "gap" theories of creation. By the 1960s many ASA members had become sympathetic to attempts to incorporate some form of evolution into a Christian viewpoint.

Thwarted in their efforts to completely overrun the ASA, which was perceived as having gone soft on evolution, the creationists turned their support to the book, *The Genesis Flood,* published in 1961 by John C.

Whitcomb and Henry M. Morris. The creationist views were widely disseminated through fundamentalist churches and organizations. Eventually, some university-trained scientists arrived in the creationist camp. The first debate I ever attended on creationism versus evolutionism featured a Christian theologian and a biology professor. The Christian theologian argued for evolution and the biology professor took the side of creationism.

Noll points out that creation science is one of the great innovations of recent evangelical history—the establishment of an alternative form of science to the form taught by the intellectual establishments of the culture.[8]

He asks why creation science exploded in the evangelical community and suggests that one answer is the increasing involvement of the federal government into local educational matters. To catch up with the USSR's space program (*Sputnik* was launched in 1957), the federal government dumped huge amounts of money on the schools in an effort to upgrade the teaching of science. One by-product of this effort was the use of biology textbooks that presented scientific consensus about human origins, but also made metaphysical claims that prompted local fundamentalist-inspired opposition.

One of the most unfortunate consequences of the battle over origins is that fundamentalists miss the powerful story found in Genesis. The Genesis stories are poetic presentations of core insights and beliefs of the Hebrew people. The ancient Hebrews were strong in their use of concrete language and weak in their use of abstract language, at least when compared to our modern culture. I will illustrate: Hunger is an abstract concept. "I could eat a horse" is a concrete way of expressing the abstract concept of hunger. The biblical writers used abstract language: grace, forgiveness, love. However, when compared to us, they were much better at using concrete language to express these abstract concepts. We might say someone is angry. The ancient Israelite might say "Their nostrils burned." Or, in one of my favorite examples, the Hebrew Old Testament sometimes refers to a male as someone who, in the words of the King James Version, "pisseth against the wall" (see, for example, 1 Samuel 25:22, 34; 1 Kings 14:10, 16:11). Unfortunately, the squeamish translators of most modern English translations soften the vivid—some say crude—concrete expression.

A good New Testament illustration of the use of concrete language is in Jesus's use of parables, which are, in effect, concrete stories designed to illustrate an abstract point. If the modern university professor were to talk about the abstract concepts of repentance and forgiveness, he or she might give a lecture that began with the etymology of the words "repentance" and "forgiveness." The professor might then give a history of the use of these concepts in Western civilization, and then proceed to distinguish them in other ways. Jesus talked to his disciples one day about repentance and forgiveness. He did it by telling them a story about a man who had two sons, one of whom took his inheritance and wasted it in loose living. The young son "came to himself" and returned to the father, asking to be accepted as a mere hired servant. The father, however, accepted him with open arms and fully as a son. The words "repentance" and "forgiveness" never occur in this parable in Luke 15:11–32, but the story is a powerful concrete expression of these abstract concepts.

This appreciation for the distinction between abstract and concrete language frees the stories in Genesis to make a contribution to our understanding of humans and their being in the world. The story in Genesis, chapter 2, about Adam and Eve being tempted by the serpent in the garden, is a powerful concrete story about the irresponsibility of human beings and our tendency to blame others. There is wonderful humor in the story (as in, an all-knowing deity asking questions to which He knows the answers) as well. All this humor and insight into the human situation is missed in the battles that necessarily arise when reading these old stories in the same way one reads a modern science book.

To say it another way, a myth is a powerful way of telling the truth, but not historical or scientific truth. Myth tells the truth of a culture, or as some might say it communicates spiritual truth. A myth, it has been said, is so true it is always true. As my University of North Carolina Bible Professor, Dr. Bernard Boyd, used to say, no one reads a 1910 physics book anymore. But after several millennia, people still read the early myths of Genesis.

While I am suggesting that the Genesis story of creation is poetic and mythological, I am not by this suggesting that the entire Bible consists of mythology. The Bible is a vast collection of books that stretches over many centuries. It contains a variety of material, including poetry, riddle, psalm, myth, gospel, letter, and apocalyptic. It is important to read each part of the Bible in a way that is appropriate for that literature. Fundamentalists think their reading of Genesis as a handbook of science saves the story of creation from destruction by liberals. The very opposite occurs. The fundamentalists end up with terrible "science," and in the process lose one of the most potent mythological stories from the ancient world.

CHAPTER 3

Fundamentalists Retreat and Advance

SHIFTING STRATEGIES

From about 1925 to about 1940, fundamentalists withdrew from the major Protestant denominations and from participation in mainstream political and cultural life. Fundamentalists separated from all secularists and modernists, and also from those who held like theological views but refused to separate from liberals. The fundamentalists stressed certain key doctrines. Several of these doctrines, detailed later in the book, were a perfect match for the separatist mentality. For example, the fundamentalist emphasis on salvation of the individual reflected and supported their decision to focus on personal morality and have nothing to do with the broader, evil society.

Even more interesting is the theological development around eschatology. Eschatology is the doctrine of the end of the world. The old-style nineteenth-century Protestant view generally was postmillennialism, the view that God will work with and through Christians to manifest the Kingdom of God. In other words, the end of time will come after (i.e., "post") the long (i.e., "millennial") work of God's people in the world. Postmillennialism reflects and supports efforts to improve society through humanitarian deeds and other social initiatives. Fundamentalists, driven by separatist mentality, advocated premillennial dispensationalism, the idea that Christ will come before (i.e., "pre") the literal thousand-year reign of God. Perhaps fundamentalists abandoned postmillennialism in favor of premillennialism because of their defeats in the larger religious and societal domains. Premillennial dispensationalism teaches that society is going to get progressively worse and more sinful.

When things hit bottom, Christ will return to overthrow the forces of evil and set up the Kingdom. During the interim before Christ comes, the job of Christians is to keep pure in the midst of an increasingly sinful world and win as many souls to God as possible. In this pessimistic view of history, there is no need for intellectual engagement, social reform, or political involvement, since the world is doomed to destruction anyhow. As we know and as I will detail later, the stance on political involvement shifted radically in the 1980s.

Fundamentalist ethics were consistent with the above theological and separatist mentalities. In their view, a special moral code distinguished true Christians from the "worldliness" of mainstream society. Early fundamentalist Christians did not dance, smoke (with some exceptions in tobacco states), drink alcohol, gamble, shoot pool, play cards, or wear improper clothing. These prohibitions, along with particular religious practices involving church life, helped fundamentalists maintain a separate religious identity in the midst of American life in general, and religious life in particular. Slogans like "separatism" and "no compromise" and "secular humanist" became energizing slogans, and separatist fundamentalism soon found organizational expression. Fundamentalists created a viable infrastructure of schools, theological training centers, institutes, churches, and parachurch organizations. Fundamentalists tend to avoid new experiences by remaining isolated in their fundamentalist networks, thereby avoiding the various novel influences that flow into an emerging identity.

While detailed attention would take me too far afield from the historical sketch I am providing, the history of fundamentalist higher education is interesting and relevant and merits brief comment. As should be clear by now, higher education was not the forte of the separatist fundamentalists we are following in this early period. Yet, even in that era, fundamentalists founded Bob Jones University. Still operating, it is arguably the exemplar of separatist fundamentalist ideology. It has been billed as the "world's most unusual university," and its leaders gladly embraced the 1967 *McCall's* magazine award, based on a survey of college newspaper editors, for providing the "most square university." Founded in 1926 in Florida, and now located in Greenville, South Carolina, the institution has to date refused to seek formal accreditation, a move that usually spells doom for educational institutions. Bob Jones University sees accreditation as yielding to the worldly systems. In his introduction to a recent undergraduate catalogue, President Stephen Jones says,

> Standing firmly for and aggressively contending for the great foundations of the Christian faith, Bob Jones University is proud to be known as Fundamental in its position. We oppose all atheistic, agnostic, and humanistic attacks on Scripture.[1]

Every day, in chapel, students and professors recite the University Creed, which affirms major fundamentalist doctrines:

> I believe in the inspiration of the Bible (both the Old and the New Testaments); the creation of man by the direct act of God; the incarnation and virgin birth of our Lord and Savior, Jesus Christ; His identification as the Son of God; His vicarious atonement for the sins of mankind by the shedding of His blood on the cross; the resurrection of His body from the tomb; His power to save men from sin; the new birth through the regeneration by the Holy Spirit; and the gift of eternal life by the grace of God.[2]

I visited Bob Jones University in 2005. Visitors are allowed to tour the school grounds when assigned a student guide. My day visit confirmed what I knew about the school from accounts provided by historians of fundamentalism. The school requires acceptance of the fundamentalist doctrines, regulates the personal life of the students, and insists that all academic subjects worth teaching should be taught by fundamentalists from a fundamentalist viewpoint. One thing in particular caught my attention. During my day on the campus I had several conversations with students. In almost every case, at the point at which my comments began to reveal that I was not a fundamentalist, I noted a distinct shift from a warm and friendly disposition to a cool, professional courtesy that closed down any kind of dialogue. While this reluctance to engage with non-fundamentalists is certainly understandable, especially given that the school has endured so much criticism in recent years, the degree and quickness of this shift was, in my mind, remarkable. I say this in spite of the fact that I was well aware of the separatist mentality of old-style fundamentalism.

Many Bob Jones University graduates end up working in fundamentalist churches, Bible colleges, and Christian schools. For separatist fundamentalist institutions, there is no one better to hire than a person trained at Bob Jones University. In the summer of 1971, when I was still a fundamentalist, I studied for a summer academic term at the fundamentalist Free Will Baptist Bible College in Nashville, Tennessee. This particular Bible College is illustrative of dozens of such colleges around the country. Many of the faculty at this typical Bible College received one or more degrees at Bob Jones University. One of the courses in particular illustrates the separatist and dogmatic approach of old-fashioned fundamentalism. The course was on the doctrine of the Holy Spirit, but most of the class time consisted of the professor attacking "heretical" views of the Holy Spirit by non-fundamentalist groups. I should add that the other course, a study of the Dead Sea Scrolls, was, for the most part, a respectable, though conservative and cautious, study of the subject. Because the Dead Sea Scrolls derive from a Jewish desert community, and do not directly impact fundamentalist doctrine of the Bible or theology, it was much easier for the professor to follow the mainstream academic position than with some subjects. The campus tone and environment of the Free Will Baptist Bible College was reflective of what I saw on my day visit to Bob Jones University. Both were committed to the "be ye separate" philosophy, and there are plenty of rules at such institutions to ensure the students are not polluted by worldly ways.

Around the early 1940s, a group of young reformers began to question the separatist strategy of "mainstream" fundamentalism, igniting a major wave of political and cultural involvement. The National Association of Evangelicals was founded in 1942 and became an important coalition in the evangelical resurgence. Prominent names in this evangelical revival include Harold Ockenga, Edward Carnell, Carl Henry, Harold Lindsell, Charles Fuller, Gleason Archer, Everette Harrison, Bernard Ramm, and Billy Graham.

These revisionists believed strongly in evangelism and many of them worked hard and effectively to deliver the invitation to salvation through mass campaigns and "crusades." All fundamentalists believed in spreading the good news of Jesus Christ, but the old guard had put so much energy into doctrinal and ethical purity that it left little time and room for effective evangelistic efforts. These new guard evangelicals were so successful that they can be seen as carving out a place for themselves distinct from both liberalism and fundamentalism. A specific concern of many of these evangelicals was fighting alleged communist infiltration into the United States and her institutions. The involvement into the national life of politics and culture went far beyond this one issue, however.

The evangelical institutional expressions were effective and many of the creations are still with us. On the publication front, the magazine *Christianity Today* became evangelicalism's flagship journal, with the involvement of mass evangelist Billy Graham. It was followed by *Eternity, Christian Life, Christian Herald,* and the scholarly *Journal of the Evangelical Theological Society* (in which I have published, I'm sure to the surprise of many fundamentalists). Publishing houses flourished, including William B. Eerdmans, Zondervan, Inter-Varsity, Baker, Thomas Nelson, and Fleming H. Revell. Music production and recording companies also sprouted up.

A variety of youth ministries were established, including Youth for Christ, Campus Crusade for Christ, Young Life, Inter-Varsity Christian Fellowship, The Navigators, Teen Challenge, Fellowship of Christian Athletes, and World Vision, all of which are still active as far as I know. While evangelical and not explicitly fundamentalist, these organizations serve as theologically safe places for young people to move through the important developmental years. Most of these organizations hold, essentially, to central fundamentalist doctrines.

Billy Graham, more than any other person in the public eye, embodies the evangelistic spirit of evangelical Protestantism. Graham certainly holds key fundamentalist beliefs, but he is more accurately understood as an evangelical. In the late 1940s he began a series of crusades that stressed cooperation among willing churches. Fundamentalist churches sometimes cooperate with other non-fundamentalist churches, but usually only with other fundamentalist churches. Graham was widely criticized by fundamentalists for his cooperative efforts with "liberals." The evangelical participation in public life is perhaps most strikingly symbolized by Graham's access to the White House.[3] Consistent with their attempt to become socially and politically involved and make an impact in the world, many of these evangelical reformers around mid-century felt that efforts should be made to make the true faith academically respectable. In 1947 Charles E. Fuller worked to promote this agenda through his fundamentalist radio program. He was a founder of Fuller Theological Seminary in Pasadena, California, which boasted star evangelical academics among its first faculty. This institution was followed by a host of others, at the undergraduate and graduate level, and many are still thriving. At the graduate level they include Gordon-Conwell Theological Seminary, Trinity Evangelical Divinity School, Calvin Theological Seminary, and Asbury Theological Seminary. At the undergraduate level they include Gordon College, Westmont College, Calvin College, Bethel College, Azusa Pacific University, and Wheaton College.

Various evangelical scholars have attempted to maintain conservative positions on the Bible and other issues, while working with methods accepted by mainstream academics. George E. Ladd is an example of a biblical scholar who worked very hard, though with mixed results at best, to produce biblical scholarship that would be accepted by non-evangelical scholars. The attempt to marry fundamentalist doctrine of the inerrancy of the Bible with critical scholarly method was not always a happy one. The 1982 publication of Robert Gundry's commentary on Matthew is an example of a conservative who, in the minds of hard-core fundamentalists, went too far and fell into modernist heresy. A few details of this controversy will illustrate the point and anticipate my more involved discussion of the Bible later.

Redaction criticism is a scholarly method of studying the gospels that uncovers how and why the author chose and modified materials available to him in the tradition. Drawing upon the insights of mainstream academic redaction critics, Gundry took the position that redacted (i.e., edited) sections of the gospel were Matthew's divinely inspired contributions to the meaning of Jesus's ministry. In this way he accommodated critical study but maintained, at least in his mind, the inerrancy of the Bible. Gundry was a member of the Evangelical Theological Society, which required of its members a belief in inerrancy. A "heresy trial" was conducted at one of the Society meetings and Gundry was eventually asked to resign.[4]

The above-mentioned schools and scholars are evangelical. Turning to higher education in the fundamentalist camp, I have noted earlier the fundamentalist Bob Jones University, which has for most of the life of the movement exemplified separatist, uncompromising fundamentalism. It has been argued that fundamentalist higher education has evolved a new face that now exists alongside the old-style separatist approach of Bob Jones University. The new approach is exampled at Jerry Falwell's Liberty University and M. G. "Pat" Robertson's Regent University. The new face of these and other fundamentalist schools is that many of them pursue academic quality and dialogue with mainstream scholarship. Faculty at such institutions usually have to sign fundamentalist doctrinal statements, but as long as they adhere to these fundamentals they can pursue activities within mainstream academic routes.[5]

The new fundamentalist approach to higher education carries with it two quite different possibilities. First, and perhaps initially, the new model will likely have more of an impact on society and its intellectual life than the separatist approach of its forebares like Bob Jones University, which, only indirectly through its graduates, has had much of an impact. In academic circles, Bob Jones University is usually dismissed as an indoctrination center that has little to do with education. The new fundamentalist schools allow their faculty and students to participate in the larger society, without compromising the fundamentalist principles, so that they can influence that society. The new schools are well organized and better financed, often in association with some television ministry. Both Falwell's Liberty University and Robertson's Regent University are closely associated with the television ministries of the founders. The same was true for Oral Roberts University, founded by longtime evangelist and faith healer Oral Roberts. These broadcast-related schools follow in the path laid out by the early success of Fuller Theological Seminary, founded by radio evangelist Charles Fuller.

The "downside" of fundamentalist higher education participating in the larger intellectual and societal context is that the schools will themselves be changed. Hiring faculty with degrees from mainline schools (unlike the intellectually incestuous Bob Jones University), seeking academic prestige by encouraging faculty to develop a professional life in the standard scholarly contexts, and allowing students to engage mainstream ideas will likely take its toll on the doctrinal and ethical purity of the fundamentalist schools.

I can illustrate this point by reporting an encounter I had with a student of Falwell's Liberty University. I visited the campus of Liberty University about 20 years ago and was surprised even then at the liberal ideas and practices of some of the students who, when they put their guard down, admitted they were not fundamentalists. I distinctly recall, in particular, a conversation with a young man who revealed to me that he was gay. I am sure he felt safe to reveal this information because I told him straight out that I was a professor at a secular university and was studying fundamentalism as a historical phenomenon. I asked why he was attending Liberty University, where homosexuality is not embraced. He replied that it was really a quite simple matter. Liberty University was one of the best places in the state to study the particular music field in which he was interested. He said there were other gay students at Liberty and emphasized that they kept their sexual orientation a secret at school. He considered it an acceptable trade-off—four years of secrecy for a quality degree in music.

The new fundamentalist schools, engaging with mainline educational systems in order to change society, are an integral part of another wave of conservative Christian activism that emerged prominently in the Ronald Reagan 1980s and continues today. One of the reasons these current efforts have been successful is that a broad coalition, which moved beyond the confines of fundamentalism and even evangelicalism, organized around common interests in particular moral issues. It is important to realize that the old style fundamentalism, best exemplified by Bob Jones University, continues its separatist ways and has not participated in the politically connected movement with other socially active branches of the "religious right." However, the majority of today's fundamentalists have worked and do work, in varying degrees, with non-fundamentalist groups on a common moral and social agenda to "take back" America for God. The most visible organization during the 1980s was the Moral Majority, an organization associated with Rev. Jerry Falwell. Rev. Falwell's goal was to bring fundamentalists into political life and impact elections. The Moral Majority strongly supported Ronald Reagan and so came into prominence along with the conservative Republican political movement in the 1980s. Bob Jones University, always the model of strict separatism, faulted Falwell's program because its pragmatic approach allowed for cooperation with all sorts of "infidels," including Jews and Catholics.[6]

The issues of the religious right are many but almost always include evolution, homosexuality, the role of women, prayer in the schools, abortion, and more recently, stem cell research. This most current wave of activism that began around the 1980s is different from previous waves in that there is a more intense, organized, and successful attempt to directly influence the political structures of the executive, judicial, and legislative branches of government by pressuring government officials and electing candidates who support the "morals and values" agenda. The final chapter has not been written on how successful this phase of right-wing religious activism will be.

One final aspect of the evangelical-fundamentalist story merits discussion. The "electronic" revival that began in earnest in the 1970s contributed to the success of the religious right and its moral and political agenda. A 1979 national Gallup poll said there were 1,300 evangelical radio and television stations that reached 130 million fundamentalists and fundamentalist-leaning Christians. This latest version of the old-time revivals elevated television ministers like Oral Roberts, Jimmy Swaggart, Jim Bakker, Paul Crouch, Pat Robertson (who has his own network and ran for president), and, of course, Jerry Falwell. These television and radio preachers, and dozens more, had or have huge budgets. While funding ministries is a legitimate activity, with some of the ministers the message of Jesus has degenerated into a "prosperity gospel," whereby naïve parishioners are promised material blessings or physical healing if they send contributions. The several well-publicized sex and money scandals of some of the preachers, amazingly, seem not to have seriously compromised the role and influence of the electronic church.

A good current example of the evangelical/fundamentalist success in the electronic realm is the radio empire of Salem Communications, the second-fastest-growing radio chain in America. The company owns 103 stations in some of the largest markets and broadcasts to nearly 2,000 affiliates. Stuart Epperson and Edward Atsinger, III, founded the company 30 years ago. Epperson is a graduate of Bob Jones University and both Epperson and Atsinger are major contributors to right-wing politicians and causes, such as banning gay marriage.[7]

Although the extensive use of television by evangelists is now several decades old, we probably are yet to discern the subtle, but significant, impact on the religion of partially moving the Christian experience from the traditional community church building to the individual's living room. Also, I suspect that scholars do not fully appreciate the influence of conservative Christian networks and programming. My guess is that many more people than the experts know are gaining their principle understanding of world events, not to mention their theology, from the news they get from the Christian "reporters" on the Christian stations.

CHARISMATIC AND PENTECOSTAL FUNDAMENTALISTS

Up to this point, I have not written about the difference between fundamentalists who "speak in tongues" and those who do not. For the sake of accuracy, it is important to draw this distinction. I have not done so up to this point because, for my purposes, the difference is not as important as understanding the psychological and historical commonalities between the "charismatics" and the "pure" fundamentalists. It is an intriguing slice of the fundamentalist story. In the history of fundamentalism that I have presented, Pat Robertson and Oral Roberts are examples of fundamentalist charismatic Christians. I am using "charismatic" here not in the secular sense of an engaging personality, but rather in referring to Christians who practice speaking in tongues.

"Speaking in tongues" or "speaking in unknown tongues," or *glossolalia* (from two Greek words, *glossa*=tongue and *lalein*=to speak), refers to an ecstatic type of religious expression in which the practitioner utters a "language" that is nonsensical to others. Actually, the phenomenon has been documented in religions outside Christianity. Christian practitioners have explained this language in at least a couple of ways: as a "heavenly" language that is known only to God or as the special spirit-inspired ability to speak real languages that the person has never studied. There are, as one might expect, many biblical and theological nuances, but the main point is that some fundamentalist Christians speak in tongues and some do not. Both camps hold to fundamentalist doctrines but think the other camp is deficient in their understanding and practice of the faith. As I pointed out in my account of the Bible College I attended one summer, "pure" fundamentalist condemnation of the charismatics can be rather severe.

The charismatics tend to have more of an ecumenical bent than the pure fundamentalists, in that the ecstatic experience has a way of bringing together Christians of otherwise disparate orientations. For example, a charismatic (i.e., tongue talking) parachurch group, such as the Full Gospel Business Men's Fellowship, might include persons who are members of various Protestant denominations, as well as Catholic churches. In addition to the parachurch organizations, there are Protestant denominations where the tongue-talking experience is considered central. Such denominations often include the word "Pentecostal" in their name. In the New Testament book of Acts, Pentecost was the Jewish festival where Christians first experienced the speaking in tongues phenomenon, as a result of the indwelling work of the Holy Spirit.

While it may seem unfair to discuss the topic of snake-handling and poison-drinking under the headings of "charismatic" or "Pentecostal," a case can be made that this is the most appropriate way to understand the tradition. In any case, it should be understood that while all snake-handling and poison-drinking sects speak in tongues, as far as I know, not all tongue-talking groups engage in these dangerous practices. The snake and poison groups are actually rather small, located for the most part in Appalachia, a region in the Southern highlands. Snake and poison practices derive from Mark 16:17–18, which reads,

> And these signs will accompany those who believe: by using my name they will cast out demons; they will speak in new tongues; they will pick up snakes in their hands, and if they drink any deadly thing, it will not hurt them; they will lay their hands on the sick, and they will recover.

The strange practice of handling snakes as an expression of Christian religiosity and faith began in 1909 with George Hensley, of Grasshopper, Tennessee. Hensley was a member of the Church of God denomination that later, in 1922, decided to no longer sanction the practice. In these snake-handling churches, the snakes are usually kept in wooden boxes and taken out at an emotional high point in the service, or when the preacher or lay handler feels "anointed." The snakes are wrapped around the head, placed inside an unbuttoned shirt, rubbed over the face, and sometimes tossed to willing fellow worshippers. The snakes, by the way, are indeed venomous and potentially deadly. Rattlesnakes and copperheads are common. There are about 80 documented deaths due to this practice, including Hensley, who died from a bite in 1955. The occasional deaths are seen to have a silver lining for the snake-handling sects, in that it proves to the skeptics that, indeed, poisonous serpents are being used. Snake-handlers disagree as to whether or not emergency medical services should be used in case of a bite. All agree that being bitten means that the worshipper's faith "wavered." The American Civil Liberties Union has gone on record, based on the First Amendment freedom of religion clause, defending against governmental attempts to outlaw the practice. It is much less common, but some snake-handlers also follow the biblical reference to drinking poison. Usually strychnine or lye is used.[8]

As a New Testament scholar, I have to get one point out of the way, even though in the scheme of things I suppose it is not that important. At the very least, however, given that there are Christians in Appalachia who orient their whole religious life around handling snakes and drinking poison, it is an extremely interesting point. The point is that the verses on which the practices are based are not found in the Bible. Yes, you read this correctly, these verses are not found in the Bible. I can give the short version of what I mean by this now; the more detailed explanation of the larger issue will come in Part Two of the book.

Here is the short version. We do not have the original manuscripts of any book of the Bible. What happened before the original Gospel of Mark, for example, was lost is that copies were made of it, and copies were made of the copies, and so on. What we have located are the later copies. So, the earlier the copies, the more likely they provide an accurate reading of what was in the lost original. Almost every verse of the Bible has some question about it in terms of what, exactly, the original manuscript contained. There are, however, two places in the New Testament where there is a substantial part of the text that is found only in later, and therefore unreliable, manuscripts. One of them is the snake-handling and poison-drinking passage which, given our best textual evidence in the oldest manuscripts, was not in the original manuscript of Mark, the one written by the author of that gospel. More specifically, in some of the later and unreliable manuscript copies, we have the so-called longer ending of Mark found in the version included in the New Testament; this extended passage, Mark 16:9–20, contains the snake and poison references. A likely possibility is that later copyists added an ending because the original version seemed to come to a conclusion abruptly. In fact, in the oldest and best manuscripts the Gospel of Mark ends with the preposition "for" (Greek *gar*), not something we would expect. In any case, I find it interesting, ironic, and even humorous, if it were not so sad, that the explicit scriptural basis for the central practices of the snake-handlers and poison-drinkers is, in this sense, not in the Bible.

RECONSTRUCTIONISTS AND THEIR PLAN FOR AMERICA

Given that we have just discussed the increasing involvement in the political domain by fundamentalists, it is a good place to make note of the Reconstructionists. The Reconstructionist movement is, I suppose, not strictly fundamentalist in that it does not hold to all the doctrines I discuss in the next part of the book. Specifically, it does not embrace premillennial dispensationalism because this futuristic program encourages Christians to hang on until God comes and takes them away from the evil world. Reconstructionists are interested not in escaping society, but in taking it over. So it differs from traditional fundamentalism on this important point of end-time views. However, the Reconstructionist movement is certainly in the fundamentalist "family" and, because the implications of this movement are enormous, it is worth much more attention than it is getting.

Reconstructionists want to restore Christian civilization and work toward controlling the established political and governmental structures so that restoration can occur. The principle of separation of church and state is anathema because this long-standing American doctrine stands in the way of establishing the Christian system. My guess is that most fundamentalists are "reconstructionist" in their general outlook. However, Reconstructionists with a capital "R" are part of a defined movement with a well-considered ideology, clear goals, specific strategies, a viable organizational structure, and prospects for significant impact.[9]

Rousas John Rushdoony, who died in 2001, was the founder of Reconstruction and the author of the 1973 800-plus page *Institutes of Biblical Law.* The movement he founded heavily influences the conservative Presbyterian Church in America, definitely not to be confused with the moderate to liberal Presbyterian Church USA. Many

Southern Baptists, whose denominational machinery and theological seminaries are now controlled by fundamentalists, also lean toward Reconstruction theology and ideology. George W. Bush has called Marvin Olasky, strongly influenced by Reconstruction and a key adviser for the creation of Bush's Office of Faith-Based and Community Initiatives, "compassionate conservatism's leading thinker." Reconstructionist Jack Hayford, well known in the conservative Promise Keepers group, gave the benediction at Bush's first inaugural.[10]

Reconstructionists have an active plan to establish the Kingdom of God on earth, which in practical terms means imposing the Mosaic (i.e., Old Testament) law as the basis for society's laws. Every aspect of life will be ruled according to the approximately 600 Mosaic laws. Their "dominion theology" teaches that true Christians must rule over nonbelievers in a society constituted around God's law. Only after this Kingdom of God has been on earth for 1,000 years (the millennium) will Jesus return in the second coming. Conservative Christians who take the name Reconstructionist range from those who work nonviolently in the established political process to those who are associated with militant and racially motivated agendas. Because they are more thoughtful, better financed, and eager to mainstream their ideas, the Reconstructionists who operate nonviolently inside the political process are more likely to achieve their goals.

Whether this movement will be able to thrust its agenda on the nation or not is uncertain at this point. However, it if does, the implications are incredible. One only has to consider that according to the Mosaic law, persons who engage in the following activities would be executed: rape, murder, adultery (women only), lying about one's virginity (women only), incest, witchcraft, homosexuality, blasphemy, marriage without an intact hymen, and talking back to parents. Unemployment benefits, Social Security, and environmental protection laws would cease to exist. Reconstructionists work hard to promote home schooling because they believe that government should not be involved in public education. Most people have not even heard of this group. However, the scary possibility exists that a few decades from now America will be a quite different country with regard to the official role of religion in our public life. If that occurs, historians will likely look back and assess the Reconstructionists as playing a key role.

In researching and writing this book, one of the most alarming bits of information I found has to do with the work of the National Council on Bible Curriculum in Public Schools. This organization is successfully placing its curriculum, based on the Council's textbook, *The Bible in History and Literature* ($150, discounted to $120 if more than five are ordered), into public school classrooms. I do not know if there is formal or informal cooperation between Reconstructionists and this Council, but the continued success of the Council would certainly move the Reconstructionist agenda significantly forward. At least two prominent Christian Reconstructionists, Rus Walton and Howard Phillips, have served on one of the Council's boards. As a biblical scholar, I am appalled at the misinformation about the Bible being disseminated; as a taxpayer I am incensed that my tax dollars would be used to promote a far-right view of the Bible to students in public schools; and as an American citizen I am nervous about the threat to freedom and democracy entailed in the Council's work.

According to the Council's Web site,[11] 312 school boards in 37 states have approved the curriculum, now being used in over 1,000 schools. Ninety-two percent of school boards approached with this curriculum approve it for use in their schools. The Council's Web site claims that 175,000 students have taken the course. The Council's Board of Directors and Advisory Board consists of prominent religious and political conservatives and activists, including two U.S. representatives and fundamentalist preachers like James Kennedy, Charles Stanley, and Joyce Meyer.

The U.S. Supreme Court has properly ruled that teaching the Bible in public schools in a nonsectarian manner is legal and appropriate. I get paid by the taxpayers of North Carolina to teach courses about the Bible in a public university. The Bible unquestionably has played a significant role in the history of Western civilization, including the United States, and as such it most certainly should be studied. The crucial word, however, is "nonsectarian." To teach a course on the Bible in the public schools in a way that promotes a particular narrow theological agenda is both illegal and dangerous. The Council's curriculum is, without question, sectarian. It is, essentially, a fundamentalist presentation of the Bible.

An excellent, short analysis and critique of the Council's curriculum is provided by Southern Methodist University biblical scholar Mark A. Chancey. He points out numerous features of the curriculum as examples of its sectarian orientation. Jesus is presented as fulfilling Old Testament "prophecy," archaeological findings are cited as evidence of the Bible's complete historical accuracy, the Genesis flood story is assumed to be literal, and miracle stories are accepted uncritically. For resources, the curriculum refers teachers to various fundamentalist-type organizations, such as the Creation Evidence Museum in Glen Rose, Texas, where one can learn that creation occurred in six days, the world is 6,000 years old, and humans and dinosaurs coexisted. While much in the curriculum simply reflects a narrow, fundamentalist view, Chancey points out some outright mistakes. The curriculum states that fragments of New Testament books were found among the Dead Sea Scrolls, that the Scrolls make reference to Jesus, and that some of the Jews at Qumran, where the Scrolls were found, accepted Jesus as Messiah. Study questions given to students include "Describe the impact of this discovery on those who do not accept the authenticity of the Bible," and "Determine the evidence from the Dead Sea Scrolls confirming the claims of Jesus as the Bible describes him." Chancey documents how the curriculum is designed to persuade students that America is a Christian nation.[12] The Council's Web site has a page entitled "Founding Fathers" that begins with "The Bible was the foundation and blueprint for our Constitution, Declaration of Independence, our educational system, and our entire history until the last 20 to 30 years."

Of course, because the Council's curriculum has to be approved by school boards, much of the language in the curriculum is carefully constructed to sound legitimate, and the Web site makes statements like this: "The program is concerned with education rather than indoctrination." All this is similar to the "intelligent design" language being used to sneak the old biblical creationism into science classrooms.

With the historical framework in place, we can now turn to Part Two where we consider the core beliefs that emerged out of the fundamentalist movement. The historical and theological stories will set the context for our investigation in Part Three into the psychology of the typical fundamentalist Christian.

PART TWO

Core Fundamentalist Beliefs

CHAPTER 4

Fundamentalists and the Bible

FUNDAMENTALISTS AS RIGHT-WING RELIGIONISTS

Occasionally, a hardened and belligerent fundamentalist will show up in my classes eager to "do battle royal for the fundamentals." Daniel always sat in a front seat, and always directly in front of the podium. Making sure I was looking, he always with a flourish placed his big, black leather covered King James Bible on the corner of his desk as he sat down for class. Daniel was actually more militant than most fundamentalists. He was also more ignorant of the Bible than most fundamentalists. The literacy of many Americans about the content of the book that has played such a role in Western culture is appallingly low. When Daniel walked into class on the first day, I was actually glad to have him, because I figured that he would at least bring to the course more knowledge of Bible content than most students do. Early in the course, in an effort to connect with Daniel, I asked him to read a passage from the Gospel of Matthew. Even I was embarrassed for Daniel when he could not locate this gospel, which is the first book in the New Testament. I repeat that Daniel turned out to be much less knowledgeable about the books and stories of the Bible than most fundamentalists. However, his story illustrates what I think is a serious deficit with the typical fundamentalist. They boldly hold the Bible forth as the sole source of authority and truth, and yet they are often woefully ignorant of basic facts about the Bible, including sometimes the content of what one would think would be the most familiar stories.

Fundamentalists like Daniel place the Protestant Bible at the center of their theology and life. It is a "source of life's meaning and purpose," "provides moral certainty and stability," and "provides fundamentalists with a worldview that allows comprehensibility and manageability to an otherwise fragmented existence."[1] Unfortunately, the typical fundamentalist is woefully ignorant of some of the basic facts about how their Bible was constructed and transmitted—how it moves from the ancient authors to the English translations carried proudly into the Sunday morning worship service.

I am advocating for a healthy and productive approach to interpreting the Bible. Ironically, the fundamentalist program of biblical interpretation usually imposes on the Bible expectations drawn from the modern world that ultimately disrespect the text. I have spent much of my adult life acquiring the necessary tools and engaging in disciplined study in order to better understand this old text that has played such a role in Western culture. What ultimately is the saddest for me is that the endless arguments over the Bible keep people from appreciating the riches it has to offer.

As we have seen, fundamentalism is a movement within Christianity that has an identifiable origin and development. As with related movements around the world, and consistent with the Marty and Appleby definition I quoted in the introduction,[2] American fundamentalism is best understood as a militant reaction against modernity. It arose during a time of intellectual ferment and cultural and social change in this country; fundamentalism would not exist without these developments. The American Christian version of fundamentalism is best understood against the background of the revivals conducted by traveling preachers, especially the Second Great Awakening. The psychological profile in Part Three will explain how the historical and cultural forces find expression in a typical fundamentalist Christian in this country. The fundamentalist theological system, to which we now turn, is the ideological expression of the history we have provided and the psychology to be examined later.

The Bible is the center of the fundamentalist theological system. The theological story of fundamentalism emerges from the various conferences, publications, and doctrinal battles described in the previous part of the book. In those chapters, we set the fundamentalist movement in its historical context. As with the historical story, I want to view fundamentalist doctrine in a larger theological context.

While labels are often libels, doing more harm than good, sometimes labels and broad generalizations can be useful in beginning to understand a movement that is ideologically based. Before looking closely and specifically at the fundamentalist belief system, I want first to place it in the larger and more general right-wing/left-wing context. "Right" and "left" are terms that can characterize political as well as religious orientations; my concern here is primarily with the religious. In general, by "right-wing" I mean conservative religion, and by "left-wing" I mean moderate and liberal religion. The bias of some might have them read "conservative=Christian" and "liberal=non-Christian," but one of my main points is that fundamentalism is only one of many versions of Christianity. In light of the long history and reach of this religion, fundamentalism is a small minority version at that. So, all the descriptions in the table below, both conservative and liberal, describe viewpoints of people who are legitimately regarded as Christians in the world today.[3]

Before stepping into the theological world of the fundamentalist, one qualification is in order. Fundamentalists do not agree with each other on all points of theology. By its very nature, fundamentalism is absolutist in its outlook, and this has led to many splits and factions within the movement. There are, for example, wings of the movement that are quite Calvinistic, that is, emphasizing the sovereignty of God and predestination and minimizing human free will. Another wing, however, is strongly Arminian, emphasizing human free will.

While there are theological differences among fundamentalist groups, individual fundamentalists within each group or church tend toward a common set of beliefs. This tendency is best explained by the research on authoritarianism to be discussed in Part Three, the psychological section of this book. So, while there are differences, fundamentalism, more

	Conservative	**Liberal**
The Divine	Theocentric (God-centered), low view of human beings as sinful and weak.	Anthropocentric (human centered), higher value placed on human ability given by God, optimistic about human capability, God works through the created order.
The World	Otherworldly, emphasizing the reality and importance of the realm above and beyond the natural, such as heaven, hell, and the afterlife.	This-worldly, emphasizing the here and now, more occupied with the immediate, present problems, rather than with the future spiritual destiny of human beings.
Revelation	Religious truth comes from God through some special communication, such as sacred writings (fundamentalist), institutions and traditions (Roman Catholic), or personal religious experience (Pentecostal/charismatic traditions).	While traditions and texts are important, truth in them is appropriated and discerned by the God-given rational ability of human beings.

than any other brand of Christianity, is marked by a common allegiance to a core set of beliefs. All fundamentalists, most evangelicals, and most other conservative Christians profess the five fundamentalist beliefs I will now discuss. Fundamentalists in other religions have comparable beliefs about scripture and other core doctrines.

All elements of the basic fundamentalist doctrinal system fit the definition of fundamentalism given by Marty and Appleby that I quoted in the introduction.[4] Using Marty and Appleby's terminology, the doctrines I discuss are either "selectively retrieved" from the Christian past, revised and modified, or "unprecedented claims and doctrinal innovations."

INSPIRATION OF THE BIBLE

All of the other doctrinal "fundamentals" I will discuss are derived from the fundamentalist reading of the Bible. In one sense, the fundamentalist system lives or dies on the fundamentalist view of the nature of the Bible. So, a relatively careful explanation and critique of the fundamentalist view of the Bible is in order.

To say that the Bible is inspired is a rather common assertion by Christians. The fundamentalists, however, assert the plenary, verbal, and inerrant inspiration of the Bible. These three adjectives—plenary, verbal, inerrant—give the fundamentalist position on inspiration a quite specific and, I will show, extreme and indefensible formulation.

"Plenary" simply means full or complete and is used in the fundamentalist lexicon in different ways.[5] It has been used to mean that every word in the 66 books of the Protestant Bible is inspired. Now, to be sure, fundamentalists, like all Christians, have a "canon within the canon," that is, sections of the Bible that support their positions and are used much more than other sections of the Bible. While the fundamentalist locates revelation and authority in the Bible, moderates and liberals tend to locate revelation in God. For a more liberal view, the question becomes, Through what texts has God revealed truth? The liberal will be more open to considering the revelation of God wherever it occurs, rather than limiting it to the Bible. While it is an extreme and unlikely example, to make my point I could say that in an extremely liberal view there is a sense in which one can be reading a telephone book and if God is ready and you are ready, revelation will occur. For the fundamentalist, the Bible itself has a special status that transcends other sources of truth and inspiration.

The adjective "verbal" refers to the actual words of the text. Fundamentalists do not believe the ideas or the writers are ultimately what is inspired, but rather the actual words of the text. Moreover, they believe that every word of the text is inspired. It is here that the fundamentalist bumps into a serious problem in his or her theology. The problem is that we do not have the original words of the various books of the Bible. We call the original manuscripts "autographs." To our knowledge, all of the autographs of the Bible long ago disintegrated in the hot sands of that ancient land. The books of the Bible were written on papyri, a material not designed to last through the centuries. So, the fundamentalist position is that the only and absolute source of truth is the very words of the Bible, but these very words exist only in books that have not survived from the ancient period. The typical fundamentalist is unaware of these issues, thinking something not far from the notion that God delivered the Bible from heaven directly into the hands of the church.

However, for fundamentalists, there are two damaging, and I think fatal, problems with their view. First, the fact that the manuscripts contain differences leaves the fundamentalist with a Bible based on manuscripts that contradict one another. As pointed out above, knowledgeable fundamentalist scholars are aware of this issue and the usual claim is that what is inerrant is the autograph of a book, not the later copies. The second issue, however, is that a claim that only the autographs are inerrantly inspired by God, and not the copies resulting from the scribal copying process, paints the fundamentalist into a corner. The ironic effect of such a view is that the fundamentalist is left with no authority because, as all knowledgeable people understand, we have only later copies. Some fundamentalist thinkers attempt to get out of this problem by suggesting that God in some general way has ensured that the manuscript transmission process is fundamentally trustworthy. It may be true that the transmission process is essentially sound, but it does not successfully address the problems raised by the extreme position of the inerrantists.

Informed fundamentalists, of course, are well aware of these difficulties. They address them in two ways. First, as noted, they argue that God's hand was at work protecting the scribal process of copying the text through the centuries. Second, scholars of a conservative theological persuasion have been active in the science of textual criticism. Textual criticism is a specialized branch of biblical scholarship charged with analyzing the various copies we have of a Bible text, in an effort to determine the most likely reading in the autograph. Fundamentalist apologists argue, rightly, that we can be fairly certain that what we read in the reconstructed text is pretty close to what was written by the author. While that is correct, and presents no problem to a moderate or liberal position, the extreme fundamentalist position on this issue is logically indefensible, because their view of authority rests on the assertion that every single word of the Bible is inspired.

The moderate and liberal positions on inspiration move away from the emphasis on the exact wording of the Bible. One might find a moderate or liberal saying that the ideas in the Bible are inspired and those ideas can be communicated in different words. Or, they may say that the writer of the Bible book is inspired, and the product of his inspiration can take different verbal forms. This view is more consistent with what is actually found in the Bible, because it is clear that the personality and experience of the individual biblical writers shine through in the various books. A trained eye will readily recognize Luke's version of the Christ event, as opposed to Mark, Matthew, or John's version.

Finally, there is the notion of inerrancy. If there is one pivotal word on which fundamentalists hang their whole program, it would be inerrancy. The theological, historical, and, as I will show, psychological weight and significance attached to this one word is truly astounding. Again, as with plenary and verbal, the fundamentalist has a particular and extreme notion of inerrancy. For the fundamentalist the Bible is without error not only in terms of what it says about religious faith and practice, but also in terms of science and history. This extreme position is what underlies the fundamentalists' hostility towards modern developments in science and scholarship. One simply cannot blindly accept literally all the notions found in an ancient and prescientitic book, and be open to modern developments in science and history. But that is the fundamentalist agenda.

The more moderate and liberal perspective on inerrancy is that the Bible provides Christians with a sound and authoritative guide to faith and practice. The Bible contains the profound reflections of a people who were responding to their sense of God's presence. However, the Bible is not a science or history book and so when it speaks on those matters, it is not to be held to the same standards as books written by modern scientists and historians.

The fundamentalist notion of inerrancy plunges the fundamentalist into a tortured program of trying to explain all the perceived discrepancies in the text. It would seem to be so easy to back off of the extreme position of the literal inerrancy of every word of the text. Fundamentalists might then be able to enjoy the inspiring message of the text more, rather than having to always defend it, but that is not possible with the fundamentalist position. Looking at it purely from the theological angle, it would seem possible. However, I will show that fundamentalism cannot be understood from only the theological angle of vision. The psychological issues are such that the fundamentalist extreme view of inerrancy is almost a necessary doctrinal piece.

The fundamentalist argument is simple and logically circular. The Bible is inspired because the Bible itself says so. In this simple statement of the fundamentalist view, no particular definition of inspiration is given. Most fundamentalists, however, when they make a claim to inspiration assume (even if they do not have access to the terms) plenary, verbal, and inerrant inspiration. Fundamentalists claim several passages support their view of inspiration, but two are quoted most often. Given the critical importance of this doctrinal point, careful attention to the verses is in order. The most important one is 2 Timothy 3:16, which reads in translation, "All scripture is inspired by God and is useful for teaching, for reproof, for correction, and for training in righteousness." (All quotations from the Bible are from the *New Revised Standard Version*, unless otherwise noted.)

Clearly, this verse cannot support the fundamentalist ideology of inspiration, with the strong and specific adjectives plenary, verbal, and inerrant. There are several problems and it does not take an expert in biblical Greek or the New Testament to understand them. First, this keystone verse is, obviously, found in one particular book of the New Testament. Taking the conservative view, the book of 2 Timothy was written by Paul around the middle of the first century. There is absolutely no evidence that by "scripture" the author meant the 66 books of the Protestant Bible that the fundamentalists claim as inspired, and only these as inspired. Two considerations are relevant here. First, some of the books that fundamentalists claim as inspired were not even written when fundamentalists say the author of 2 Timothy penned his words. This would include the four gospels, Revelation, and other books, all written in the second half of the first century. Second, it was not until centuries later that the Christian church came to some consensus about which books were to be "in the Bible." So, even the books that were in existence at the time 2 Timothy was composed were not at that time ordered into a collection recognized as scripture by the community of faith. To complicate matters for the fundamentalist, the authors of the inspired 66 books sometimes quote non-biblical books, as in the case of Jude 14, which quotes the apocryphal book of 1 Enoch 1:9. The fundamentalist does not include 1 Enoch in the list of inspired books, but why not? It was quoted by an inspired writer. The problems surrounding which books 2 Timothy 3:16 refers to are such that attributing the fundamentalist notion of inspiration to this verse is ludicrous.

Fundamentalists make a lot over the word "inspired" (Greek *theopneustos*), for which the most literal translation is "God-breathed." The literal meaning does evoke a powerful and beautiful image. However, it does not by any stretch of the imagination, or a plain reading, yield a plenary, verbal, and inerrant text.

Finally, taking the verse literally and exactly, which is what the fundamentalist always wants us to do, the scripture (whatever books are being referred to) that is inspired (whatever that means) is to be used for "teaching," "reproof," "correction," and "righteousness training." If I understand things, this is pretty much the moderate and liberal position on inspiration. Moderate and liberal Christians usually state that the Bible can be trusted when it speaks on matters of faith and practice, but not necessarily science and history. So, to make the point clear, 2 Timothy 3:16 does *not* say that scripture is to be used as science and history.

The second verse often used to support fundamentalist inspiration is 2 Peter 1:21, which reads: "No prophecy ever came by human will, but men and women moved by the Holy Spirit spoke from God." Again, taking the conservative view, this book was written shortly before the apostle Peter's martyrdom in Rome in 64/65 CE. Are fundamentalists saying that Peter is referring to books in existence at that time? The gospels were not yet written, along with a number of other books that are now in the New Testament. Or, is the author talking also about books to be written, and if so, what are the limits of his reference? The problems are just too numerous to take seriously that this verse means anything like what the fundamentalists want it to mean.

For the sake of argument, let us grant the fundamentalist view that 2 Timothy 3:16 and 2 Peter 1:21 make the claim for fundamentalist inspiration for the 66 books of the Protestant Bible. So, to reiterate the fundamentalist view, the Bible is inspired because it says it is. Sometimes the fundamentalist will turn to some usually vague defense of inerrant inspiration by referring to the accuracy of biblical predictions. Usually, however, the claim will be a simple, circular argument.

Many fundamentalists, when it comes to matters of their religious faith, are deficient in applying the most basic elements of logical thought. I do think the psychology of their faith commitment blinds them to discrepancies in their positions. I sometimes become exasperated in conversations with fundamentalists about their circular logic on the issue of inspiration. On one occasion, to make the point about circular reasoning, I wrote on a piece of paper the following statement: "Whatever Calvin Mercer says is inspired and without error in every way." On another occasion, I think I wrote something like: "This statement is God's true and final word: the Bible has been superseded by whatever Mercer says." In both cases I gave the paper to the fundamentalist and pointed out that to believe what the piece of paper says simply because it says it is as ridiculous as basing inerrant inspiration of the Bible on something the Bible says. At this point both my fundamentalist conversation partners saw the light, but they quickly retreated to some other justification. Of course, as I later point out in the psychological profile of the typical fundamentalist, larger issues are at stake than the mere use of circular logic on this theological point.

With regard to the circular nature of the claim for inerrancy, James Barr suggests the argument is meant to be this way. "It forms a tight circle into which the outsider can break only by totally abandoning his objections and accepting in entirety the world-view of those within."[6] I think Barr gets to the heart of the matter. The core fundamentalist theological ideas constitute a "circle the wagons" kind of mentality. No one point of the "fundamentals" can or will be sacrificed, or the whole house of cards will come tumbling down, along with the Christian identity of the fundamentalist, who would then be destined for the burning hell.

With regard to the claim to inerrancy, many fundamentalists will make the mistake of thinking that inerrancy requires specific fundamentalist interpretations of the Bible. The point that can often be made with fundamentalists is that a particular passage, even if inspired and even if inerrant, can be interpreted different ways.

CHAPTER 5

Problems with Fundamentalism's View of the Bible

HARMONIZATION

Strict adherence to inerrancy requires the fundamentalist to solve apparent discrepancies in the Bible. Such a requirement leads to a massive program of harmonizing passages that seem to contradict each other. Professional exegetes who hold fundamentalist views on inerrancy are well aware of the extent of harmonization necessary to fulfill an inerrancy claim and they spill much ink to accomplish this. I give just a few examples below to illustrate. It may seem cruel to bring these discrepancies to the attention of fundamentalists, but it is their doctrine of inerrant inspiration that creates the problems and it is appropriate to have them see the issues involved.

In some situations, the harmonization approach can work even though it yields a result that is forced and improbable. Other discrepancies present greater challenges for the fundamentalist. Was Jesus crucified four times? We have four accounts of the crucifixion in the gospels and all are slightly different. Was Paul converted three times? We have three accounts of his conversion in the Bible and all are slightly different. Slight differences are not an issue for most Christian readers, but fundamentalists believe the Bible is without error and so slight differences in detail are relevant. The fundamentalist attempt to harmonize discrepant texts becomes ridiculous after a time.

Here below are a few problem passages, and the specific references, that the intellectually honest fundamentalist must explain.[1]

- How many pairs of birds was Noah to take into the ark?
  Genesis 7:3: Seven.
  Genesis 7:8–9: Two.
- Who killed Goliath?
  1 Samuel 17: David killed Goliath.
  2 Samuel 21:19: Goliath was killed by Elhanan.
  1 Chronicles 20:5: Elhanan killed Lahmi, the brother of Goliath.
- What did God say about the Sabbath?
  Exodus 20:8–11: Remember the Sabbath because God created the world in six days and rested on the seventh.
  Deuteronomy 5:12–15: Observe the Sabbath because God liberated the Israelites from Egypt.
- How many men were taken by David?
  2 Samuel 8:4: 1,700 horsemen and 20,000 foot soldiers.
  1 Chronicles 18:4: 1,000 chariots, 7,000 horsemen, and 20,000 foot soldiers.
- How many mercenaries were there of the Ammonites?
  2 Samuel 10:6: 20,000 plus 1,000 plus 12,000.
  1 Chronicles 19:7: 32,000 chariots plus the army of the king of Maacah.
- How many men were killed by David?
  2 Samuel 10:18: 700 charioteers pus 40,000 horsemen.
  1 Chronicles 19:18: 7,000 charioteers plus 40,000 horsemen.
- Who incited David to take a census?
  2 Samuel 24:1: The Lord.
  1 Chronicles 21:1: Satan.
- What were the census figures?
  2 Samuel 24:9: 800,000 in Israel and 500,000 in Judah.
  1 Chronicles 21:5: 1,100,000 in Israel and 470,000 in Judah.
- What was the price of the threshing floor?
  2 Samuel 24:24: 50 shekels.
  1 Chronicles 21:25: 600 shekels.
- How many stalls were there for chariot horses?
  1 Kings 4:26: 40,000
  2 Chronicles 9:25: 4,000
- What was the capacity of the "sea"?
  1 Kings 7:26: 2,000 baths.
  2 Chronicles 4:5: 3,000 baths.
- How many generations are there in Jesus's genealogy?
  Matthew 1:1–17: 42
  Luke 3:23–38: 76
- Who was the son of David that carried the messianic line?
  Matthew 1:6: It was Solomon.
  Luke 3:31: It was Nathan.

- What was the name of Jesus's grandfather?
  Matthew 1:16: It was Jacob
  Luke 3:23: It was Heli.
- Where was Jesus born?
  Matthew 2:11: A house.
  Luke 2:12: A barn with a feed trough.
- Where was Jesus standing when he delivered the beatitude sermon?
  Matthew 5:1: A mountain.
  Luke 6:17: Down on a level place.
- When did the temple cleansing occur?
  Matthew 21:10–17, Mark 11:15–19, Luke 19:45–48: Jesus cleanses the temple near the end of his public ministry, at the beginning of the passion week.
  John 2:13–17: Jesus cleanses the temple at the beginning of his public ministry.
- When did the miraculous catch of fish occur?
  Luke 5:4–7: During the Galilean phase of Jesus's ministry.
  John 21:4–8: Following the resurrection.
- What kind of meal was the last supper?
  Matthew 26:17, Mark 14:12, Luke 22:7: It was a Passover meal.
  John 13:1–9, 12–16: It was a preparation for the Passover meal.
- How did Judas die?
  Matthew 27:3–10: He hanged himself.
  Acts 1:15–19: He fell.
- Who visited the tomb of Jesus?
  Mark 16:1: Mary Magdalene, Mary the mother of Jesus, and Salome.
  Matthew 28:1: Mary Magdalene and the other Mary.
  Luke 24:10: Mary Magdalene, Mary the mother of James, Joanna, and some other women.
  John 20:11: Mary Magdalene.

Discrepancies that arise from the clear contradiction between two passages in the same "inerrant" Bible are seemingly impossible to overcome, though fundamentalist commentators satisfy their mind and the minds of their constituencies that, indeed, the discrepancies are adequately explained. No one, who does not have the fundamentalist inerrancy doctrine as a presupposition, is convinced.

I must admit to being a bit hesitant in blatantly providing a list like this. It is not my intention to poke fun at fundamentalists. However, as I said, it is the very fundamentalist doctrine and agenda that invites investigation into this problem. Fundamentalists should not be allowed to be vague or evasive about these very precise questions about the text. As Barr points out, the fundamentalist is "responsible for . . . the problem of manure in Noah's Ark," referring humorously to the question of how Noah handled the logistics of waste disposal on the ark.[2]

While the typical fundamentalist is vague and evasive about these questions—because, in my opinion, there are no good answers—thoughtful and informed fundamentalists, indeed, fully recognize what is at stake. Fundamentalist commentaries on the Bible are filled with ingenious (and sometimes not so ingenious) "solutions" to these discrepancies. The real problem is that there are so many inconsistencies and there are definite patterns among them. If there were only a few such instances in the Bible, then one appropriate approach might be to seek some sort of harmonizing solution to the apparent discrepancies. However, it is the high number of discrepancies and consistent patterns among them that show the fundamentalist view of inerrancy to be an alien imposition onto the text. Furthermore, the patterns themselves suggests a more appropriate solution to the "problem." I will illustrate.

Consider the discrepancies in the flood story, for example. The number of animals Noah takes into the ark is but one of several blatant contradictions in the story. In the Genesis story Noah is clearly commanded by God to take two of every kind of animal into the ark:

> "And of every living thing, of all flesh, you shall bring two of every kind into the ark, to keep them alive with you; they shall be male and female. Of the birds according to their kinds, and of the animals according to their kinds, of every creeping thing of the ground according to its kind, two of every kind shall come in to you, to keep them alive." . . . Noah did this; he did all that God commanded him.
>
> (Genesis 6:19–20, 22)

> Of clean animals, and of animals that are not clean, and of birds, and of everything that creeps on the ground, two and two, male and female, went into the ark with Noah, as God had commanded Noah.
>
> (Genesis 7:8–9)

The text could not be much clearer. Two of each kind of animal were brought into the ark. However, between the above two passages (i.e., Genesis 6:19–20, 22 and Genesis 7:8–9), we find God giving these instructions to Noah.

> Then the Lord said to Noah, "Go into the ark, you and all your household, for I have seen that you alone are righteous before me in this generation. Take with you seven pairs of all clean animals, the male and its mate; and a pair of the animals that are not clean, the male and its mate; and seven pairs of the birds of the air also, male and female, to keep their kind alive on the face of all the earth." . . . And Noah did all that the Lord had commanded him.
>
> (Genesis 7:1–3, 5)

So, in a plain reading of the text, the first two passages quoted say that two of every kind of animal was brought into the ark. "Every kind" includes clean animals and birds. In the second passage seven pairs of clean animals are brought in and seven pairs of birds are brought in.

Fundamentalist interpreters work long and hard to construct sophisticated explanations of this kind of problem. The scholarly interpretation of this "problem" easily explains the discrepancies. Here is how. Critical scholarship on the Pentateuch, the first five books of the Hebrew Bible (what Christians call the Old Testament), has determined that we have several sources behind these books. The various sources, written at different times and places in Israel's history, were woven into a single narrative by later editors. Although there is debate among scholars about the details, there is general agreement that there are several main sources for the Pentateuch.

The "J" source originated in the southern kingdom of Judah. It uses a particular name for deity, namely, "Yahweh." It is highly anthropomorphic, that is, attributing human characteristics to deity. "God came walking through the garden in the cool of the day" (Genesis 3:8) is a line from the "J" writer. The "E" source originated in the northern kingdom of Israel. "E" saw God operating in individual human concerns, employed the dream motif a lot, and preferred the Hebrew word "Elohim" for deity. The "P" writers were the priests and this source reflects an interest in things priests would have focused on, like the Sabbath, circumcision, and sacrifice.

Before the written sources came into being, the stories were transmitted orally through the generations. In our culture where paper is so prevalent and writing so common, it is difficult to appreciate the long and rich oral tradition of ancient cultures.

The issue of the different sources in the Pentateuch is similar to the four gospels about Jesus, except that in the case of the Pentateuch someone wove the sources into one long narrative. Actually, in the ancient period there was an effort to weave the accounts from the four gospels into one long narrative about Jesus. This project never took hold and so we are left with four different and separate accounts of the life of Christ: Mark, Matthew, Luke, and John.

The source-critical view of the Pentateuch, called the documentary hypothesis, is opposed by fundamentalist teachers of the Bible. The traditional view for centuries was that Moses wrote the first five books of the Bible. Calling into question this traditional view is staunchly opposed by fundamentalists. However, it was the critical scholars—not the fundamentalists—who read the Pentateuch carefully and were required by the evidence to construct a hypothesis that fits the evidence.

Nowhere in the Pentateuch does it say Moses wrote the Pentateuch as we have it. It is claimed that he wrote parts of it, but the fundamentalist claims Mosaic authorship of the entire Pentateuch. Also, Moses is consistently referred to in the third person (e.g., "The Lord said to Moses," Exodus 20:22); if Moses were the author, we would expect him to be referred to in the first person. There is a record of Moses's death, burial, and epitaph in Deuteronomy 34. Most people do not write their own obituary. There are numerous other pieces of evidence that challenge the Mosaic authorship and support some version of the documentary hypothesis.

Applying the documentary hypothesis to the problems in the flood story illustrates both the weakness of the fundamentalist position and the value of careful, critical analysis. Genesis contains the accounts of the flood from at least two different sources. Looking closely at the specific problem of how many of each of the animals, and specifically birds, Noah was to bring into the ark, we see that at the very point in the story that we find shifts from two to seven, and then back from seven to two (Genesis 6:10–20, 22, then Genesis 7:1–3, 5, then Genesis 7:8–9), something else happens. The name by which the deity is called changes from *Elohim* (English translation "God") *to Yahweh* (English translation "Lord") and then back to *Elohim,* a sign that two different sources are behind the story. So the documentary hypothesis provides a reasonable explanation of the discrepancies in the flood story. In my mind, the scholarly source theory only makes the story that much more interesting. It was a story that was so powerful in its theological and human meaning that it registered a lasting impact on various segments of the Israelite population. Meaning aside, however, the point I am making here is that the fundamentalist inerrancy claim requires an untenable position on this and many other biblical passages.

Again, if the flood story discrepancies were the only ones in the Bible, I might be open to a different way of addressing the problem. However, the flood story contradictions are not alone. As the representative examples I gave earlier show, the Bible is filled with discrepancies that can, nevertheless, be made sensible by way of the critical method. I will summarize one more pattern, and take the example from the New Testament. Like the Old Testament, early Christian literature reflects a long history of oral tradition and the confluence of many oral and written sources. The different perspectives of the four gospels can be illustrated by looking at the birth stories. Actually, only the Gospels of Matthew and Luke provide birth stories. In Matthew, Jesus is born in a house and is visited by wise men who bring gold, frankincense, and myrrh (Matthew 2:11). Luke's Jesus is laid in a feed trough (Luke 2:12); the translators use the fancy word "manger," but it is what in normal language is called a feed trough. In Luke, he is visited by shepherds (Luke 2:15–16). Matthew and Luke bring differing and, indeed, valuable perspectives to the story. Matthew's Jesus is the king of the Jews; in Luke Jesus's heart goes out to the poor and sick. Interestingly, in the manger scenes at Christmas, we harmonize the birth accounts of Jesus by picturing Mary holding baby Jesus. The Christ child is surrounded by Joseph and both the shepherds and wise men, perhaps presumed to be three in number because of the three gifts of gold, frankincense, and myrrh. While this scene portrays a warm and comforting image, it does not accurately convey the message of the gospel stories.

I would like to again point out that moderate and liberal Christians are not disturbed by such critical conclusions, because these Christians are not bound to an extreme doctrine of inerrancy that mandates a certain conclusion about the text. Moderate and liberal Christians are theologically and psychologically free to allow critical study to open up the text in all its wonderfulness and complexity. Fundamentalists, however, are required by their theology and psychology to resist any perceived dent in their artificially constructed inerrant text.

Discrepancies that arise in the contradictions between the fundamentalist reading of the Bible and science and history can be just as devastating as contradictions between two biblical passages. Perhaps it is easier for fundamentalists, who distrust science and history in the first place, to dismiss these contradictions than it is to handle contradictions within the text itself. In any case, to illustrate the kinds of appropriate and rational questions that are asked of fundamentalist readings, I will mention a few things about the flood.

The usual fundamentalist literal reading of the flood story is that it was a flood that covered the whole earth. Some commentators who believe in inerrancy do hold that it was a local Mesopotamian flood, but that is not the clear meaning of the text. Here is part of the account:

> The flood continued forty days on the earth; and the waters increased, and bore up the ark, and it rose high above the earth. The waters swelled and increased greatly on the earth; and the ark floated on the face of the waters. The waters swelled so mightily on the earth that all the high mountains under the whole heaven were covered; the waters swelled above the mountains, covering them fifteen cubits deep.
>
> (Genesis 7:17–20)

I suppose we could say that the unofficial fundamentalist account is that the flood was universal. In 1961 two fundamentalists, Henry M. Morris, a hydraulic engineer at Virginia Polytechnic Institute, and John C. Whitcomb, Jr., a Bible teacher at Grace Theological Seminary, set forth the new flood theory in *The Genesis Flood.* According to this theory, fossils and evidence from geology, when seen in light of a worldwide flood, show that the earth is not older than about 10,000 years. In this reading of the Bible, God created all life in six literal days. Morris and Whitcomb clearly tapped into a widespread desire for support of the fundamentalist position. The book sold over 200,000 copies and its teachings were popularized in other books (*The Early Earth, The World that Perished,* and *The Moon: Its Creation, Form, and Significance*) and many other formats, including articles, pamphlets, tapes, charts, and Sunday School lessons.

There are enormous historical and logistical complications of positing a worldwide flood. The highest mountain in Mesopotamia was Mount Ararat, which is about 17,000 feet. I have climbed the Himalayas. They are much higher, soaring to 29,000 feet. A universal flood that covered the whole earth would be eight times more water than is currently on the planet and six miles of water above current sea level. Where did all that water drain? What about the effect on marine life from mixing fresh and salt water? How did the kangaroos of Australia and polar bears of Alaska make the long journey to Noah's ark? How would they have been fed and cared for? And how did they get back to their natural habitat, keeping in mind that after the flood for many species there were only two of each of the animals. One has only to reflect just a bit about life on the ark to sense the complexities involved in explaining how all the animals were fed and cared for. Indeed, what about the manure? Of course, Noah and his family could have just shoveled the manure overboard. But does the story really intend to convey a picture answering all these questions? Is this what this old story is about? These kinds of questions are so problematic for the fundamentalist that the usual response is to dismiss them with a wave of the hand and some comment about God being able to do anything. The problem is that the fundamentalist reading of stories like the flood invites the kind of inquiry I am making.[3]

A more reasonable, and I think respectful, reading of the flood story goes like this. Floods were quite common in the ancient Near East along the Nile River and Delta and the Tigris and Euphrates Rivers in Mesopotamia, the birthplace of the ancient Sumerians, Assyrians, Babylonians, and Persians. It is no surprise that many other cultures, from all around the world, developed flood stories. Ancient cultures used familiar images and experiences to express their values and hopes. The Israelites were no different in this regard. They lived in the ancient Near East and were no doubt familiar with stories about local floods from the region. They adopted these stories and adapted them to their own theological outlook on the world. Is the theology in the biblical flood story different from the theology in, say, the Mesopotamian flood story? Yes. The biblical flood story conveys the Israelite understanding of God and God's relationship to the human community. This is what makes the biblical flood story special. Attempts to turn this old story into a modern scientific and historical account is wrongheaded, and I think ultimately disrespectful to the Bible.

I cannot count the times students in my Bible courses have asserted, "but they have found the remains of Noah's ark." Upon questioning, of course, their assertion withers to some vague claim their fundamentalist preacher or Sunday School teacher made. Apparently, there is a report that someone saw a ship or a part of a ship sticking out of Mount Ararat's south glacier.[4] I really do think I am open to new evidence about any aspect of the Bible, but I always encourage my students to refrain from constructing their view of the Bible on vague, unproven assertions. The standard response I give to such student comments about the ark is to ask the student to provide for me the documentation for this alleged sighting of Noah's ark. I point out to them that a radiocarbon dating of the wood from the ship would certainly be an important piece of evidence as we proceed to evaluate the claimed sighting and its relevance. Radiocarbon dating is based on the fact that all organic materials have amounts of carbon in them, including radioactive carbon. When the organic material dies, no more radioactive carbon is added and what is present begins to decay at a fixed rate. By comparing the percentage of the radioactive carbon with the more common carbon isotope, scientists can determine the approximate age when the tree, bone, food, or textile material "died." My challenge to the student sometimes turns into an opportunity to explain something about scientific dating methods used by archaeologists. The point of this story, however, is that to date no student has ever returned with any data that I can review.

HOW WE GOT THE BIBLE

As pointed out earlier, in our brief look at the snake-handlers and poison-drinkers, we do not have any original manuscripts (autographs) of any book of the Bible. I might add here that, given advances in scholarly understanding of the role of oral tradition and in the complex questions of ancient authorship, the concept of a single original manuscript may be naïve. However, for our purposes we can speak somewhat simplistically of a point in time when a particular Bible book came into existence in written form. All of the Bible books were written on papyri, ancient paper, and all of the papyri autographs have been lost. Fortunately, before the autograph of a particular book was lost or destroyed, one or more copies were made. The early copies, too, have perished, but copies were made of the copies before they perished, and so on. What we have, in libraries and museums around the world, are thousands of copies and fragments of copies made many years, and text generations, from the original. The earliest copies or fragments we have of many books of the Bible date to hundreds of years after the original.

"Textual critics" are critical scholars who use rational methods to examine the surviving manuscript copies and from them reconstruct a hypothetical original. The evidence, and it does not serve our purposes here to elaborate, is that textual critics of the Bible have done a good job. We can be reasonably certain that modern Hebrew and Greek editions of the Bible constructed by textual critics are pretty close to what was written by the ancient authors. To say it in a more technical way, we are generally confident that the hypothetical reconstructed biblical texts are generally conveying what the autographs conveyed. While this conclusion is sufficient for most scholars who work on the Bible and for most Christians who hold the Bible to be, in some sense, the word of God, the conclusion presents serious logical problems for the extreme view of inspiration held by fundamentalists.

The facts are that the manuscript copies we have and can study contain differences. That is not a liberal or conservative view. That is a fact that all knowledgeable persons, liberal or conservative, agree on. Anyone who can read Hebrew and Greek can, theoretically, go to the libraries and museums around the world and see the differences. To make clear exactly what I am talking about, I will give a couple of representative examples.

At Luke 8:26, the best (meaning, most reliable) manuscripts of this gospel read that "Then they arrived at the country of the Gerasenes." However, some other ancient manuscripts of this gospel spell this location as "Gadarenes" and still other manuscripts spell it "Gergesenes." For sure, the import of the story is what happened at this place, not the exact spelling of the location. The point, however, is that we do not know with certainty how this location was spelled. Another example is found in Luke 7:11, which reads: "Soon afterwards he went to a town called Nain." However, some ancient manuscripts read: "Next day he went to a town called Nain." Again, there is virtually no difference in the meaning between the two, but it does illustrate the fact that we do not know exactly what the Bible said at this point.

One can use the word "error" or the milder word "variations," but the point is that the manuscripts of the same book or passage differ. In fact, most verses in the Bible contains some textual variation. Many English translations of the Bible give as footnotes some of the textual variations. These variations are usually given as a comment on a verse that goes something like this, "Other ancient authorities read . . . ." Most of the variations in the Bible do not impact the basic meaning of the passages in the Bible.

How did the differences creep into the manuscript tradition? The answer is that the persons making the copies made mistakes. Mistakes of the eye included misspelling words. Many of the Hebrew and Greek letters are very similar and it is easy to see how the scribes made mistakes. Sometimes they left out words or even sentences. Sometimes marginal notes made by an earlier scribe were erroneously inserted into the text, making the new copy longer. These differences present no surprises for scholars who work with ancient texts from any culture. The differences present no theological problem for Christians who are not locked into a verbal and inerrant inspiration claim.

Once the textual critics have done their work on the various copies of a book of the Bible, they produce a critical edition of that book in the original language. The text is the critics' best judgment about what was in the autograph. Unless one can read Hebrew or Greek, the reconstructed text must be translated into the language of the reader. Translation is a step in the process that knowledgeable fundamentalists understand. Unfortunately, many fundamentalists, who have not the capability and/or the opportunity to learn about their sacred scripture, may apply their notion of inspiration to an English translation, always the cherished King James Version of the Bible. While the allegiance is breaking down, up until about mid-twentieth century, fundamentalist commitment was almost exclusively to the King James Version. There is a report of a preacher who used a blowtorch in his pulpit to burn a copy of the new *Revised Standard Version* (RSV) of the Bible that was published in the early 1950s. Such extreme reactions, and pamphlets entitled "The Bible of the Antichrist" or "The New Blasphemous Bible," reflect the once harsh reaction to anything but the King James Version.[5] Most evangelicals understand the basic concept of translation, and I dare say only a handful of evangelicals today would be attached to the King James Version as inspired over some other translation. Most fundamentalist college students, also, will be aware of the issue and will make use of various modern translations. Unfortunately, however, there are still a few fundamentalists who claim that the King James Version is the only inspired translation, and, therefore, the only one Christians should use.

Because there are fundamentalists who are not knowledgeable of the translation process, those who wish to communicate with them should understand the basic ideas. Language is like a person—it grows over time, changing with the seasons; thus, the perennial need for rendering the source text in language that is current. Sometimes the change in the meaning of a word, and the consequent need for a new translation, are obvious. Paul's claim to the Corinthians that "once I was stoned" (2 Corinthians 11:25) and the Psalmist's "I will accept no bull from your house" (Psalm 50:9a) potentially connote something very different today than when the *Revised Standard Version* New Testament was published in pre-hippie America of 1946. Notice that the *New Revised Standard Version* translates these verses in ways that take account of the evolution of language. 2 Corinthians 11:25 reads "once I received a stoning" and Psalm 50:9a reads "I will not accept a bull from your house."[6]

In a work of translation, a choice must be made between literal translation and paraphrase. The array of differing responses can be couched in the terminology of equivalence used by translators. "Formal equivalence or correspondence," roughly what is commonly called literal translation, seeks, as far as is possible, a one-to-one formal correspondence with the source text. "Dynamic equivalence," or paraphrase in its extreme form, seeks to have the message received by the modern reader be as close as possible to the message believed to have been intended to be received by the original reader. Since the original message is often disputed, dynamic equivalence can be understood as involving a larger degree of interpretation than formal equivalence.

To illustrate the translator's dilemma, let's explore the gender bias issue. Issues surrounding the question of gender and translation are much more complex than the simple evolution of words like "stoned" and "bull." A male bias has apparently influenced some translations where the Greek New Testament text itself does not contain gender-bound terminology. Romans 16:1 reads, literally, "I commend to you Phoebe, our sister, being a deacon of the church." Keep in mind that in a conservative and traditional church setting women are usually not allowed to serve as deacons, high officials in the church. So, here, we have a woman named Phoebe called a deacon. The *King James Version* calls Phoebe "a servant of the church." It is true that the root meaning of "deacon" is "servant." However, the bias of the translators is clear when, elsewhere, in various places in the letters of Paul, the *King James Version* translators chose either "deacon" or "minister" to render the same Greek word that, in reference to the female Phoebe, is translated "servant." The *Today's English Version,* also titled *Good News for Modern Man,* also avoids the official term deacon by saying she "serves the church." The *Revised Standard Version* calls her a "deaconess of the church." There is no separate Greek word for deaconess, and so the *New Revised Standard Version* translates the word as "deacon," as it would normally be translated if referring to a man, although the *New Revised Standard Version* contains a note with the alternate translation of "minister."

The male bias of *The Living Bible Paraphrased,* a popular version among evangelicals and some fundamentalists, is particularly evident here in rendering deacon "a dear Christian woman." For those who care about what the Bible actually says, *The Living Bible* has done a great disservice to the Christian community. It originated from one man (Kenneth Taylor) who read the Bible in English translation and then paraphrased it in his own words. It has been published under various names and covers. As we have seen, any English translation, however competently done, is a step removed from what the biblical authors wrote. To paraphrase an English translation is to move the Bible yet another step from the original words, and do it via the theological outlook of one man. *The Living Bible* is worse than a bad translation. It is one man's interpretation of the Bible marketed as the Bible.

As is becoming clear, the typical fundamentalist is unaware of some of the elemental aspects of the very book he or she considers the word of God. The issue of canon is another example of something many fundamentalists know practically nothing about. "Canon," as it is used by scholars of religion, when applied to sacred texts, refers to a collection of books that a religious community considers authoritative. So "canon" is, in effect, a "collection" or "list" of sacred books. We can and do speak, for example, of the Buddhist canon, meaning the books that Buddhists consider in some sense authoritative.

"Canonization" is the process by which a particular book came to be viewed as authoritative by a religious community. With respect to the biblical tradition, when an ancient book was written by a devout Jew or Christian, there were, theoretically, four possible scenarios for the book. One, the book was immediately recognized as authoritative and, so, was "in the canon." The Israelite books associated with the great lawgiver Moses were in this category. They include Genesis, Exodus, Leviticus, Numbers, and Deuteronomy. Two, the book was neither widely read nor accepted by the religious community and so we can say it never made it into the canon. Examples include Apocalypse of Zephaniah, Fourth Book of Ezra, and Testament of Job.

Three, the book was in and out of the canon at different time periods and eventually ended up either in or out. Finally, a book could be both in and out of the canon at the same time, in different geographical regions. Books would be in favor or out of favor, in different times or places, depending on how they lined up with the prevailing theology or sentiment of the time and place. The book of Esther was considered problematic because it never mentions the name of God or refers to any of the religious rituals of ancient Israel. However, it tells such a powerful story about survival in the face of adversity that it was allowed in the text.

The Song of Songs (sometimes known as the "Song of Solomon") had a difficult time making it into the canon because of its sexually bold language. Here are some examples of the beautiful, but in some quarters problematic, poetry:

> As an apple tree among the trees of the wood,
> so is my beloved among young men.
> With great delight I sat in his shadow,
> and his fruit was sweet to my taste. (Song of Songs 2:2)
>
> How fair and pleasant you are, O loved one, delectable maiden!
> You are stately as a palm tree,
> and your breasts are like its clusters,
> I say I will climb the palm tree and lay hold of its branches.
> Oh, may your breasts be like clusters of the vine,
> and the scent of your breath like apples,
> and your kisses like the best wine
> that goes down smoothly,
> gliding over lips and teeth. (Song of Songs 7:6–9)

This book was eventually accepted by Jews, because the language about lovemaking was viewed as symbolic of the relationship between God and Israel. Christians viewed the language as symbolic of the love between Christ and the church and so allowed it into the Christian canon.

Our knowledge of the history of the New Testament canon also reflects these four possible scenarios. Here are some of the key episodes in the development of what came to be a New Testament canon of 27 books. The Muratorian Canon is a list of books considered sacred in the late second-century CE. This list contains the following books: Matthew, Mark, Luke, John, Acts, Romans, 1–2 Corinthians, Galatians, Ephesians, Philippians, Colossians, 1–2 Thessalonians, 1–2 Timothy, Titus, 1–2 John, Jude, and the Wisdom of Solomon. Persons familiar with the New Testament will recognize that the list does not include several books that eventually made it into the New Testament, namely, Philemon, Hebrews, James, 1–2 Peter, and 3 John. The list contains the Wisdom of Solomon, a book that was deleted from later lists. This Muratorian Canon mentions the Revelation of John (a book that finally made it in) and the Revelation of Peter, which was highly regarded by many second-century Christians.

A glance at the canonical lists of some of the important theologians and church leaders in the late second-century CE reveals differences of opinion about what books are sacred. Irenaeus knows about Hebrews, James, 2 Peter, 3 John, and Jude, all books that finally made it into the canon, but Irenaeus is uncertain about their status. Irenaeus quotes as scripture a book called the Shepherd of Hermas, not now in the canon. Clement of Alexandria accepted as inspired a number of books that did not make it into the New Testament canon: Revelation of Peter, Preaching of Peter, Epistle of Barnabas, 1 Clement, the Didache, and the Shepherd of Hermas.

Eusebius, around 325 CE, in his book *Ecclesiastical History,* divides certain books into three categories. The "acknowledged books" are Matthew, Mark, Luke, John, Acts, Paul's letters (presumably including Hebrews), 1 John, 1 Peter, and Revelation of John, with the note that Revelation "may" be placed in the acknowledged group "if it seems desirable." The "disputed books" are James, Jude, 2 Peter, 2–3 John, Acts of Paul, Shepherd of Hermas, Revelation of Peter, Barnabas, Didache, and Revelation of John "may" be placed here "if this view prevails." Finally, Eusebius makes reference to a number of books that he categorizes as "heretical."

So the contents of the canon continued to be debated for several centuries following the establishment of the church. The earliest list we have of what eventually came to be the 27 books of the Christian New Testament came in the 367 CE Easter letter of Athanasius, bishop of Alexandria. In this letter he names those "books that are canonized and handed down to us and believed to be divine."

It should be pointed out that even as late as the sixteenth-century Protestant Reformation, there was debate about the status of certain books. The Roman Catholic church accepted, as having some canonical status, a group of books referred to as the "apocrypha." This category of books was not finally accepted by the Protestants. Fundamentalists are usually unaware of even the existence of these books.

ARCHAEOLOGY: A FUNDAMENTALIST MISREPRESENTATION

I have reviewed public school and college textbooks and other literature written by fundamentalist writers. In the books I have seen fundamentalist writers often impress upon their readers that archaeology has proven the scientific and historical truth of the Bible. Some general statement like this is made and then, usually, one or two examples are provided that demonstrate this "proof." Students with a fundamentalist or evangelical background often make this kind of comment as well. I am not a professional archaeologist, but it is one of my academic "hobbies." I have hung around many digs in Israel and try to keep up with the literature in this specialized field. I understand things well enough to know that archaeology in no way supports, much less proves, the fundamentalist system.

Biblical archaeology, or what is sometimes called Syro-Palestinian archaeology (the proper terminology is a matter of controversy), is a vast field of study with wonderful ongoing debates about method, the relationship between archeology and the Bible, and conclusions. It is simply a misstatement to claim that archeology has proven the Bible. There are specific instances where archaeologists have dug something out of the ground that appears to support what the Bible says in some account of the past. There are many other instances where the biblical text is not supported, and even contradicted, in what has been retrieved from the archaeological dig.

Sometimes, in their enthusiastic use of archaeology to prove an inerrant Bible, the fundamentalists will invoke the name of William F. Albright (1891–1971), the Johns Hopkins University professor who for so long was the dean of American archaeology, whose prodigious writings set the agenda for the field, and whose students are still influential in the field. Albright, admittedly, often came to rather conservative conclusions about the dating of biblical books and the historicity of events they tell about. However, by no stretch of the imagination did Albright hold a fundamentalist view of the Bible or can his work be used in the main to support the extremist fundamentalist agenda.

Fundamentalists are being extremely naïve in using archaeology to defend their view of the Bible. For the sake of making a point, let us assume that archaeology currently does support the biblical account. What if next year archaeological research revealed something that flatly contradicted the Bible? To be consistent and intellectually honest the fundamentalists would have to revise their position on biblical inerrancy. Of course, no one expects that they would do this, because archaeological findings are by no stretch of the imagination the basis for their view of inerrancy. Their view of inerrancy is rooted in psychological and historical factors. That this is true is made clear by the fact that archaeology, in fact, has shown that the biblical record at points is not a historically accurate one, but fundamentalists continue to misrepresent Albright, latching on to bits and pieces from the field of archaeology, ignoring the general consensus of the field, and reporting unfounded sightings of Noah's ark.

CHAPTER 6

The Jesus Question

WHAT ABOUT MIRACLES?

The two doctrines next discussed (virgin birth and resurrection) fall into the general category of miracles in the Bible. These doctrines, along with a number of other topics I have discussed and will discuss (flood, creation, prediction of the future), open up the general question of supernatural intervention. As I have explained, fundamentalism is a modern movement, tied to modernity in that it is a reaction against change and new ideas that are threatening to the fundamentalist psyche. So, before we continue with the doctrines that have a miraculous basis, a review of the larger issue is in order.

By now the reader is fully aware of the fact that people are prone to fight over the Bible, and the question of miracles is one of the most favorite things to fight over. Let us consider some of the issues. By miracles, what I refer to are stories in the Bible that, taken literally, contradict what we understand to be the natural workings of the universe. Miracles generally cluster around pivotal events in the biblical story, for example, the exodus from Egypt and the life of Jesus. With respect to Jesus's life on earth, there are four types of miracle stories: exorcising demons, curing the sick, raising the dead, and controlling nature.

The typical fundamentalist, who is not well informed about fundamentalism and how the movement and doctrines fit into the larger picture of Christianity and the modern world, will usually simply revert to some general defensive statement to the effect that God can do anything and, so, the miracles in the Bible are accepted on faith. A more sophisticated position, advocated by conservative apologists, is that critical scholars of the Bible dismiss *a priori* the possibility of miracles and, therefore, disregard the "evidence" of the Bible for miracles. Actually, I am not going to here disagree with this charge. However, the fundamentalist also has some difficult issues to face if he or she is going to engage in an honest debate about miracles.

While the question of miracles is really a matter for philosophers of religion (not my specialty, and so I do not intend an in-depth discussion), there are several things that are useful to keep in mind in terms of basic perspectives. First of all, miracle stories are not unique to the Bible. The Greco-Roman world and the Jewish tradition were filled with stories of miracles and miracle workers. In our secularized world, a miracle story stands out. In the first century, such stories were not so special. Likewise, miracle stories are found in the early written traditions of most religions. One needs to realize that scholars are going to approach all miracle stories in all religions with the same standards of analysis. If the fundamentalist decides that the miracle stories in the Bible are to be believed as reported, but the miracle stories surrounding the birth of the Buddha are legendary, then to be intellectually honest, the fundamentalist should be forthcoming about why the stories in one tradition are accepted and stories in the non-Christian religion are rejected. The answer, of course, is that the fundamentalist is bringing a biased look to the Bible stories. I like the way Barr puts this point:

> It is this confinement to a zone identical with the Bible (excluding the Apocrypha) that makes the supernaturalist argument, as it is used by Protestant fundamentalists, a superstition. Their use of the supernatural is occasionalistic and opportunistic. They do not have and do not advocate a general supernaturalist outlook; the supernaturalist argument is one upon which they fall back at those points where it is the only way of establishing a necessary conservative position.[1]

In understanding the scholarly analysis of miracles, it is important to be clear about the definition of a miracle. Persons on the street will report that a miracle is an event that occurs that is contrary to the natural laws of the universe. If the person is a person of faith, they will add that God caused the event to occur. However, notice that this definition presupposes a natural universe, a world that operates regularly and consistently according to certain natural laws. It is crucial to realize that this concept was foreign to the people who wrote the Bible. In the ancient and prescientific world, events occur because of some divine power. If it is a good event, it is a good god that caused the event. If it is a bad event, then it was caused by a bad god. I love the quote by Gilbert Chesterton that in the ancient world the sun did not rise in the morning by natural law, but because God said, "Get up and do it again!"

Consider this example: For an obstetrician the birth of a baby is likely to be experienced as a very natural occurrence. The doctor has seen hundreds of such events and will likely report any particular one in very medical, even mechanical terms. Ask the doctor to tell you about baby number 14, born on Tuesday at 4 P.M. If he or she even remembers the delivery at all, the description will likely include technical information about heart rate, procedures used, and complications. However, if you speak to the mother of baby number 14, she will likely describe it in poetic and miraculous terms. If she is a person of faith, she may call it a gift from God. So the same event can be interpreted in purely naturalistic terms, or as a divine act, depending on one's perspective.

Tonight I will sit down in my den and switch on the television. I cannot explain how it works, but I am not surprised when the picture appears because I know there are experts down the street who can explain the workings of a television as a very natural occurrence. My great grandfather fought in the War Between the States. If you were to place a television in front of him and switch it on, he would exclaim it to be a miracle, or maybe some devilish contraption.

If one of my students falls down in the aisle, jerks, and bites their tongue, most persons, informed by the science of medicine, will interpret that as some sort of seizure. In the first century, that behavior would have quickly been interpreted as demon possession. Hurricanes in the first century would be interpreted as caused by an angry wind god, not by air currents and atmospheric pressures.

Please understand that I am not suggesting that modern science has the final and complete answer to everything. In fact, I have studied enough history to be confident that in 100 years, what is today called seizure will likely be called something else. Perhaps they will be talking about the inefficient transfer of energy or some such thing. In any case, the notion of seizure may very well be seen to be as primitive as demon possession appears to the modern university trained medical doctor. The point is that the same event/behavior can be interpreted in quite different ways, depending on one's perspective.

The miraculous events in the biblical stories serve to indicate something special to the people of faith in that day. The stories were told and retold in the community and passed on orally for generations until they reached the form in which we read them in the Bible today. The people were slaves in Egypt and God freed them. A miracle, a wonder, for them was some event in which they, the people of faith, experienced God working on their behalf. This view does not mean the stories have to be interpreted literally and as contradicting the known laws of the universe. The biblical authors had a theological and devotional agenda, not a scientific one. In the New Testament Gospel of John, the author states his purpose, one that is clearly nothing like that of a modern author of a science or history book:

> Now Jesus did many other signs in the presence of his disciples, which are not written in this book. But these things are written so that you may come to believe

that Jesus is the Messiah, the Son of God, and that through believing you may have life in his name.

(John 20:30–31)

Sometimes the fundamentalist defends miracles in the Bible in a way that, unknowingly to them I am sure, actually works in the direction of undermining their supernaturalist worldview. Fundamentalists, in supposedly learned books and commentaries on the Bible, will sometimes defend the biblical account of some miracle by showing how the account could have actually occurred in the natural course of events. They see this as proving the Bible. I am sure the fundamentalist does not realize that what they are doing is rationalizing the miracle story, and in effect adopting a technique used by critical scholarship. Use of these "natural" explanations of the biblical miracle stories reveals that proving the Bible takes precedence even over supernatural intervention by God.

An example of this "proving the Bible by science" approach is how the creation story in Genesis, the first book of the Bible, is handled. Here the "days" of creation in the Genesis account are viewed as "ages." To give another example, Exodus (chapter 16) recounts the miracle of how God fed the Israelites in the Sinai desert by sending numerous quails and other food (namely, manna). A popular evangelical commentary at Exodus 16:13, reads:

The common quail migrated across the Red Sea in large numbers at this time and, faint after a long journey, could be caught with ease. The miraculous element consists in the time of their arrival.[2]

Exodus 16:14 records the miraculous arrival of the manna, providing food for the people. The commentary on that verse reads:

Each morning after the dew there was found on the ground a fine, flake-like thing like hoar-frost with a honey taste, which could be ground and used in cooking and baking. Several partial parallels to this are known to exist in the Sinai peninsula, e.g. honeydew-producing insects leaving sweet, light-coloured drops on tamarisk twigs.[3]

In Exodus 11:31, the conservative commentator writes:

The outcome of the people's demand for flesh is now described. The Lord sent a wind which brought quails from the sea, probably the gulf of Aqabah. This is a natural phenomenon and still today the quails migrate in the spring (March, April) from Africa and return in the autumn (September). They travel up the Red Sea and cross the Sinai Peninsula toward Palestine and often fall exhausted to be picked up by the local inhabitants for eating or for sale.[4]

A slight variation of this general approach is that various passages in the Bible are seen as anticipating scientific findings. The phrase "When he gave to the wind its weight" (Job 28:25) anticipates discoveries about the weight of air; "the silver cord is snapped" (Ecclesiastes 12:6) refers to the discovery of spinal marrow; and "the wheel broken at the cistern" (Ecclesiastes 12:6) refers to the heart's role in the circulation of blood.

The problem that many fundamentalists are unaware of here is that they are going down a path that potentially defeats them. Let us look carefully at what they are doing. By arguing that specific things in the Bible have been proven by scientific discoveries, fundamentalists, if they are intellectually honest, are saying that they are willing to give credence to scientific discoveries. So, what if tomorrow scientists discover something that contradicts the Bible? Does this mean the fundamentalists are going to give up their respect for the Bible? Of course not, because what is happening here is that fundamentalists are using science only when they think that it supports the biblical text. However, their methodology is clearly flawed, given their goals and beliefs in the Bible.

VIRGIN BIRTH AND DIVINITY OF JESUS CHRIST

There are actually two claims here, but they are often related in the minds of fundamentalists and so I treat them together. The virgin birth of Jesus Christ is one of the doctrines that fundamentalists see as worth defending at whatever cost. Fundamentalists defend mightily this teaching, probably for a couple of reasons. One, it is one of the more prominent miracles in the life of Christ and the fundamentalist system requires defense of a literal reading of all miracle stories. Second, fundamentalists interpret the virgin birth as proof of the divinity of Christ, which for them is crucial.

When examined carefully, and without the imposition of the inerrancy notion, the virgin birth has thin support. The author of the Gospel of Matthew indeed states that Jesus was born of a virgin. Matthew was interested in relating Jesus to his Jewish background as much as possible and to that end looked for anything in the Jewish scriptures that could be related to Jesus. On the virgin birth Matthew quotes from the Old Testament book of Isaiah. In 1:23, he quotes from Isaiah 7:14:

> Look, the virgin shall conceive and bear a son, and they shall name him Emmanuel.
>
> (Matthew 1:23)

Matthew here was quoting from a Greek translation of the Hebrew scriptures. Because of the spread of Greek culture by Alexander the Great, many Jews in Jesus's day read their scriptures in Greek translation.

Matthew used the Septuagint, sometimes referred to as the "LXX" translation. Unfortunately, the Septuagint translators mistranslated Isaiah 7:14. The Hebrew of that verse reads that a young woman (Hebrew *'almah*) will bear a son. The Hebrew word for virgin is *betulah,* but Isaiah did not use that word. The Greek word for virgin is *parthenos,* and for whatever reason the Septuagint translators chose that word to translate *'almah* (young woman) from the Hebrew. So, naturally, Matthew, using the Septuagint, quoted Isaiah as referring to a virgin. Because of Matthew's translation, conservatives often judge a translation of the Bible based on whether the translation uses *'almah* (young woman) or *betulah* (virgin) at Isaiah 7:14. This controversy over the translation of Isaiah 7:14 fuels the debate about the virgin birth of Jesus.

As for the divinity of Jesus Christ, the nature of Jesus Christ was early and extensively debated by Christians. Christianity settled on the paradoxical view that Jesus Christ is both fully divine and fully human. The typical fundamentalist accepts this orthodox formulation.

The interesting thing about the teaching that Jesus is divine is that this claim plays differently in the modern world than it did in the first century. In the modern world of science and reason, supernatural occurrences, assuming they occur, are unusual. To the degree that we are informed by the modern, scientific worldview, we live in a secular universe. However, in the first century the opposite was true. Gods and divine men populated a universe filled with the supernatural. My point is that in the modern age, fundamentalists argue for the virgin birth because it is seen as proof that the secular perspective is in error. However, in the first century, the virgin birth and the divinity of Jesus would not have been nearly as remarkable as it is today. To illustrate this point, I turn to a wonderfully crafted quotation from New Testament scholar Bart Ehrman. This quotation is taken from his textbook on the New Testament, in a section where he is setting Jesus Christ in the context of his day.

> From the beginning his mother knew that he was no ordinary person. Prior to his birth, a heavenly figure appeared to her, announcing that her son would not be a mere mortal but would himself be divine. This prophecy was confirmed by the miraculous character of his birth, a birth accompanied by supernatural signs. The boy was already recognized as a spiritual authority in his youth; his discussions with recognized experts showed his superior knowledge of all things religious. As an adult he left home to engage in an itinerant preaching ministry. He went from village to town with his message of good news, proclaiming that people should forgo their concerns for the material things of this life, such as how they should dress and what they should eat. They should instead be concerned with their eternal souls.
>
> He gathered around him a number of disciples who were amazed by his teaching and his flawless character. They became convinced that he was no ordinary man but was the **Son of God.** Their faith received striking confirmation in the

> miraculous things that he did. He could reportedly predict the future, heal the sick, cast out demons, and raise the dead. Not everyone proved friendly, however. At the end of his life, his enemies trumped up charges against him, and he was placed on trial before Roman authorities for crimes against the state.
>
> Even after he departed this realm, however, he did not forsake his devoted followers. Some claimed that he had ascended bodily into heaven; others said that he had appeared to them, alive, afterward, that they had talked with him and touched him and became convinced that he could not be bound by death. A number of his followers spread the good news about this man, recounting what they had seen him say and do. Eventually some of these accounts came to be written down in books that circulated throughout the empire.[5]

Ehrman then points out, probably to the surprise of most of the readers, that the miracle-working "Son of God" he described is the first-century CE neo-Pythagorean teacher Apollonius of Tyana. Apollonius worshipped the Roman gods and we know of his life and teachings from *The Life of Apollonius,* written by one of his followers, Philostratus. Apollonius of Tyana is by no means the only such miracle-working divine man in the Hellenistic world. We have many accounts of such persons, illustrating the supernatural character of the ancient worldview.

As pointed out, the fundamentalist view of Christ as divine and human is the orthodox Christian position. However, I think that the fundamentalist has not fully explored the implications of this orthodox teaching. Here is what I mean. The fundamentalist, with their otherworldly orientation, easily aligns with the notion that Christ was God. In a modern world where science has steadily encroached on the supernatural domain, it is understandable that the fundamentalist fight would focus on preserving the supernatural. In their emphasis on the divinity of Christ, fundamentalists have often ignored the human Jesus. It was the human Jesus whose heart went out to the poor, sick, and dispossessed. Just as liberals have perhaps downplayed the divinity of Christ, fundamentalists have failed to fully appreciate the theological implications of a God who chose to come in human form to work in the world.

In addition to the virgin birth, fundamentalists point to the resurrection as further proof of the divinity of Jesus. Fundamentalists love to quote the New Testament writer Paul, who says that if Jesus was not raised from the dead "your faith is in vain" (1 Corinthians 15:17). While fundamentalists take resurrection as physical and literal, it is not at all clear that this is what Paul had in mind. Paul calls the resurrected state a "spiritual body" and says that "flesh and blood" cannot inherit the Kingdom of God (1 Corinthians 15:50).

EVANGELISM AND THE NEED TO BE "BORN AGAIN"

The doctrine of "atonement" refers to theological discourse on how Christ effects salvation for human beings. Moving from the nature of

Christ to the work of Christ, we find that fundamentalist doctrine, while related to traditional Christianity, is certainly not the only legitimate option. With this doctrine, unlike some of the others, it is more difficult to draw distinctions between the fundamentalist view and the traditional views in Christianity. When they present their view, many fundamentalists, without having the options distinct in their mind, will draw upon elements and terminology from various traditional options.

The usual understanding of atonement among the founders and early theologians of fundamentalism is called the "substitutionary" or "penal substitution" theory. The view here is that the death of Christ was designed to propitiate God, that is, to regain the favor of God by having Christ bear the penalty for human sin. This view was advocated by the great Protestant Reformer John Calvin. It echoes the Old Testament notion of sacrifice as a substitution.

Fundamentalists today, however, when they speak about atonement, will often use ideas and terminology from the "satisfaction" view, which, admittedly, is somewhat similar to the substitutionary theory. The satisfaction theory is one with a long history in Christianity, with formal articulation going back at least as far as Anselm of Canterbury (ca. 1033–1109). The basic idea is that sin has dishonored God and offends God's justice. Reparation or satisfaction is due to God so that justice can be maintained. At the cross, God's justice and grace are both expressed; God became a man in Christ and satisfied the debt.

In fundamentalist circles, one will also hear elements of yet a third theory of the atonement. The "Christus Victor" theory, also called the classic, patristic, or Greek theory, is that Christ's death on the cross was essentially God's victory over sin and the devil. Jesus voluntarily gave his life as a ransom for humanity. Because this theory is set forth against the dualistic backdrop of a cosmic struggle between good and evil, its portrayal appeals to fundamentalists. In its formal articulation, this interpretation goes back at least to Ignatius of Loyola (1491–1556).

Finally, the moral influence theory of the atonement goes back to at least Peter Abelard (1079–1142). This theory appeals more to moderates and liberals. Here, the death of Christ is a demonstration of God's sacrificial love, which provides a model for our lives and, hopefully, elicits the human response of repentance and love. Admittedly, the moral influence theory, while important, has been less characteristic of mainstream Christianity than the other theories.

Fundamentalists, along with evangelicals, assert that all people are either saved or lost, and that people must individually convert to God through Jesus Christ in order to be saved. Fundamentalists use various terms for this conversion experience: "getting saved," "giving one's heart to Jesus," and, perhaps the most used, "being born again." The phrase "born again" or "new birth" is derived from a conversation between Jesus and Nicodemus in the Gospel of John (3:1–7).[6]

The markedly individualistic nature of this conversion has often been noted. Fundamentalist ethics are oriented toward personal morality, rather than structural and broad social change. This ethical orientation flows from the individualistic theology of conversion. Likewise, sin for the fundamentalist has to do with private moral failures. Fundamentalists, in general, have not participated in organized attempts to address the underlying structural causes of poverty, hunger, and racism. For the fundamentalist, the problem and the solution lies with the individual and his or her status before God.

Because the eternal fate of one's soul is at stake, this core belief in the necessity of personal conversion is what consciously motivates fundamentalists and evangelicals in their many evangelistic and missionary efforts for which they are so well known. The most important thing a Christian can do for a lost person is to lead them to Christ. Of course, it is easy to speculate about unconscious motives that may also be at work, such as increasing the size of a church or organization, or the desire for cultural domination.

All fundamentalists and most evangelicals contend that salvation is available only through faith in Jesus Christ. The implications are significant—heaven for the saved and a literal burning hell for the unsaved. This central belief is at the heart of the significant Christian missionary enterprise that has spanned the globe and the centuries. Fundamentalist organizations and television preachers boast of the "souls saved" by their various worldwide missionary efforts. What fundamentalists do not understand is that the high conversion numbers for non-Western cultures like India and Africa are due to the inclusive, even polytheistic nature of the religion of these cultures. If you believe in a dozen deities, you probably will not have much difficulty accepting one more god into your pantheon. Muslims, like fundamentalist Christians, are absolutist in their orientation and this is why conversion rates in Muslim countries are always low.

Despite the difficulty of missionary work among Muslims, evangelical groups targeting Muslims for conversion has been ratcheted up since 9/11. The Window International Network is a campaign to target Muslims for conversion. Southeastern Baptist Theological Seminary, my alma mater that is now a fundamentalist training school, has created a master's degree to train missionaries in how to convert Muslims. The number of missionaries in Islamic countries has increased several fold. The impact of all this increased missionary effort is yet to be seen.

Many concerned Christians, especially students still in the process of formulating their ideas, do not want to believe that everyone who does not profess Christ will burn in hell. However, they feel locked into this view. They think this is the only Christian view and are both surprised and relieved when they learn that devout Christians have and do hold other views.

While the exclusivism and finality of the fundamentalist view of salvation characterize most of conservative Protestant Christianity, this is by no means the only formulation found among Christian thinkers. Several positions have been distinguished and a number of them are advocated by thoughtful Christian theologians.

- "The Replacement Model." There is no value in other religions and it is God's will that Christianity replace all other religions. This is the fundamentalist position.
- "The Fulfillment Model." God is present in other religions. However, Jesus will enhance those religions and provide a fuller revelation of what persons of other faiths already know in some fashion.
- "The Mutuality Model." Persons of any faith, including Christianity, can benefit from knowledge of other religions. This model promotes genuine interreligious dialogue in the service of promoting spiritual growth.
- "The Acceptance Model." All religions are legitimate spiritual paths. Diversity is fully embraced in a postmodern world.[7]

With the fundamentalist view of the Bible, Jesus, and salvation in place, we now turn to what most fundamentalists think about what is going to happen in the future.

CHAPTER 7

The Rapture

AN UNUSUAL FUNDAMENTALIST DOCTRINE

For many non-fundamentalists, the fundamentalist doctrine of premillennial dispensationalism is the most peculiar part of the fundamentalist belief system. The enormous popularity of the *Left Behind* series of novels, selling more than 50 million copies to date, and with spin-offs in comic books, movies, and children's books, is evidence of the importance of end-time speculation in the fundamentalist scheme of things. The *Left Behind* series is written by Tim LaHaye and Jerry Jenkins. LaHaye, a prominent fundamentalist advocate of premillennial dispensationalism and right-wing fundamentalist political causes, provided the "theology" of the series and Jenkins, a fiction writer, constructed the plot line.[1]

As with fundamentalism in general, and, for that matter, any movement or ideology, I think it is useful to place premillennial dispensationalism in its historical and ideological context. The fundamentalist doctrine of the end of time is a peculiar and minority perspective in the long history of Christianity and in the theology of most Christians around the world. In my New Testament classes, I have a section on the book of Revelation, one of the favorite books of the Bible for fundamentalists. When I describe the premillennial dispensationalist interpretation of Revelation, I can look at the faces of my students and with near certainty discern which students grew up in a southern, conservative Protestant church, and which ones grew up in, for example, a Roman Catholic church.

"Of course, this is what the book of Revelation means and this is the way things will unfold in the end of time," say the faces of the southern, conservative Protestant students. When I present premillennial dispensationalism, the faces of the Roman Catholic students, however, depict utter puzzlement. "What in the world are you talking about?" their faces ask.

For those who have not been exposed to the futuristic scenarios of the fundamentalists, I now give a summary. If you choose to dip for yourself into some of the literature produced by premillennial dispensationalists, I warn you in advance that it takes a patient and ingenious critic to come to grips with the confusing maze of distinctions and scenarios that constitute the dispensationalist program. The premillennial dispensationalist authors often fill their books with so many elaborate charts and diagrams so as to make advanced scientific treatises look tame. I have wondered if my own obsessive tendencies played a role in my youthful fascination with these programs for so long.

First, here is some beginning terminology. "Eschatology" is from two Greek words that mean "end" (*eschaton*) and "discourse about" (*logos*). Let me be clear. Christians have traditionally believed that Jesus Christ will return to earth; this teaching can be found in the New Testament and early creeds. That said, Christians have formulated a number of ways of thinking about the second coming of Jesus and eschatology in general.

"Apocalyptic" is an adjective derived from a Greek word (*apokalypsis*) that means "revelation," and in an eschatological context, "apocalyptic" refers to an unveiling of truths that are ordinarily hidden. In fact, the title of the last book of the Christian Bible is "Apocalypse," and most people know the book by the translated word "Revelation." By the way, the title of this book is singular; it is "the" revelation of Jesus Christ. In any case, apocalypticism, broadly conceived, is the belief that the struggle between good and evil will climax in some sort of imminent end of the world as we know it. Almost always, the ethic appropriate for an apocalyptic program is an "interim" ethic, that is, it is in place only until the soon end of the world. The interim ethic is usually one that called the believer to a strict holy life as a way of preparing for God's soon intervention. This general apocalyptic program is an important element in the three "Western" or Abrahamic religions of Judaism, Christianity, and Islam and all three traditions share common sources for some of their apocalyptic notions.

Premillennial dispensationalism is the particular apocalyptic eschatological periodization program promoted by fundamentalists. It is questionable on many counts, as I will show. There are many variations but the basic scheme is as follows. There are several dispensations or succeeding ages through which God relates to the human community. In each age or dispensation God offers human beings a different plan of salvation. Humans rejected each offer with disastrous consequences (for example, expulsion from the Garden of Eden, worldwide flood). We are currently in the church age, and we are also now heading toward catastrophe and God's radical intervention.

Fundamentalists talk about the "signs of the times." By this phrase, they mean that the Bible gives us clues about events that will transpire in the "last days," the days immediately before the end-time scenario unfolds. All Christian futurists believe that the "signs of the times" prove that we are nearing the end. The "signs of the times" that fundamentalists talk about include an increase in natural disasters. Events like the 2004 tsunami that struck Indian Ocean nations prompt dispensationalists to renew their insistence that the end is near.

In most futuristic scenarios, the very next event to occur in the premillennial dispensationalist scenario is that Christians will be taken from the earth in the "rapture," a concept that has excited the imaginations of fundamentalists. When Christians are suddenly raptured from the earth, the world is left in chaos. This is the "theology" behind the sensational fundamentalist portrayals of planes and cars crashing when the Christian pilots and drivers are raptured. This scene, depicted in fundamentalist novels, movies, paintings, sermons, and bumper stickers, provides an exciting and spectacular chapter in the futuristic end-time scenario. It is important to keep in mind that the transportation of Christians from the evil world in the rapture is referring to "true" Christians and certainly not the liberal, apostate Christians.

Unfortunately for the fundamentalists, the actual word "rapture" is not found in the Bible. The English word is derived from *raptura,* the Latin word used by the Roman Catholic translators of the Vulgate for what is loosely translated into English as "caught up" (1 Thessalonians 4:17). The New Testament texts most often used to promote the rapture concept are Matthew 13:25–52; 24; 1 Thessalonians 4:13–17, 5:1–4; 2 Thessalonians 1:7–10; and 1 Corinthians 15:51–53. "Rapture" may very well be an appropriate word to use in English translations; however, given the centrality of this concept to fundamentalist doctrine about the end-time, I think it is worthwhile to note the paucity of biblical material on the rapture.

Dispensationalists believe that the bulk of the biblical book of Revelation describes a distressing and chaotic future time that will occur after the rapture. This period of distress is called the tribulation. The ones "left behind" will endure the terrible tribulation inflicted on the world by the Antichrist. The Antichrist figure is one of the more intriguing personalities in the end-time speculations. The term Antichrist occurs only in two minor New Testament epistles, 1 and 2 John, where the meaning of the term is unclear. The popular Christian imagination, however, has exhibited great interest in the concept through the centuries. Every futuristic generation of interpreters has its own notion about the identity of the Antichrist. In past times, individual Roman Catholic popes made the list. The Protestant Reformer Martin Luther saw the institution of the papacy as the Antichrist. Hitler was an obvious choice during the World War II era. In fundamentalist circles the futurist teachers explained to their flocks that the Antichrist could be identified by assigning numbers to the letters in the alphabet in the following pattern: A=100, B=101, C=102, and so on.

Using this code, the name H-I-T-L-E-R is the numeric equivalent of 666, the number of the dreaded beast in the apocalyptic book of Revelation (Revelation 13:18). Never mind that the arithmetic did not work out in German. Others identified as the Antichrist have included Henry Kissinger, Mikhail Gorbachev, and, more recently, Saddam Hussein and Osama bin Laden. Barack Obama has drawn attention because one of the winning lottery numbers in his home state was 666. Currently, the Antichrist is usually predicted to be some world leader who appears as a prince of peace, but is really, of course, the devil in disguise. If I were a premillennial dispensationalist, I would certainly have my own idea about who on today's world scene might fit the bill.[2]

During the tribulation, the Antichrist will rule via some kind of world government or system. Futuristic interpreters have traced the threat of world domination by the Antichrist to the formation of the European Economic Community, the Susan B. Anthony dollar, fiber optics, bar codes used at checkout counters, and many other modern developments. This belief in a world takeover explains why many fundamentalists, inspired by futuristic thinking, are wary of the United Nations. They see the UN as a likely candidate for the world system that the Antichrist will use to rule the world during the tribulation. The Antichrist will be opposed by true believers who will have converted during the tribulation. The worldwide good versus evil conflict taps into the same fascinations that have made popular everything from old westerns to the more recent *Star Wars* series.

Following the tribulation, Jesus Christ will return to the earth in the "second coming." The great, final battle between the forces of good and evil will occur at an ancient site called Armageddon. Jesus Christ will win this literal battle. The final age will see the establishment of a literal kingdom in Jerusalem with Jesus ruling for 1,000 years. The notion of the millennium is central in the futuristic program. It is, however, based on this rather obscure text in the New Testament book of Revelation:

> Then I saw an angel coming down from heaven, holding in his hand the key to the bottomless pit and a great chain. He seized the dragon, that ancient serpent, who is the Devil and Satan, and bound him for a thousand years, and threw him into the pit, and locked and sealed it over him, so that he would deceive the nations no more, until the thousand years were ended. After that he must be let out for a while. Then I saw thrones, and those seated on them were given authority to judge. I also saw the souls of those who had been beheaded for their testimony to Jesus and for the word of God. They had not worshiped the beast or its image and had not received its mark on their foreheads or their hands. They came to life and reigned with Christ a thousand years. The rest of the dead did not come to life until the thousand years were ended. This is the first resurrection. Blessed and holy are those who share in the first resurrection. Over these the second death has no power, but they will be priests of God and of Christ, and they will reign

with him a thousand years. When the thousand years are ended, Satan will be released from his prison and will come out to deceive the nations at the four corners of the earth, Gog and Magog, in order to gather them for battle; they are as numerous as the sands of the sea. They marched up over the breadth of the earth and surrounded the camp of the saints and the beloved city. And fire came down from heaven and consumed them. And the devil who had deceived them was thrown into the lake of fire and sulfur, where the beast and the false prophet were, and they will be tormented day and night forever and ever.

(Revelation 20:1–10)

As indicated in the text quoted above, the author of the book is reporting a vision. Visions like this, especially when occurring in apocalyptic texts, are never easy to interpret and a review of how Christians throughout history have interpreted the millennium reveals a wide variety of approaches. Unfortunately, most futurists have latched onto these few verses in a very large Bible, exaggerated their significance, and interpreted them literally. Part of the problem is that futurists are not consistent in their interpretation. Read literally, this passage states that those who have been beheaded will rule with Christ in the millennium, although most futurists teach that all Christians will rule with Christ.

Significant for their political implications, the final events will involve a restored Jewish kingdom and conversion of Jews to Christ. Dispensationalists believe these events will entail a literal return of Jews to Israel. Following this period, the final judgment will occur and then the eternal state—heaven or hell.

Disagreement exists among futurists about a number of things. For example, "pretribulationists" believe that Christians will be evacuated from the earth by a preliminary coming of Christ before the terrible tribulation. "Posttribulationists" have argued that the church will have to endure the tribulation. "Midtribulationists" cannot decide this question and so have convinced themselves that there will be three and one-half years of tribulation, the church will be evacuated, and then the final three and one-half years of tribulation will be endured. There are futurists who argue for a "partial rapture," where only the godly part of the church will be evacuated. And so on and so on. The main point is that all futurists believe that the Bible describes events that are soon to take place.

THE PROBLEMATIC NATURE OF FUNDAMENTALIST ESCHATOLOGY

Now for the history lesson. Given the role which premillennial dispensationalism plays in fundamentalism and has played in the thinking of some leaders in our government, it is important to get everything out on the table.

As I will show, premillennial dispensationalism with its rapture and other odd notions is a clear invention of modern fundamentalists and fundamentalist precursors. The irony is that while he was by no stretch of the imagination a premillennial dispensationalist, Jesus was very possibly an apocalypticist. I warn the nonfundamentalist Christian reader, even the moderate or liberal Christian, that what I am about to report may be theologically uncomfortable for you. Jesus was a Jewish preacher and, to say it straight out and more specifically, he may very well have been a Jewish apocalyptic preacher who thought the world as he knew it was coming to an end in his lifetime. If so, he was wrong, of course. Here are some sayings attributed to Jesus from the gospels that, at the very least, suggest that Jesus thought the end-time was near:

> "Truly, I say to you, there are some standing here who will not taste death before they see the Son of man coming in his kingdom."
>
> (Matthew 16:28)

> Jesus came into Galilee, preaching the gospel of God, and saying, "The time is fulfilled, and the Kingdom of God is at hand; repent, and believe in the gospel."
>
> (Mark 1:14–15)

> "Truly, I say to you, there are some standing here who will not taste death before they see the Kingdom of God come with power."
>
> (Mark 9:1)

> "But I tell you truly, there are some standing here who will not taste of death before they see the Kingdom of God."
>
> (Luke 9:27)

I should quickly point out that scholars disagree on this question of whether or not Jesus anticipated the end of the world. As we are treading on what for some is holy ground, I will back up and get a running start. The futuristic type of apocalyptic speculation began in earnest in the intertestamental period, that is, "between the testaments," Old and New, roughly one to three centuries before Christ. In a number of places in the Bible, we have texts that are apocalyptic, in that they predict an imminent end of history. "Apocalyptic" is a word that refers to revelation about the near end of time and also to a kind of literature that was produced during times of oppression and stress and that revealed this near end. An important part of this story, provided to us by biblical scholars and totally missed by most fundamentalists, is that the biblical apocalyptic books are not the only apocalyptic books written by persecuted Jews and Christians of that day. We have discovered other such texts, more than a dozen Jewish ones, and even more Christian texts. Often, these books are called the "lost" books of the Bible. On a slow news day, the tabloids might run some story about the "lost" books of the Bible. Of course, they are not lost. I have copies of them on my bookshelf, right next to my Bibles. Scholars have long been aware of them and use them to understand the history and context of the ancient Jews and Christians. They are "lost" to most folk who are unaware of biblical scholarship. These books are the ones we know about and, it seems likely, there would have been others that have not survived the ancient period.

These many apocalyptic texts are full of the same kinds of images and events that fill the biblical apocalyptic texts on which fundamentalists build their end-time scenario. As I write I have on my desk Second Esdras. In this Jewish apocalyptic book, that is not in the Protestant canon of scripture, the old scribe Ezra goes on a journey and meets such strange characters as a twelve-winged eagle, a talking lion, and a woman who turns into a city. All apocalyptic books, in or outside the Bible, contain depictions of strange characters and bizarre events. The following quotation is from the book of Second Esdras, a book not in the fundamentalist canon and written in the second century before Christ. The quotation illustrates that the futuristic program of the fundamentalists is built on a very selective reading of this kind of literature.

> The sun shall suddenly begin to shine at night, and the moon during the day. Blood shall drip from wood, and the stone shall utter its voice; the peoples shall be troubled, and the stars shall fall. And one shall reign whom those who inhabit the earth do not expect, and the birds shall fly away together. . . . There shall be chaos also in many places, fire shall often break out, the wild animals shall roam beyond their haunts, and menstruous women shall bring forth monsters. Salt waters shall be found in the sweet, and all friends shall conquer one another . . . these are the signs that I am permitted to tell you, and if you pray again, and weep as you do now, and fast for seven days, you shall hear yet greater things than these.
>
> (2 Esdras 5:3–13)

When we examine all these texts in historical context we gain an understanding of their origin and basic role in ancient faith communities, although scholars dispute some of the particulars. Here is one common way of looking at things. In Jewish history, the second century before Christ was a time of persecution of the Jews. This was the time of Antiochus IV, ruler of Syria, called the "madman" by the Jews. He presided over a program designed to systematically eliminate Judaism from the planet. And it was terrible. The apocryphal book of 1 Maccabees, generally an excellent historical source, provides often vivid descriptions of the persecution of Jews during this awful time. Here is an example:

> According to the decree, they put to death the women who had their children circumcised, and their families and those who circumcised them; and they hung the infants from their mothers' necks.
>
> (1 Maccabees 1:60–61)

The persecution sets up the exciting story of the Maccabean Revolt, initiated by the aged and devout Mattathias. Hollywood would do well to depict this old Jew and the revolt he inspired. The point of this digression is to show that these were hard times for the Jews. Life was felt to be dislocated, painful, and scary.

In the midst of these hard times, Jewish writers arose to encourage their fellow Jews. In the Jewish Bible, the book of Daniel is the one book that is almost totally apocalyptic. The book of Daniel is extensively used and terribly misused by the dispensationalists. The writers of apocalyptic are sending the message to the persecuted Jews, "Hang on, don't give up, God will save you and He won't tarry." The literature is written in highly symbolic language. It is full of natural disasters, strange animals, and curious events.

Closer to the time of Christ, the Dead Sea Scrolls, which came to light in 1947, were written by a Jewish monastic community that lived in the desert, near the Dead Sea. That this community was, to some significant degree, apocalyptic is reflected in, for example, one of their texts, entitled "The War of the Sons of Light and the Sons of Darkness." This fascinating text provides details about the final battle between the forces of good and the forces of evil. The text gives plans for the final great battle, including the number and kinds of soldiery, the type of weaponry, and how the attack is to be prosecuted. These people believed the battle was coming and they were getting ready! The point of this and other such texts is that it informs us about the apocalyptic nature of the Judaism of Jesus's day. To give a bit more of the flavor of these apocalyptic texts, and the way they present detailed descriptions of the future climactic battle, here are a few selections from the Dead Sea Scroll text. Brackets [ ] represent places where the text is corrupted and the translator either makes a guess about what was said or leaves it blank. Ellipses (. . .) indicate omission of sentences not relevant to the point I am making.

> [Streaks of lightn]ing will flash from one end of the world to the other, growing ever brighter until the era of darkness is brought utterly to an end. Then, in the era of God, His exalted grandeur will give light for [evermore,] shedding on all Sons of Light peace and blessing, gladness and length of days. . . . For the remaining thirty-three years of the War, the dignitaries appointed to the Assembly and all the chiefs of families in the community are to select the soldiers for service in the various foreign countries. They are to draft them annually out of all the tribes of Israel in accordance with the established conventions of warfare. . . . To form a complete front. The line is to consist of a thousand men. Each front-line is to be seven deep. One man standing behind the other. All of them are to hold shields of polished bronze, resembling mirrors. These shields are to be bordered by a wreath-like rim wrought artistically by a skilled smith . . . . Each shield is to be two and one half cubits long and two and one half cubits wide. The men are to hold in their hands a spear and a lance. . . . The seven battle lines shall be flanked

in turn, on the left and on the right, by cavalry. Each line shall be accompanied by two hundred light horsemen, so that there will be in all seven hundred of the latter on the one side and seven hundred on the other. . . . The line troops are to be forty to fifty years of age. . . . Six [times] shall the priests sound on the trumpets the signal for carnage—a sharp, insistent sound, to direct the battle. And the levites and all the people with rams' horns shall sound a loud blast. And as the sound goes forth, they shall start lashing out and felling the Kittians. All the people shall silence their war-cries while the priests are sounding on the trumpets the signal for carnage. And the battle shall be waged victoriously against the Kittians. . . . When the great hand of God is raised against Belial and against all the forces under his dominion, inflicting on them an eternal discomfiture, and when the war-cry of Israel and of the holy beings rings out, as they pursue Assyria; and when the sons of Japhet fall never to rise, and when the Kittians are cut off without [survivor]; then, when the hand of the God of Israel has indeed prevailed against all the multitude of Belial, the priests shall sound the blasts of memorial, and all the lines of battle shall rally unto them, and all shall receive their portion of the spoil [ ] to "devote" to it. And when the sun is hasting to set on that day, the high priest shall stand up, and the priests and the levites that are with him, and he shall look upon the [ ] battle array and there bless the God of Israel.

("The War of the Sons of Light and Sons of Darkness,"
in the Dead Sea Scrolls)

A later Christian example of an apocalyptic text is the Revelation of Peter, a second-century document that was widely read by Christians. Like most apocalyptic books, it contains visions of the future. It depicts extreme suffering by sinners, as exampled in these descriptions:

And this shall come at the day of judgment upon those who have fallen away from faith in God and have committed sin. Cataracts of fire shall be let loose; and darkness and obscurity shall come up and clothe and veil the whole world; and the waters shall be changed and turned into coals of fir, and all that is in them shall burn, and the sea shall become fire. . . . Then shall men and women come to the place prepared for them. By their tongues wherewith they have blasphemed the way of righteousness shall they be hanged up. There is spread under them unquenchable fire so that they do not escape it. Behold another place: there is a pit, great and full. In it are those who have denied righteousness; and angels of punishment chastise them and there they kindle upon them the fire of their torment. . . . And near this flame there is a pit, great and very deep, and into it flows from above all manner of torment, foulness, and excrement. And women are swallowed up therein up to their necks and tormented with great pain. . . . And again, other men and women, gnawing their tongues without ceasing, and being tormented with everlasting fire. These are the servants who were not obedient to their masters; and this then is their judgment for ever.[3]

The above passages from Second Esdras, Dead Sea Scrolls, and the Revelation of Peter, along with many others I could cite, show that the biblical apocalyptic writings (such as, Daniel in the Old Testament and

Revelation in the New Testament), that fundamentalists make so much of, are not by any means unique. Pious Jews and Christians from that ancient period wrote many such books.

Mainstream scholars are in general agreement that Christianity in its origins was an apocalyptic religion, at least to some degree. We have found about twice as many Christian apocalyptic books as Jewish and these kinds of Christian texts flourished into the third century. Almost no scholar of early Christianity would disagree that Christianity, like Judaism, to some significant degree held to the notion of an imminent end. There is, however, dispute about the nature and extent of Jesus as a preacher of the end-time. There are two general views among scholars.

Some scholars, reflecting a recent trend, view Jesus as a teacher of subversive wisdom, a popular sage who traveled around in an itinerate ministry to the poor and dispossessed. Members of the famous—and infamous—"Jesus Seminar," a scholarly enterprise that has received much attention in the secular press, generally take this non-apocalyptic view of Jesus. Marcus Borg is a good example of a member of this group of scholars and currently is in high demand on the public lecture circuit. He pictures Jesus as a sharp-tongued social prophet who subverts conventional wisdom. According to Borg, the "new" political Jesus is emerging from study informed by at least three perspectives.

First, recognizing the two-class peasant society in which Jesus lived locates him as a social prophet similar, in some ways, to the classical prophets of Israel. Second, patriarchy as a social context, uncovered by feminist biblical scholarship, also allows us to see Jesus as advocating an alternative social vision. Finally, in a vein particularly championed by Borg, Jesus is seen as challenging the purity structures of his day, structures which legitimized the ruling elite.[4]

A second general scholarly view of Jesus is that he was thoroughly apocalyptic in his outlook and preached the imminent end of the world. This venerable scholarly tradition includes the famous Albert Schweitzer, a remarkable man and Nobel Peace Prize recipient admired by the general public as well as academics. In his famous book, translated into English in 1910 as *The Quest of the Historical Jesus,* Schweitzer dealt a near death blow to the "lives" of Jesus written up to that point by liberal scholars. Well written and covering the whole life of Jesus, this book was read by an audience much wider than that which usually reads scholarly books. The reader will note that the book came on the American scene at the time that fundamentalism was cranking up in response to offensive intellectual ideas in the realms of science, history, and religion. Schweitzer showed that we do not have the ancient materials necessary to write a modern biography of Jesus and, perhaps more importantly, that the books on Jesus up to that point were in essence projections of the authors who were reading back into the gospels their own contemporary images of Jesus. In effect, Schweitzer dealt a blow to the liberal and optimistic portrayal of Jesus that Schweitzer revealed as a creation of the liberal social agenda.

To replace the mistaken liberal portrayal, Schweitzer argued that Jesus expected the eschatological kingdom in his immediate future. Jesus operated out of a conviction that he was God's instrument for hastening the end-time events. Jesus sent out his disciples to preach about the coming Kingdom of God in order to speed up the process. Jesus lived in such anticipation of the end that he expected God to bring in the end before the disciples returned. "You will not have gone through all the towns of Israel before the Son of Man comes" (Matthew 10:23). When the disciples did return and still no Kingdom, it was devastating to Jesus and at this point he made the decision to personally die in order to force the coming of the Kingdom. When Jesus died, there was no sign that the Kingdom was any closer and Schweitzer concludes that Jesus died broken and disillusioned.

Now, what is fascinating and remarkable to most is that somehow Schweitzer was motivated by this despairing Jesus, this pitiful defeated figure dying on the cross, to give his life in service as a medical missionary in Africa. For Schweitzer, the historical Jesus is irrelevant to theology and Christian life; it is the heroic spirit of Jesus that lives on in a powerful way.[5] The most famous paragraph Schweitzer ever penned was the last paragraph in his *Quest of the Historical Jesus* and bears repeating:

> He comes to us as One unknown, without a name, as of old, by the lake-side. He came to those men who knew Him not. He speaks to us the same word: "Follow thou me!" and sets us to the tasks which He has to fulfill for our time. He commands. And to those who obey Him, whether they be wise or simple, He will reveal Himself in the toils, the conflicts, the sufferings which they shall pass through in His fellowship, and, as an ineffable mystery, they shall learn in their own experience Who He is.[6]

Did Jesus think the world was coming to an end in his lifetime? Many very careful scholars think very likely so. Schweitzer's general apocalyptic interpretation of Jesus framed the scholarly discussion, until the last few decades with the arrival of the new perspective that sees Jesus as a wandering teacher of morality and a critic of the establishment (scholars such as Borg and others). I personally like that picture of Jesus as a subversive prophet and critic of the religious and political establishments. We will see how well it survives continued rigorous examination of the historical Jesus. It is not my purpose in this book to weigh in on this particular debate. I'll just say that as with many scholarly disputes that run deep, my guess is that both major camps—apocalyptic Jesus and moral teacher Jesus—zero in on an important piece of the truth about the historical Jesus. In any case, there are these two major positions about Jesus on this issue that are, at least explicitly, based on an unbiased examination of the evidence rather than some theological agenda. In neither case does Jesus emerge in a way that supports the fundamentalist program.

The question of the relevance of the historical Jesus for Christian faith is one that has long been discussed in the theological community. How much history is enough? Predictably, the extreme positions are that the historical Jesus is crucial for faith and that, as with Schweitzer, the historical Jesus is totally irrelevant, and there are formulations all along the spectrum between these extreme points. Fundamentalist theology obviously champions the first view. Liberal Protestantism also wants to look to the historical Jesus as a model, although liberals who believe the historical Jesus was an apocalypticist and are more open to scholarship than fundamentalists find ways to tone down the apocalyptic aspects of Jesus. For example, nineteenth-century liberals argued that the apocalyptic elements were the "husks" of Jesus's teaching and not its true "kernel."[7]

CHAPTER 8

"Left Behind" Theology

THE ORIGIN OF A STRANGE IDEA

The doctrine that Christ will return to the earth to reign for a thousand years is an old notion, going back to early Christianity, and probably has origins in Jewish apocalyptic. The eschatology of Protestant Christianity, through most of the eighteenth century, was "postmillennial." Postmillennialism taught that God is at work in the world and the second coming of Christ will occur after the "millennium," hence "post" millennialism. Postmillennial thinking is optimistic and encourages Christians to work as instruments of God in the world in order to reform society. The premillennial futuristic interpretation, especially in its premillennial dispensationalist form, has its roots in the early nineteenth century in Ireland and England, and some have suggested that it can be related to the disillusionment following the French Revolution. Rather than a better life, the people got the guillotine and more wars.[1] Premillennial dispensationalism is probably also related to the attempt by Christians in certain parts to understand what was judged to be the heresy and decline of the Church of England. The futuristic scenario does provide a convenient framework for distinguishing the true church (of the fundamentalists) from the liberal, apostate church.

John Nelson Darby (1800–1882) was the important early proponent of premillennial dispensationalism. He was originally ordained as a priest in the Church of Ireland, which he eventually rejected. He joined a group of dissenters called the Plymouth Brethren and preached in America and Canada on several mission trips between 1862–1877, bringing with him the dispensationalist scheme. This was, of course, a trying time of war and ugly aftermath for the "United" States, hence, a time of hardship when people were looking for some way to understand their lives, exactly the kind of atmosphere ripe for apocalypticism.

Perhaps the most widespread dissemination of Darby's scheme came through the *Scofield Reference Bible,* first published in 1909 by Cyrus I. Scofield. Scofield used the *King James Version* of the Bible and added extensive divisions, notes, and cross-references implementing the Darbyite dispensationalist framework. Scofield was an attorney who was associated with the influential evangelist Dwight L. Moody, and Scofield also gained financial support from Lyman Stewart, who with his brother funded *The Fundamentals* pamphlet series we encountered in Part One. The solid fundamentalist orientation of the *Scofield Reference Bible* is indicated in the *Reference Bible*'s statement that the author follows

> the plenary inspiration and inerrancy of the Scriptures; the triune Godhead composed of the Father, the Son, and the Holy Spirit; the virgin birth and Deity of Christ; the necessity and efficacy of His atoning work; Christ's bodily resurrection and ascension; His imminent coming for His Church and His visible, premillennial return to the earth; the everlasting felicity of the redeemed; and the everlasting punishment of the lost.[2]

The *Scofield Reference Bible* sold millions of copies and a full generation or two took the interpretation contained in the notes of this Bible as normative. In fact, most readers of the *Scofield Reference Bible* were likely unaware that the dispensationalist framework was actually just another interpretative approach. Fundamentalist and evangelical students today will likely not own or know about the *Scofield Reference Bible.* They use "modern" translations. However, the *Scofield Reference Bible* will be the Bible their grandparents, and maybe parents, have on their shelf back home. Current *Left Behind* enthusiasts have inherited the teachings of Darby and Scofield, whether they know it or not.

The dispensationalist scheme was expanded and propagated through popular Bible conferences and by numerous evangelists, beginning in the last half of the nineteenth century. Bible Institutes, which proliferated during this period, and most notably the Moody Bible Institute, jumped on the bandwagon. *Jesus is Coming,* authored in 1878 by William Blackstone, helped spread the dispensationalist word. Lewis Chafer, a Presbyterian minister, was among the converts. He founded Dallas Theological Seminary, which became the leading theological school devoted to premillennial dispensationalism. While the institution has a long and deep history of allegiance to the Darby-Scofield dispensationalist program, I am told, informally, by one of my students who attended, that there are shifts away from a strict premillennial dispensationalism among some of the newer faculty. Graduates of the school in the earlier years who were leading apostles of dispensationalism include John Walvoord, later president of the Seminary, and Hal Lindsey, popular author.

The solid implantation in America of the Darby premillennial dispensationalist scheme occurred during the early decades of the twentieth century when our involvement in the war in Europe was a stark reminder that all was not well with the world. The dispensationalist notions became even more embedded in the psyche of the evangelical/fundamentalist wing of American Christianity during the time of the Holocaust and World War II. While a detailed examination is outside the scope of this book, the general time period around the middle of the century saw the rise in Christianity of what is called "neo-orthodox theology," associated with the names of theologians like Karl Barth and Dietrich Bonhoeffer. The latter was imprisoned and hung by the Nazis for his involvement in a plot to assassinate Hitler. Premillennial dispensationalism and neo-orthodoxy both took seriously traditional notions of human sinfulness and the need for God's grace. Both were responding to the same deeply felt anxiety about the ability of human beings to find their way out of the chaotic mess that characterized the world in this age.

In my college generation of the 1970s, Hal Lindsey was the most popular proponent of the dispensationalist program. His books, *The Late Great Planet Earth* and *There's a New World Coming,* and later *The 1980s: Countdown to Armageddon* (1980), sold tens of millions of copies. *The Late Great Planet Earth,* his first one, has alone sold over 19 million copies. They are the ideological and publishing father of the current *Left Behind* series. In Lindsey's day, before the end of the cold war, the villains were the Soviets. Lindsey made much of the rebirth of Israel, Middle Eastern turmoil, and interest in Satanism. With the collapse of the USSR, today's future enemies are more likely to be Muslims. In his most recent book, *Planet Earth 2000* (1994), Lindsey also weaves in environmental concerns. I suppose that is progress of a sort.

In the spirit of futurism, this seems like as appropriate place as any to formally place into print a prediction of my own. In the 2004 U.S. presidential election, in which Republican George W. Bush defeated by a narrow margin Democrat John Kerry, security was a major concern, understandable in light of the 9/11 attacks on the New York Twin Towers. Along with the economy, security was a major issue in the 2008 election of Barack Obama as president. At this writing, in January 2009, it would seem with Bush's war dragging on in Iraq, in the context of worldwide terrorism, that security will continue as a major concern for the foreseeable future. Our leaders continue to remind us that we should brace ourselves for more terrorist attacks, perhaps more devastating than 9/11.

I have little doubt but that terrorism and security will remain high on our list of worries, but I have a prediction. In the tradition of those futurists who have set dates for the second coming, I will give a specific date. On the presidential election date of November 8, 2020, polls will show that the top three concerns of Americans will be global climate change, human germline genetic engineering, and radical life extension. The last two refer to developments in science that are now underway. Germline genetic engineering, sometimes referred to by the popular term "designer babies," refers to manipulating the genetic material in ways that are inherited by future generations. Radical life extension is another term for solving the aging process so that the human body can live indefinitely and be healthy. While the possibility of "practical immortality" sounds far-fetched to most people now, as medical and biological science pushes toward the goal, there will be intense focus on the many astounding cultural, economic, sociological, legal, religious, and other implications of reaching the goal.[3] Security from terrorism will be the number four concern of Americans. My prediction is for the presidential election about a decade from now. I actually think global climate change, germline engineering, and radical life extension will be major concerns before the year 2020, but I am not as bold as some futurists. I want to give myself some wiggle room. If my prediction comes true, then by 2020 premillennial dispensationalists will be writing books, selling tapes, preaching sermons, plastering bumper stickers on their vehicles, and filling up Web sites with "signs of the times" and predictions of the end-time that are oriented around, you guessed it, global climate change, designer babies, and radical life extension. The Soviets and communists of the mid-twentieth century were replaced by the Muslims of today who will be replaced by these new issues in the wild-eyed end-time speculation of the fundamentalist premillennial dispensationalism.

Ironically, fundamentalists who argue strongly for a literal reading of the Bible go wild in their symbolic interpretations of the apocalyptic texts, relating these old symbols to contemporary world events. My point, of course, is that given their seemingly inflexible assignment of referents to the various symbols in the biblical apocalyptic literature, the dispensationalists can be amazingly flexible and nimble when world events shift. Paul Boyer captures it well, speaking about the collapse of the Soviet Union, for so long a staple in the futurist predication.

> These dramatic events [fall of the Soviet Union] initially threatened an epistemological crisis in the world of prophecy belief. An end-time scenario that for half a century had mirrored in lurid apocalyptic terms the central realities of a world divided between two nuclear-armed superpowers suddenly seemed out of date. Some elements of the system remained in place, of course, notably those relating to Israel and the Jews, but the alarming predications of global thermonuclear war and the destruction of the Soviet Union that had enlivened countless prophecy popularizations for decades now seemed embarrassingly passé.
>
> But the prophecy popularizers barely missed a beat. One of the great strengths of literalistic apocalypticism over the centuries has been its resourcefulness in adapting to new realities. The Emperor Saladin gave way to Napoleon, and

Napoleon to Mussolini, as the prime candidate for the Antichrist. The Ottoman Empire gave way to Russia as the doomed kingdom of the north.[4]

The social and psychological significance of the dispensationalist program is certainly worth exploring. Historically, we have seen that the emergence and early popularity of premillennial dispensationalism via Darby, the *Scofield Reference Bible*, and other avenues were in the latter part of the nineteenth century and the beginning of the twentieth. Premillennial dispensationalism carries a pessimistic outlook on the possibilities of this world. It thrives during times of crisis, as in the period after the Civil War. During the troubling social shifts of those days, the futuristic interpretation provided hope that conservative values would in the end win out. After the 9/11 attacks on the Twin Towers, sales of the *Left Behind* novels increased 60 percent.[5] The Darby-Scofield-Lindsey-*Left Behind* group rejects the more optimistic, hopeful postmillennialism that sees God working through people to bring about spiritual and moral progress in the world. Postmillennialism was a theological tool that moderate and liberal Protestants used to adjust the (perhaps) embarrassing biblical apocalyptic language and concepts to Enlightenment notions of reason and social progress.

Dispensationalism is a program made to order for the psychological uncertainty and threat that fundamentalists must feel during stressful periods, such as the time after the Civil War and 9/11. As discussed in Part One, the fundamentalists emerged fighting in a time of immigration, urbanization, the spread of Darwin's ideas, and other threatening intellectual and social developments. American society was changing, schools were converting to the new ideas, and mainline denominations were being won over. In this context, Darby's novel notion of the rapture served an important psychological purpose, albeit in a neurotic manner. Darby believed the rapture was a "secret" rapture. The institutional church is populated by infidels; only God knows the true Christians and only they will be taken up in the rapture. So, Christians who were intimidated by the social, intellectual, and religious changes of the day could believe that in the rapture they would be vindicated as the true Christians. The false and hypocritical Christians would be left behind to continue running the government, institutional church, and other organizations.[6]

Fundamentalist dispensationalists, who have heard nothing all their life but the premillennial dispensationalist scheme, are usually surprised to learn that there are other ways Christians have interpreted those old apocalyptic texts. My view, which I embed here and there in the following paragraphs, as I critique specifics of the futuristic program, is mild—even boring—by comparison with the futuristic scenarios, but it does reflect an interpretation informed by scholarship and held by most Christians.

For the dispensationalists, a key passage is Daniel 9:24–27. Amazingly, the fundamentalist interpreter often asserts that God's entire plan for the end of time is laid out in these four verses at the end of Daniel. Here are the verses, which report a vision given to Daniel, that are so crucial to the dispensationalist program:

> Seventy weeks are determined for your people and for your holy city, to finish the transgression, to make an end of sins, to make reconciliation for inequity, to bring in everlasting righteousness, to seal up vision and prophecy, and to anoint the Most Holy. Know therefore and understand, that from the time that the word went out to restore and rebuild Jerusalem until the time of an anointed prince, there shall be seven weeks; and for sixty-two weeks it shall be built again with streets and moat, but in a troubled time. After the sixty-two weeks, an anointed one shall be cut off and shall have nothing, and the troops of the prince who is to come shall destroy the city and the sanctuary. Its end shall come with a flood, and to the end there shall be war. Desolations are decreed. He shall make a strong covenant with many for one week, and for half of the week he shall make sacrifice and offering cease; and in their place shall be an abomination that desolates, until the decreed end is poured out upon the desolator.

This vague apocalyptic vision most likely refers to the period of the Maccabean revolt (168–64 BCE), a time of terrible persecution for the Jews, and their revolt against the Syrian oppressors. Dispensationalists, of course, see the final seventieth week as an unfulfilled prediction of our near future. To illustrate the arcane and, I think, groundless dispensationalist interpretation of these verses, one needs only read the commentary on these verses from the dispensationalist "Bible," the *Scofield Reference Bible.* The commentary rambles on for a page, piecing together passages from various parts of the Bible to "prove" that "during the interim between the sixty-ninth and seventieth week there must lie the whole period of the Church set forth in the NT . . . "[7]

Just as persecution of the ancient Jews provided the occasion for this and other Jewish apocalyptic writing, a background of persecution also exists for the New Testament apocalyptic texts, namely, Mark 13, and the book of Revelation. The Christians were being persecuted by the Roman emperor. The persecution was severe, the challenge was great, and the need for "hard times" literature to encourage the faithful was enormous. Revelation, like all apocalyptic books, contains its share of wild imagery and events, like the talking altar, beasts with many heads, and bottomless pits.

These symbols can be understood in the historical context of the apocalyptic writer. The beast, for example, likely refers to one of the Roman emperors who persecuted the Christians. Throughout history, those who have tended toward futuristic views have interpreted the beast in light of the tyrants of their day. Today, as mentioned earlier, the beast is sometimes seen as some person, perhaps now born, who will rise to the world stage and take control of some world governmental system, such as the United Nations.

For persons of faith who see the Bible as in some sense the word of God, the futuristic program has the benefit of offering these old apocalyptic texts in a way that is relevant for today's world. Of course, the key issue is how they are relevant. Futurists see the texts as referring to specific developments that are beginning to unfold in today's world. It seems to me that this benefit entails a huge problem. If the futurists are correct, then the book of Revelation and other apocalyptic texts had no real relevance for the Christians and Jews who lived in ancient times. If you tell me that something is going to happen 2,000 years into my future, I may have some curiosity, but it does not relate to my life directly. Every book in the Bible can be understood as emerging out of the real experience of human beings in those communities of faith. To come to Daniel in the Old Testament and Revelation in the New Testament, and see those books as having no relevance for the lives of Jews and Christians who lived when the books were written, seems an inadequate way of approaching the Bible.

We have information about a number of religious groups throughout history who have predicted a specific time for the end. The particular reading and prophetic calculations of farmer-preacher William Miller led him to predict that the world would end around 1843. Like all futurists, Miller zeroed in on particular texts of the Bible, to the exclusion of those that might not fit his scheme. Miller was enamored with the Jewish biblical book of Daniel, and specifically Daniel 8:14, the second part of which reads, "For two thousand three hundred evenings and mornings; then the sanctuary shall be restored to its rightful state." A common tactic of futurists is to convert biblical "days" into years, because the literal meaning would not serve their purpose of seeing the end-time as approaching in our future. The 2,300 years, starting, conveniently, from 458 BCE, a date when the King Artaxerxes I of Persia authorized the priest Ezra's mission to rebuild the Jerusalem temple, left Miller with the prediction that Jesus would return around 1843.

Miller had nearly a million disciples in various northeastern states. When the end did not materialize, a new date, October 22, 1844, was set by his followers and accepted by Miller. In his failure and downfall, Miller actually influenced in a major way later futurist programs. Unlike Miller, most later futurists have been careful not to predict a specific date, hence the popularity of Darby's "secret" rapture, the time of which no one knows, although the "signs of the time" make clear it will likely be soon. This approach conveniently allows the fundamentalist futurist to live on the "edge of time" but not have to be accountable for the exact location of that edge.

While futurists learned from the failed Miller policy of setting a specific date for the great end, futurists are excitable types and occasionally cannot contain themselves. Margaret Rowan, a young girl from California, reported that the angel Gabriel told her the world would end on February 13, 1925. Her report was widely disseminated. A New York housepainter, Robert Reidt, believed the report and urged people to gather with him on a hilltop to await the end of time. Gathered in white robes for the rapture, a crowd chanted "Gabriel" until sundown on February 13. When nothing happened, the delay in the second coming was attributed to interference from photographers' cameras.

Even the usually steady revival preacher Billy Graham, in what was, perhaps, the more unsteady early years of his ministry, proclaimed the imminent coming of Christ and, while he did not set a definite date, Graham talked in the early 1950s about the end being a short time away, "two years," "another year," "next few months."[8]

Hal Lindsey walked perilously close, if not over, the date setting line when he predicted that the rapture "might" come in 1981. Like Miller, Lindsey applied his calculator to some old apocalyptic texts. Connecting vague references in Mark 13 (for example, verse 30, "until all these things have taken place") to the 1948 founding of the state of Israel, and taking the word "generation" as a literal 40 years, Lindsey concluded that the great final battle, the Battle of Armageddon, could occur by 1988 (1948 plus 40). Of course, in the premillennial scheme, one has to subtract seven years, the length of the tribulation, because Christians will be spirited away before this awful time. So, in 1981 (1988 minus 7) many in the evangelical and fundamentalist camps were doing their best to live holy lives, just in case the Lord came back that year.

We have other such instances of apocalyptic date-setting. I am reminded of an old Jewish story about a man whose job was to sit at the village gate and wait for the Messiah. The man complains to the village elders that the pay is too low. The elders reply, "You are right. The pay is low, but the work is steady."

When the predicted time comes and goes and the end-time scenario does not occur, it throws the apocalyptic group into crisis. The people are disillusioned, the leaders are discredited, and the theology is called into question. When this occurs, there can be several outcomes. The group may not be able to effectively address the crisis, causing the group to disintegrate. Jim Jones's People's Temple is an example of an apocalyptic group where this occurred. In other cases, the group recalculates the end of time. Typically, the recalculation pushes the end of time farther into the future.

Yet another solution is that the group rethinks their whole understanding of eschatology. In early Christianity, as I have said, there is good evidence that many of the early Christians really did think the world as they knew it was coming to an end in their lifetime. In the apocalyptic chapter 13 of Mark, Jesus tells his disciples, "Truly, I say to you, this generation will not pass away before all these things take place" (Mark 13:30). The apocalyptic book of Revelation begins and ends with this sense of the imminent return of Christ. The book begins, "The revelation of Jesus Christ, which God gave him to show to his servants what must soon take place . . . " (Revelation 1:1). It ends, "He who testifies to these things says, 'Surely I am coming soon.' Amen. Come, Lord Jesus!" (Revelation 22:20). The unexpected and unexplained delay in the coming of Jesus was very confusing to the earliest Christians. From a purely historical perspective, it could have spelled the doom of the little movement.

Several early Christian leaders stepped up to the crisis and led the young church through this difficult period. Luke wrote Luke-Acts, a two-volume work that included Acts, a kind of history of the early church. Luke pushed the time of the coming of Jesus into the indefinite future. In effect, Luke was saying to the Christian apocalyptic enthusiasts of his audience that they were putting their time frame on God, and that God would come back when God was ready. Their job was to go about the business of being the church in the world.

Paul, too, dealt with the problem of Christians in his churches standing around with their hands in their pockets, waiting for the end of time. Paul, or whoever wrote the text, told them to get back to work (2 Thessalonians 3:6–13). Clearly, many of the first-century Christians were caught up in the futuristic fervor and to some degree were reined in by leaders whose books are in the New Testament canon.

Before leaving the biblical material, I would like to address a final point about terminology. The fundamentalists usually refer to their futuristic scenarios as "prophecy." If you go downtown and ask people on the street to give you a definition of prophecy, they will say things like "predicting the future." This is a misuse of a wonderful Hebrew word. The root of the words "prophecy," "prophesy," and "prophet" has to do with the basic idea of communication. One could loosely translate the verb "prophesy" as "preach." The great Israelite prophets, such as Isaiah, Micah, Hosea, and Amos, were prophets in the sense that they spoke forth the word of God. Their job was not to give some mysterious prediction of future events. If you read the books left by these men, you will see that they spent their time proclaiming the truth of God to the unjust social conditions and abuses of political power of their day. The reader may have noticed that when talking about Christian futuristic programs, I use terms like apocalyptic eschatology. Perhaps it is a minor point, given the misreading of things by the premillennial dispensationalists, but I think it is worth the effort to correct this terminology.

FUNDAMENTALISTS AND JEWS

One might ask, why worry about the fundamentalist dispensationalist program. Many people hold strange views, and so what. Even though I think the premillennial dispensationalist theology and interpretation are incredibly misguided, I really do not care what fundamentalists believe about the end of time. But I am very concerned about the implications of this belief in premillennial dispensationalism.

First, a strong futuristic emphasis in eschatology fits nicely into what scholars call an otherworldly religion, as opposed to this-worldly. Liberals tend to be this-worldly, focused on God's work through human beings in the here and now. Fundamentalists tend to think of this world as caught in the grip of evil and, so, the focus is on escaping to another world. I regret otherworldly religion to the extent that it takes people away from addressing the present suffering of their fellow human beings.

Secondly and more importantly, I am very concerned when a particular eschatological formulation from any religion begins to influence public policy. Barbara Rossing's book, *The Rapture Exposed,* gives specific examples of how public officials have been influenced by dispensationalist scenarios about Israel.[9] The influence comes from "Christian Zionism," a dangerous program promoted by a relatively small but energetic and influential group of fundamentalist dispensationalists. The apocalyptic scenario of many futurists includes the restoration of Israel as God's primary instrument in history. Belief in this piece of the scenario has resulted in political alliance between Christian futurists in the United States and the right-wing Likud Party in Israel, both of which are united, for different reasons, in promoting Israel's control of the Holy Land. Given the potential mischief of Christian Zionism, a brief explanation is in order.

Zionism refers to a movement within Judaism that can be understood as the secularization of the traditional Jewish messianic dreams. The Jewish Zionists urged the renovation of Jewish national life—rather than assimilation—under the ideological and programmatic influence of Theodore Herzl's *The Jewish State,* written in 1896. The organized movement that followed encouraged Jews to immigrate to Palestine and ultimately resulted in the creation of the state of Israel as a national home for the Jewish people. Obviously, the Holocaust, the Nazis' systematic extermination of millions of Jews, fueled the Zionist movement. The Zionist impulse and fervor are deep, strong, and understandable. I remember walking into a Jerusalem synagogue service on the Sabbath with my Jewish friend. Just before we entered, he paused and said, "Where are the Nazis, where are the damn Romans now? We're still here. We know what we're doing. We remember the prayers. And we've come back to stay."

From the early years of Zionism (Herzl, in the late 1800s), Christian futurists were attracted to the movement.[10] Herzl, the father of Jewish

Zionism, made his contribution at about the same time that Darby had spread his futuristic Christian views to America. Many fundamentalist dispensationalists have adopted some of the Jewish Zionist ideas, but adapted them to their own dispensationalist ideology and program. Fundamentalist dispensationalist magazines have long published news on developments in Israel and the Zionist movement, and fundamentalists were enthusiastic when the state of Israel was established May 14, 1948.[11] The zeal and commitment the Christian Zionists bring to their program now rivals that of the Jewish Zionists. The Christian Zionists promote a conservative Middle East political agenda that encourages Israeli expansion and is leery of any moves toward peace with Arabs. Such a position has direct political implications when applied, for example, to the Israeli settlements in the West Bank. I have walked through some of these settlements with my Arab friend and can understand why they are at the center of the tension and disagreement between Israel and the Palestinians. The settlements are problematic enough when put in the context of the Israeli-Palestinian conflict. Adding the Christian Zionist dispensationalist end-time scenario to the mix only complicates a very bad situation. What is important to realize is that the Christian Zionist support of Israel is based on the dispensationalist framework that sees Israel as playing a key role in the end-time scenario.

The founding of the nation of Israel in 1948 and the capture of the Old City of Jerusalem, where the original temple stood, are the kinds of events futurists interpret as a sure sign of the "fulfillment of prophesy." According to dispensationalists, the rapture of the Christians can now occur at any moment. After that event, before Christ returns for the final thousand-year rule, the evil Antichrist will head up a one-world government. A peace treaty with Israel will precede the tribulation, the seven years of terrible persecution that provide the plot for the *Left Behind* series. The rebuilding of the Jerusalem temple will also precede the thousand-year reign of Christ.

As one can see, the next thing to take place in the dispensationalist scenario is the rapture. Because the one-world government and the rebuilding of the temple will occur soon after the rapture, world events have to be lining up so that these "prophesies" can be fulfilled. When fundamentalists talk about the "signs of the times," they are referring to world developments that they see as proof of the nearness of the rapture.

Some might view as benign these dispensationalist notions of the Antichrist heading up a one-world government and the rebuilding of the temple. On the contrary, these dispensationalist notions have significant political implications for the Middle Eastern region and for American policy. Opposition to the United Nations, among fundamentalists, is strong and often based on the suspicion (some fundamentalists would call it fact, not suspicion) that the United Nations will be the one-world government vehicle the Antichrist will use during the awful tribulation period.

To me, one of the puzzling things about the dispensationalist view is that certain things, like the emergence of a one-world government, is required for the end-time scenario to unfold. Since the final chapter includes heaven for the true (presumably fundamentalist) Christians, it would seem fundamentalists would not oppose something like the United Nations that could provide a key piece of what must develop in the end-time story. I have asked dispensationalists this question. Everyone I asked replied the same way, saying that (1) God will bless countries that support Israel, and (2) God will judge countries that "come against Israel." These countries to be judged include, of course, Arab countries and the United States, if they do not support Israel. Hence, the push for the United States to hold firm in pro-Israel policies.

As for rebuilding the temple, the temple area in the Old City of Jerusalem is one of the most special and most politically and religiously sensitive sites on the planet. In ancient times, in the tenth century before Christ, King Solomon built the first temple on a site that was the location of the traditional story of Abraham's aborted sacrifice of Isaac, recorded in Genesis 22. The temple that Solomon built was destroyed by the Babylonians during their invasion of the country in 597 BCE. The temple was rebuilt in 520–515 BCE and destroyed again in 70 CE by the Romans. The Jews have lived without a temple since the first century. As seen from this historical sketch, the place where the old temple stood is a holy place rooted deeply in Jewish consciousness. The Wailing Wall, near where the temple stood, is the holiest site in Judaism today. The Wailing Wall is actually a part of the retaining wall built in ancient times to support the Temple Mount, where the actual temple was located. Today, devout Jews go to the Wailing Wall to make prayers. Regardless of one's religious orientation or lack thereof, a visit to the Wailing Wall should make evident the special energy of this holy site.

The dispensationalist belief that the temple will be rebuilt is supported, in the fundamentalist mind, by Daniel 9:27 that says,

> He shall make a strong covenant with many for one week, and for half of the week he shall make sacrifice and offering cease.

In the futurist scenario, this verse refers to the tribulation period at the end of time. I suppose for sacrifices and offering in the temple to "cease," there has to be a temple there. While rebuilding the temple is mostly a Christian Zionist idea,[12] there are fringe Jewish groups in Jerusalem that are now preparing temple furniture and priestly garments in preparation for the rebuilt temple. The best known is the Temple Mount Faithful, begun in the 1970s.[13] Such efforts, of course, fit nicely into the Christian Zionist program.

Since the temple was last destroyed in the first century by the Romans, the religion of Islam emerged in the seventh century in that part of the world. Jews and Muslims share the same history that includes Abraham, Isaac, and Solomon. For Muslims, the site where the Jewish temple stood is the place where Muhammad, the Muslim prophet, ascended into heaven. This site, which Muslims call *Qubbat al-Sakhra* (Dome of the Rock), is the third holiest site in their religion and the location today of an important shrine that has stood there since 691 CE. Here lies the problem.

Support for rebuilding the temple is extremely problematic because the site where the temple is to be rebuilt is the location of the holy Muslim site. In the fundamentalist mind, the holy Muslim site must be removed in order for the Jewish temple to be rebuilt. Muslims around the world would die for this holy place. The difference between the current status of Muslims worshipping at the Dome of the Rock, and the Christian Zionist insistence that this holy place must be removed before the final rule of Christ, seems irreconcilable and volatile. The *Left Behind* novels depict Muslims as agreeing with the Antichrist to move the Dome of the Rock to another location in Iraq. There is, to my knowledge, no evidence that this is seriously considered by a single practicing Muslim anywhere.

To illustrate the level of ridiculousness that religion can inspire, here is a plan I heard about on one of my visits to Israel. As a way of having both Jews and Muslims physically connected to this holy site, some ingenious minds advocated installing a pillar in the holy rock. The pillar would rise two stories into the sky. Muslims, whose structure is currently in place, would control the first story. Jews would construct their holy site on top of the Muslim structure, but would be connected to the holy rock by way of the pillar.

The ideas of one-world government and a rebuilt temple are but two of a number of odd dispensationalist notions. Fortunately, some of them may be strange, but are not doing mischief in the region, at least directly. These more benign notions include the idea that, according to Numbers 19, a red heifer is needed to reinstitute the sacrificial system in the rebuilt temple. No pure red heifer has been born in recent years, a problem prompting American dispensationalist cattle breeders to invest much energy into breeding a pure red heifer.

It is not my goal here to give definitive or exhaustive consideration of the fundamentalist views of the end of time. As I have noted, others have done an excellent job detailing the weak biblical interpretation, questionable political stance, and historically conditioned rise of premillennial dispensationalism. However, since one of my main interests is to apply a psychological interpretation to fundamentalism, I would like to applaud Professor Rossing for a couple of intriguing suggestions she makes.[14]

Rossing correctly notes that dispensationalists are especially fascinated by Armageddon, the climactic battle that all dispensationalists see as the "main event" (Lindsey's term) in the end-time scenario. The final battle and defeat of the Antichrist and his evil forces will occur at Armageddon, a large plain in the northern part of Israel. In ancient times, it was an important passage for armies moving from one part of the Fertile Crescent to the other, from Egypt to Mesopotamia (namely, the general area of Iraq) and back again. I have been to Armageddon and looked out over the plain where once marched mighty armies from the two sides of the Fertile Crescent, Egypt and Mesopotamia. If one is going to pick a spot for some future end-of-the-world battle, Armegeddon is an excellent choice. Dispensationalists, of course, believe the battle will be a literal one, with the blood flowing to the horses' bridles and other such gore, all imagery taken from the book of Revelation. As Rossing points out, the word "Armageddon" occurs only once in Revelation (16:16), the book that is so central to the dispensationalist scheme. As with the rapture and other dispensationalist themes, fundamentalist interpreters have unduly exaggerated the importance and role of Armageddon. Rossing suggests that dispensationalists emphasize Armageddon because the rapture of Christians into heaven places them in a front row and safe seat, in heaven, from which to view the war unfolding on earth below. It is a voyeuristic impulse, Rossing suggests. She further suggests that our culture's addiction to the "television version of war today—a spectator sport" may lie behind the fundamentalist fascination with Armageddon. To support her interpretation, Rossing cites a revealing passage from the eleventh *Left Behind* novel. The hero, Rayford Steele, is led to fly his plane over the battle so that he can have the same view that raptured Christians will have from their heavenly box seat:

> That old curiosity was back. Rayford couldn't shake it. No way he could be this close to Armageddon—he guessed less than seventy miles—and not do a flyover. It was crazy, he knew. He might find himself in an air traffic jam. But the possibility of seeing an aerial view of what he had been hearing and reading and praying about drew him like an undertow.[15]

One could, I suppose, conclude that my treatment of things eschatological has consisted in the main of a dismissive judgment on the fundamentalist program, and that assessment is, I think, a fair one. Perhaps my various biblical, theological, and historical impressions have left some readers, who identify with the Christian tradition, perplexed at just how these old, strange apocalyptic texts in the Bible can be interpreted by thoughtful, modern Christians. I will briefly explain one approach that can be considered.

How might the thoughtful, modern Christian think about the biblical apocalyptic language and worldview? History, as is often the case, yields possibilities. In the history of Christianity we find several interpretative strategies for handling apocalyptic texts. If there is one dominant reading in the Roman Catholic Church, it is the "amillennial" or "nonmillennial" view, which teaches that the essential meaning of these old texts is a spiritual one. We might loosely think of a text like the apocalyptic book of Revelation as a poetic account of the struggle between good and evil and the ultimate triumph of good over evil. This approach, certainly not limited to Roman Catholics, allows the apocalyptic poetry to apply to the struggle between good and evil, wherever and whenever that occurs, whether it is on the world stage with the murder of millions in gas chambers, or whether it is in the heart of a student tempted to cheat on an exam. Origen (ca. 185–ca. 254), Augustine (354–430 CE), and others in the Roman Catholic Church can be seen as amillennial, along with the Lutherans and other groups in Protestantism.[16]

I would be pleased, and I think Christianity would be a more authentic witness in the world, if fundamentalists would take to heart this amillennial notion, or some other more reasonable approach. There are those who are pessimistic that this will ever occur. Boyer, in the article I have quoted earlier, concludes his excellent piece, written just before the turn of the last century, as follows:

> As the twentieth century ends and the portentous year 2000 looms, all evidence suggests that fundamentalist apocalyptic interpretations, endlessly refashioned, infinitely adaptable, and seemingly impervious to intellectual challenge, will retain their grip on the popular imagination, as they have for centuries.[17]

I remain hopeful, although mindful of the difficulty fundamentalists have in altering their end-time views. I am aware of the historical currents and contexts that foster futuristic religious speculation and make it difficult to accept some sensible spiritualized or symbolic interpretation of the old apocalyptic texts. Even more problematic is that something very profound, and fragile, is at stake—personal and social identity. I will, of course, address this point in Part Three.

WHAT ABOUT SATAN, HELL, AND ANGELS?

The intensity of the fundamentalist speculations on the end-time is in part explained by the fact that their doctrine is set in the larger context of a cosmic struggle between good and evil. To understand this severe context helps to explain the psychological intensity of the fundamentalist's fascination with things apocalyptic. The fundamentalist belief in the devil goes beyond the notion of temptation. For the fundamentalist, there is an active, intelligent personage out there working to do human beings harm.

An analysis of the biblical material on these subjects clearly indicates that there is a development of ideas through time. Looking at the books of the Bible in chronological order, we see a development from tribal polytheism to monotheism and finally to the extension of monotheism in the form of a Satan figure, angels, demons, and hell. The early books of the Bible contain no clear presentation of the personification of evil in a Satan figure. The figure of the serpent in Genesis 3:1–7 is often pointed to as evidence that Satan existed during this early period. The problem here is that the story does not mention Satan. It plainly says that a serpent (meaning, snake) tempted Eve in the Garden of Eden. The details of the story make my point. Given the adverse consequences of the encounter between Eve and the tempter, if the tellers of this story had a concept of the personification of evil, then surely Satan would have been used in the story. The fact that they did not have this concept is why they used the snake, a lowly and despised animal in many cultures, and therefore a good candidate as the source of temptation.

Exodus 7:1–3, 13 is an interesting passage that reflects the fascinating theological tension that drives the development of Satan. God told Moses to go tell the Egyptian pharaoh to "Let my people go!" Moses goes to Egypt and tells the pharaoh just that. Then, the text says something very interesting—God hardened the heart of pharaoh so that he would not let the people go. Does that make any sense? It does not make sense from the fundamentalist framework. Why would God keep the pharaoh from doing something that God wanted the pharaoh to do? If the Israelites had at this time a notion of Satan, then certainly the text would have said that "Satan hardened the heart of pharaoh."

Other texts point to the strict monotheism and lack of a Satan figure. In Deuteronomy 32:39 God proclaims,

> See now that I, I am He, and beside me there is no other god. It is I who deal death and life; when I have struck it is I who heal (and none can deliver from my hand).

In Isaiah 43:13, we read:

> I am God, and there is no other. I form light, and I create darkness; I produce well-being and I create evil; I God do all these things.

The theological dilemma is clear. God is good and something bad happens, as in, the pharaoh will not let the people go. Since God is all-powerful, then God must be the one hardening the pharaoh's heart. The situation is ripe for the development of a Satan figure as an explanation for why bad things happen.

A striking example of the change in perspective that comes is found in 2 Samuel 24:1–2, which is a story about the taking of a census in Israel. The story begins this way:

Again the anger of the Lord was kindled against Israel, and he incited David against them, saying, "Go, count the people of Israel and Judah." So the king said to Joab and the commanders of the army, who were with him, "Go through all the tribes of Israel, from Dan to Beer-sheba, and take a census of the people, so that I may know how many there are."

In 1 Chronicles 21:1–2 we find this account of the census:

Satan stood up against Israel, and incited David to count the people of Israel. So David said to Joab and the commanders of the army, "Go, number Israel, from Beer-sheba to Dan, and bring me a report, so that I may know their number."

Clearly, the two accounts are about the same census in ancient Israel. The striking difference between the two accounts is that in 2 Samuel 24:1 the "Lord" tells David to count the people. However, in 1 Chronicles 21:1 "Satan" incites David to count the people.

Exegetes who are bound by a view of inerrancy are required by their theology to find some way to explain this obvious discrepancy. As with many other perceived discrepancies in the Bible, fundamentalists force an unnatural reading on the text in order to harmonize the two stories. Critical scholarship has a more natural reading of the stories and gives a reasonable explanation for the shift from "Lord" to "Satan." The book of Chronicles was written about 500 years after Samuel. The census was apparently something that was not viewed with favor by the authors and by the time Chronicles was written, the notion of Satan as an adversary or accuser had entered the tradition.

How the notion of Satan entered the tradition is not absolutely known. However, one possibility is that it occurred during the Babylonian exile of the Jewish people. In the sixth-century BCE, God's people were defeated by a foreign power and many of them exiled in Babylon. Certainly they must have wondered why they were suffering. Some of them thought they were being punished for their sins. The punishment, however, was so severe that some must have wondered if there was another explanation. At this time in history, the emerging religion of Zoroastrianism was promoting the idea of dualism, which in this case involved a good god and an evil god in battle with each other. It is possible that the Israelites acquired their notion of the personification of evil, at least to some degree, from the Zoroastrians.

Once the notion of the personification of evil was introduced into the tradition, however it was introduced, it developed over time. The Jewish tradition, around the first two centuries before the common era and expressed in certain noncanonical books and rabbinical writings, spoke to the question of how and why Satan and his associates came to earth. For example, 1 Enoch 6:1–6 says that 200 angels came because of their lust for beautiful earth women. Jubilees 4:15 says that God sent angels to earth to teach human beings, and that, after arriving, they lusted and fell. This Jewish tradition is perhaps based on and expresses an attempt to understand the brief and puzzling reference in Genesis 6:1–4 which speaks of the "sons of God" marrying and mating with women.

Several sketchy references in the New Testament (Jude 6; 2 Peter 2:4; and maybe Luke 10:18 and Revelation 12:7–12) probably have this Jewish material as a background and seem to assume the view that Satan and his demon-beings were created by God but, through a self-centered refusal to obey God, rebelled and were cast down from heaven. Isaiah 14:12 ff has been interpreted by some to refer to a notion similar to the view in Jude 6 and 2 Peter 2:4. Reading Isaiah 14:12 ff apart from a later Christian perspective, however, suggests that Isaiah is here speaking of the Babylonian king, not Satan.

By the time we get to the early Christian writings, we have a clearly developed Satan figure, who now has demons and presides over hell. Jesus has conversations with Satan (Matthew 4:1–11; Luke 4:1–13) and exorcises demons out of people (Mark 5:1–20). To counteract this evil structure, messengers from God early in the Bible have now become angels with names and a hierarchy.

The development continues beyond the biblical period. The pointed ears, pitchforks, and other aspects of the devil and hell are derived from the seventeenth-century Milton, Halloween, and other traditions. While it is too early to draw conclusions, the current development of the concept of evil will likely involve in some way our technological orientations. Movies like the *Matrix* (1999) embody such notions.

We have examined the main fundamentalist doctrines. Before moving to our psychological analysis, however, there are two unofficial fundamentalist "doctrines" that I think are important for understanding the fundamentalist mind.

CHAPTER 9

Two Unofficial Fundamentalist Doctrines

RIGHT-WING POLITICS

At the advent of fundamentalism in America, the primary battle was against science. While that battle is still being fought, a new front has emerged—politics. The politically active fundamentalists, in the tradition of Rev. Jerry Falwell's Moral Majority, are taking strong stands in the public square on issues they identify as a "values" agenda. The right-wing values-based political agenda of activist fundamentalists has become, one could say, an unofficial point of fundamentalist doctrine. Fundamentalist involvement in the American political system is to be expected. Marty and Appleby's massive study of fundamentalism worldwide demonstrates that again and again fundamentalists of all religions, despite separatist tendencies, are drawn into the political life of their nations. The modern state regulates so many aspects of social life that involvement in politics is inevitable.

With regard to voting patterns, fundamentalists do not usually state blatantly that God is on the side of a particular candidate. Fundamentalists may cloak their true feelings in moral language. "I'm voting for this candidate because I think moral values are important," they will sometimes say. However, fundamentalists have clearly expressed strong preferences in recent presidential elections, and many other major elections, for particular candidates. Research indicates that there is a positive correlation between fundamentalism and conservative, if not right-wing, political orientations. This correlation does not hold always and everywhere, but the general tendency is evident.

To understand the contemporary debate adequately, it is important to reach back to the beginnings of this country. Fundamentalists also reach back, but their reading of the history is often terribly flawed. Fundamentalists often marshal the names of founding fathers to prove that America was founded on Christian principles. The revisionist history is found every Sunday, especially during heavy political seasons, in many fundamentalist churches and Sunday School classes around the country. The sources for the flawed readings of our nation's past are found in books like the following: *The Light and the Glory: Discovering God's Plan for America from Christopher Columbus to George Washington* and *From Sea to Shining Sea: Discovering God's Plan for America in Her First Half-Century of Independence, 1787–1837,* both by Peter Marshall and David Manuel. These two books alone have sold nearly a million copies and their influence is surely in multiples of that number. An example of the revisionist history that circulates widely in fundamentalist circles has to do with an address of Benjamin Franklin in one of the Constitutional Convention meetings, on June 28, 1787.

Historians agree that Franklin did address a deadlocked convention on this date. In urging the delegates to find a compromise, Franklin asked why the delegates had not applied to the "Father of lights" for help, reminded them that in the fight with Britain the Continental Congress had prayed for divine protection, said he believed that "God governs in the affairs of men," and moved that the assembly pray every morning before beginning its work.[1] Unfortunately, for the fundamentalist revision, Franklin's motion was tabled and the Convention never began its sessions with prayer. However, the facts do not stop Marshall and Manuel from interpreting Franklin's address as a turning point in our nation's history and one that supposedly resulted in the founding of the nation on fundamentalist Christian principles. Here is the account from Marshall and Manuel in versions of these books for children. They report that Franklin's speech was

> clearly the most extraordinary speech anyone had delivered in the entire three months the delegates had been meeting.... They immediately declared three days of prayer and fasting, to seek God's help in breaking the deadlock among them. At the end of that time, all the resentment and wrangling were gone ... it [the Constitution] was divinely inspired.... In effect, it documents the Covenant Way on national paper.[2]

The fundamentalist revision is based on a story that can be traced back to the mid-1820s, but it is not considered credible by historians.[3]

Fundamentalists say that America was founded on Christian principles by Godly men. What they mean to communicate, however, is the message that America was founded on "fundamentalist" Christian principles by "fundamentalist" Godly men. The complexity of the historical situation cannot be captured by such a simplistic view. True, there were Protestants who were involved in the Declaration of Independence, the Revolutionary War, and the Constitutional Convention where Franklin gave his speech. However, the Protestant Christians, with few exceptions (possibly Patrick Henry and Richard Bassett), can in no way be interpreted as holding views that eventually characterized the fundamentalist movement. The founders were individuals with differing approaches to religion. For the most part, the religious views of the founding fathers were deism, traditional Anglican, and/or Congregational Protestantism. There were a few Roman Catholics here and there.

To give a few notable examples, George Washington was an active Christian layperson, but his deist orientation led him to believe that reason and revelation were incompatible. Deism is the view that God created the world and set it in motion with natural laws, and God is now not actively involved in the world. Sometimes deism is called the "watchmaker" view of God, in that a watchmaker builds the watch and winds it up, but afterward is not actively involved in the workings of the watch. Deist religion makes plenty of room for reason and science as ways of understanding the world that God created and set into motion.

Thomas Jefferson, a deist and humanist, was proud of being the author of the Virginia Statute of Religious Freedom and was a leader in the push for the First Amendment establishment clause. He edited his own version of the New Testament, entitled *The Life and Morals of Jesus of Nazareth.* It is fascinating reading. Fundamentalists would not be gratified to discover that Jefferson deleted all the miraculous passages from the gospels. In the spirit of Lyman Stewart who funded *The Fundamentals: A Testimony to the Truth,* it would be interesting to mail a copy of Jefferson's cut-and-paste job on the gospels to every fundamentalist in America. Perhaps there is some thoughtful Christian millionaire out there reading these words who will be prompted to take on this project, and counteract the damage done by Stewart's project. Fundamentalists who take the time to read his book, *The Life and Morals of Jesus of Nazareth,* will no longer so easily invoke Jefferson's name.

The final versions of the root documents of our country, and the well-documented debates around them, are widely available. Any careful and complete reading reveals that they are not Christian documents and debates, and certainly not fundamentalist Christian. The Constitution contains no reference to God, much less Jesus Christ. There are two references to God in the Declaration of Independence. One refers to the "Laws of Nature and Nature's God." The other is the famous statement that men are "endowed by their Creator with certain inalienable rights." Both references reflect a deist orientation, and certainly not a Christ-centered theology. Ironically, enlightenment deism is the very kind of liberal, humanistic religion that fundamentalism opposes.

While many fundamentalists are terribly misinformed about the religious character of the founders and the root documents of our country, one should not overstate the case in the other direction. The framers were not secularists. There is no embrace of religion in the Constitution, but it is also true that the framers of that document refrained from getting bogged down in issues with which they did not have to involve themselves. Unlike the federal constitution, religion played a significant role in the state constitutions. Over time, including the period that saw many new states added to the union, the states increasingly imitated the federal constitution with regard to religion.

The obvious references to God in our public "documents" date after the founding period. "In God We Trust" was added to our money after the Civil War. "Under God" was added to the Pledge of Allegiance in 1954 during the McCarthy communist scare.

It is true that most of the American colonies, to varying degrees, attempted to have an established church. There were those who were inclined toward some form of Protestantism as the established religion, but they did not win the argument. Those who believed that alignment of church and state had generated more mischief than good won the day. The official separation between church and state came with the First Amendment to the Constitution, the relevant section of which reads, "Congress shall make no law respecting an establishment of religion, or prohibiting the free exercise thereof." The First Amendment, as part of the Bill of Rights, was adopted in 1791. Subsequent and various court rulings have attempted to set forth the implications of this disestablishment. In our history various metaphors and phrases have been used in the service of disestablishment, including "wall of separation" (between church and state), "neutrality" (of government toward religion), and avoiding "excessive entanglement" (of state with religion).

Fundamentalists read their christological perspective into the language of what Robert Bellah called America's "civil religion."[4] "Civil religion" includes general and ceremonial references to God, values, and order. Civil religion does not, however, use specifically Christian language. Washington, Adams, and Jefferson all mention God in their inaugural addresses; none of them refer to Christ. This is the typical pattern for major national and ceremonial speeches throughout our history. It is true that, contrary to strict deist principles, our leaders often ask God's help, but those requests are made to God on behalf of America. The deity here invoked is consistent with a civil religion in the service of the national interest. Civil religion is not Christian and definitely not fundamentalist. Fundamentalists, however, hear the word "God" in a president's speech or the Pledge of Allegiance and assume that what is being referred to is the God of Jesus Christ.

The irony is that fundamentalists are shooting themselves in the foot by wanting to marry Christianity and government. They see their initiatives as promoting Christianity. However, a strong case can be made that the absolute worst thing that could happen for Christianity is to have interference by the government. In the fourth century Constantine declared Christianity the official religion of the Roman Empire and, arguably, that government involvement sapped Christianity of much of its spiritual and moral power. It is curious to me that fundamentalists, who usually vote an antigovernment, right-wing agenda, actually want government involved in their faith. That will be only the beginning of their problems. Once Christianity is endorsed (officially or unofficially), then the Christians will soon find themselves fighting about which version of Christianity gets promoted through governmental channels and programs. Will it be Pentecostal Christianity that promotes speaking in tongues, Southern Baptist Christianity that believes in baptism by full immersion under water, or the Christian snake-handlers from Appalachia? Who will write the prayers that children pray in the classroom? Which version of the Bible will they read? I believe the absolute worst thing that could happen for Christianity is for the fundamentalists to succeed in their attempts to bring religion and state closer together.

The debate about religion in the public schools is a good example of how the courts have become involved in the fundamentalist struggle to gain government sanction of a religious agenda. I will summarize the most pivotal court cases about religion in schools.

One of the earliest and most influential court cases that would set a framework for later cases was *McCollum v. Board of Education* in 1948. In an 8–1 decision, the Supreme Court declared it unconstitutional for an Illinois school to hire religious instructors of the Catholic, Protestant, and Jewish faith to give religious education to willing students once a week. The students, whose parents had given written permission, would receive religious instruction once a week, while those "students who did not choose to take the religious instructions were not released from public school duties; they were required to leave their classrooms and go to some other place in the school building for pursuit of their secular studies."[5] The Court argued that the First Amendment created a barrier between church and state and that tax-supported public schools should not be used for the spreading of religious doctrines. Thus, the Supreme Court determined that the Illinois school's action created a rift between secular and religious students in a public school setting and this rift contradicted separation between church and state.[6]

In *Engel v. Vitale* in 1962, when the state of New York implemented a prayer to be recited at the beginning of each day, the Supreme Court struck it down with a 6–1 decision. Here is the prayer:

Almighty God, we acknowledge our dependence upon Thee, and we beg Thy blessings upon us, our parents, our teachers and our Country.

The Court determined that "It would be an abuse of power by the federal government to manage or pressure the religiosity of the American people in this way. No government, whether it be state or federal, can promote by law any official type of prayer to be implemented in a government sponsored religious occurrence."[7]

A case similar to that of *Engel v. Vitale* was the court case of *Abington School District v. Schempp* in 1963. In an 8–1 decision, the Supreme Court declared unconstitutional the actions of a Pennsylvania statute requiring the recitation of at least ten verses from the Bible at the beginning of each school day. Furthermore, the promotion of religious exercises in a public school setting, such as a reading (without comment) of the Bible and reciting the Lord's Prayer, was determined to be contrary to the rules set forth by the establishment clause. In the Court's words:

While the free exercise clause clearly prohibits the use of state action to deny the rights of free exercise to anyone, it has never meant that a majority could use the machinery of the State to practice its beliefs.[8]

In the monumental 1985 case of *Wallace v. Jaffree*, the Supreme Court ruled in a 6–3 decision that it was contrary to the Constitution for an Alabama statute to state that a teacher could declare a minute of silence in which only meditation, introspection, and prayer could occur. The court felt that the major error in the statute was that it did not have a secular legislative purpose.[9]

Turning to a different example of right-wing politics, I think it is safe to say that the tendency among fundamentalists is to support the right-wing agenda for a strong, active military. Differences of opinion about military matters is one thing. To cloak a particular partisan political viewpoint with Christ, and present it as the Christian perspective, is quite another thing. There are good biblical, theological, and historical bases for a variety of legitimate Christian attitudes toward war and peace.

Pacifism, the just war, and the crusade are the three basic attitudes toward war and peace that have been advocated by the church. In general, the early church was pacifist until Christianity became the official religion of the empire in the fourth century under Constantine. Pacifism resurfaced in the historic peace churches of the late Middle Ages and Reformation period and included the Anabaptists, Quakers, and the Brethren. The varieties of pacifism range from nuclear pacifism to opposition to all war to opposition to all violence against human beings. With regard to military service, pacifism can range from refusal to bear arms to refusal to participate in any seemingly nonviolent activity that supports lethal action by others. The strongest biblical case for pacifism is found in the teachings of

Jesus, and especially sayings like these found in the famous Sermon on the Mount:

> Do not resist an evildoer. But if anyone strikes you on the right cheek, turn the other also.
>
> (Matthew 5:39)

> If anyone forces you to go one mile, go also the second mile.
>
> (Matthew 5:41)

> Love your enemies.
>
> (Matthew 5:44)

Roland Bainton, himself a World War I conscientious objector who served in a Quaker Red Cross unit in France, argues for Christian pacifism in the last two chapters of his widely respected history of Christianity on the subject of war and peace.[10]

Because of threat from barbarian invasions, and state influence on the religion, in the fourth and fifth centuries Christians practiced just war, a doctrine adapted from the classical world. Just war requires that military action is justified only when certain conditions are met. Just war conditions may require that the war be waged only as a last resort and only with state sponsorship, no military action against innocent noncombatants, and defensive goals only. Christian supporters of just war theory often turn to the New Testament texts that call for support of one's civil government (for example, Romans 13:1–6; Mark 12:17).

A primary critique of just war theory is that the modern techniques of war, and especially nuclear war, make it difficult if not impossible to avoid killing innocent people, and so just war theory is useless, even if a moral war is theoretically possible. Paul Ramsey (author of *The Just War*) is a strong and clear proponent of a Christian just war ethic.

The Crusades in the Middle Ages inspired Christians to fight a holy war under the direction of the church or some religious leader. The ancient Israelites practiced a kind of crusade by fighting in obedience to commands from God. The Israelite practice of placing an entire enemy city under the ban (*herem*) is a striking expression of Old Testament holy war. Literally, the ban meant that an entire city, including innocent women and children, were burned as a sacrifice to God. The first 11 chapters of the book of Joshua provide a detailed, and gruesome, account of the Israelite holy war assault on the Canaanites in order to take control of the land the Israelites believed God had given to them. The New Testament passage usually cited to support a crusade is the story of Jesus's cleansing of the temple (John 2:15 mentions that he did it with a whip of cords). Other crusading sayings by Jesus include "I came not to send peace, but a sword" (Matthew 10:34) and "He that hath no sword, let him sell his garment, and buy one" (Luke 12:51). These militaristic sayings, however, are minimal compared to the pacifist sayings of Jesus.

While conservative Christianity's traditional support of American right-wing politics still holds, there is evidence that some realignment is occurring. The support of evangelicals for progressive positions on social issues and accompanying social action seems to have grown in recent years. The work of respected evangelical leader Jim Wallis is a good example of this trend. Wallis was among evangelical leaders who in 1973 issued the "Chicago Declaration of Evangelical Social Concern" and in doing so pledged to

> defend the social and economic rights of the poor and oppressed . . . deplore the historic involvement of the church in America with racism and . . . challenge the misplaced trust of the nation in economic and military might—a proud trust that promotes a national pathology of war and violence. . . . As evangelical Christians committed to the Lord Jesus Christ and the full authority of the Word of God, we affirm that God lays total claim upon the lives of his people. We cannot, therefore separate our lives from the situation in which God has placed us in the United States and the world. By this declaration, we endorse no political ideology or party, but call our nation's leaders and people to that righteousness which exalts a nation.[11]

While Wallis and other like-minded evangelical leaders are careful not to identify with a particular political party, clearly there is some movement of conservative Christians toward candidates more moderate than conservative Christians have traditionally supported. The rise to international prominence and the election of Barack Obama as president of the United States is a striking example. Obama's attempt to make inroads into the conservative Christian camp began early in his campaign for the presidency. As a veteran political observer noted in 2006,

> When Rick Warren, one of the nation's most popular evangelical pastors, faced down right-wing pressure and invited Sen. Barack Obama to speak at a gathering at his Saddleback Valley Community Church about the AIDS crisis, he sent a signal: A significant group of theologically conservative Christians no longer wants to be treated as a cog in the Republican political machine.[12]

Much of this realignment may be temporary and due to the widespread unpopularity of George W. Bush's presidency. How extensive and how long the realignment will last is uncertain. For the long term, at most I think it will involve a small but significant movement of some evangelicals toward moderate politics.

THE SUBORDINATION OF WOMEN[13]

The fundamentalist agenda to make women subordinate to men involves extensive biblical, theological, and political strategies. Unlike premillennial dispensationalism, a uniquely fundamentalist doctrine, gender discrimination is a popular notion around the world. The fundamentalists, on this point, are aligned with the Roman Catholic Church and all major religions of the world. I believe this agenda of discrimination is as dangerous as it is morally flawed, and so I am going to carefully unpack what I see to be a harmful doctrine.

My own involvement in this issue goes back to a time in my life when I lived in a rural southern county. Upon investigation, a local mental health therapist and I discovered that the incidents of rape and spouse abuse in our county were alarmingly high and there was no effective program in the county to address the problem. Along with a few moderate pastors and other community people, we organized what is now a complete and reliable rape and spouse abuse program in that county. My passionate desire to challenge the fundamentalist view of the role of women is fueled by vivid memories of brutality against women, as told by them and documented by authorities, and by insights I gained while working with the rape and spouse abuse program.

The key text usually quoted by fundamentalists is, "Wives, submit yourselves unto your own husband as unto the Lord" (Ephesians 5:21). Oppressive attitudes, reflected in New Testament statements such as 1 Corinthians 14:34–35 that women should keep silent in the churches, be subordinate, and ask their husbands at home if they want to know anything, eventually carried the day for the early Christians. Those attitudes became increasingly oppressive toward the end of the first century. By that time women were also admonished to repress their sexual appeal by dressing modestly (see, for example, 1 Timothy 2:9–15).

The deeper fundamentalist paradigm is that a family ordained by God is a man and woman legally married with clearly defined roles and obligations and set within a structure of authority that is patriarchal. The husband is primarily responsible for providing leadership materially and spiritually for the family and has the final say on matters of dispute. The wife is the "helpmate" companion and supporter of the husband.

While it may at first seem to be a different issue, I think the controversy over abortion and stem cell research (the right-wing has folded the stem cell debate into the abortion issue) can be understood in the larger context of fundamentalist perspectives on family, sexuality, and the role of women. I suspect that much of the fundamentalist attention to family values is related, unconsciously, to a fear of sexual expression of whatever kind: premarital relations, homosexuality, adultery, pornography, dancing, Hollywood culture and movies, and perhaps even excessive marital passion. The issue here I think is the threat to the evangelical sexual ethic. Sexual intercourse is reserved for heterosexual legal marriage. The concern about legalized abortion, as evangelical pro-life literature often claims, is in large part due to it being a technique that enables people to have sex outside of marriage.

I want to extend my comments to an area that I admit will be controversial and, also, hard to prove. It is, however, a gender issue and an important one. If I am correct in my thesis, fundamentalism is not only a theologically odd member of the Christian religion; it is also psychologically and physically dangerous. Because this is a difficult case to make, I will do it in some detail.

The important Christian symbol "God"—especially understood as male and warrior—and attendant views of women, men, and sexuality, especially prominent in fundamentalist Christianity, foster attitudes about and behaviors toward women that are conducive for sexual violence. I am not saying that fundamentalists are more likely than liberals to abuse women sexually or otherwise. That is an empirical question that as far as I know has not been investigated. I am asking the reader to consider the possibility that the male warrior God of Christianity helps set the ideological context in society for violence against women. The male warrior God and related ideas can be traced through the Old Testament, New Testament, early church fathers, Middle Ages, Reformation, and the modern period.

While sexual abuse is, at least in major part, an expression of male violence against women, the sexual aspect *per se* is not unimportant. Although not as major a theme as maleness and violence, the repression of sexuality is common in fundamentalist theological and ethical programs. Margaret Bendroth documents how certain fundamentalist writers have equated female leadership with feminine sensuality.[14] Both female leadership and sexuality are understood as rooted in rebellion against God and his ordained social order. Such ideas provide the theological basis, at least in part, for the widespread fundamentalist teaching against sexual sins and the related admonitions toward female modesty in dress and speech.

Male violence against women, perhaps most obviously expressed in forcible rape, but often taking other forms of sexual abuse both within and without marriage, can yield to explanation at several levels and from a variety of disciplinary directions. I have isolated one aspect of the Western cultural/ideological framework, an aspect that can support, if only indirectly, man's "right" to do sexual violence to women. The aspect being isolated is the language about and imagery of God which convey the deity as male and warrior and which shows up in traditional, and especially fundamentalist, expressions of the Christian religion.

Fundamentalist Protestant Christianity in America is a current expression of the religion where the male warrior God and related ideas show up in particularly compelling ways. I do not argue that aggressors consciously justify their behavior by explicit appeals to religion; I do isolate one aspect of the cultural/ideological fabric that is consistent with male sexual violence against women and which can provide justification, at least at the unconscious level, for that violence. Society's structures, attitudes, and behaviors are undergirded by religious symbols.[15] This widely held belief motivates feminist scholars to critically analyze religion in an attempt to identify the myths, symbols, and practices that sanction sexist thinking and behavior in the larger culture.[16]

God as male and warrior may be one important image that contributes to male violence against women. It is certainly not the only one. Charles Ess has isolated another image, one that powerfully complements the male warrior God. It is that of woman as "chaos agent" who threatens the patriarchal order of male dominance. According to Ess, this image of woman can be traced from the Genesis Eve, who upsets God's patriarchal order of creation,[17] through Augustine who blames woman for introducing sin into the world, and finally to modern notions.[18]

Saying that the male warrior God of Christianity is a part of the cultural context for sexual violence against women does not preclude psychological interpretations that might demonstrate the possibility—perhaps probability—that over time the violence is projected "into the sky" and itself helps create the male and warrior image of deity.[19] The degree of influence in each direction is debatable, but that there is a noticeable and suggestive correspondence between the notion of deity and male sexual violence is evident to me.

Decades of feminist scholarship on the biblical and historical materials of Christianity have brought the usually gendered and often warlike image of God to the surface. That the Christian religion is thoroughly patriarchal, in its view of God and female-male relations, is widely recognized.[20] The religion's patriarchy is rooted in the language, images, and worldview of the Bible. The warlike nature of God and the related militant nature of the church's behavior through the centuries and in many countries, while less prominent than patriarchy, is significant. God's warlike nature is undergirded by notions of power (see 1 Chronicles 29:11–12), holiness (Exodus 3:5; Hosea 11:9; Isaiah 6:3), and judgment (Isaiah 1; Romans 14:10). The Christian God is a moral being who punishes the wicked (Psalms 58:6–11). Additionally, while overt sexual violence against women is not an explicit major fact of Christian history, the gendered and warlike images foster male dominance and attitudes toward women that can provide rich soil for such violence. Militant images and attributes do not constitute the totality of the Christian view of God. Grace and love, the so-called soft attributes, are certainly prominent. However, I am highlighting those images and attributes that can serve to justify and provide the context for male aggression. The following survey of the Christian tradition is drawn from my own reading of various texts from that tradition and from the surveys provided in Ruether, Clark and Richardson, and Carmody.

The ancient Israelite worldview was shaped in the ancient Near East during the first two millennia before the common era. With few exceptions, the major cultures of that time and place arose out of powerful absolute monarchies in which the political order of the male warrior king, who often took and maintained power violently, was divinely ordained. While they were not always able to maintain it, the Hebrew people also achieved monarchy and this model informed to a large extent the Old Testament view of God.[21] By referring to the Israelite "male" God, feminist scholars are not suggesting that God is understood as being a man in any sexual or literal sense. The God of Israel transcends sex. However, the images and language for deity are mostly drawn from masculine categories and include father, king, Lord, shepherd, and husband.

In Israel's society, men held power in every area of life (political, economic, religious); women's primary responsibility was as wives and mothers (see, for example, Proverbs 31:10–31). There is some disagreement at this point, but it has been argued that women, to some degree, were viewed as the property of their fathers and husbands. Women are named in lists of booty taken in war (Deuteronomy 20:14; 1 Samuel 30:2; 1 Kings 20:3, 5, 7) and wives were counted, along with silver and gold, as one measure of a man's wealth (1 Kings 10:14–11:8).[22] A woman's sexual fidelity to her husband was of utmost importance and it was that sexuality, understood as the exclusive property of her husband, which was her primary contribution to the family and which can explain the importance attached to being a virgin at marriage. The husband's suspicion that his wife had been unfaithful to him could prompt a trial (Deuteronomy 22:13–21). The husband's extramarital sex was treated much more lightly than that of the wife (Deuteronomy 22:28–29). These Old Testament attitudes, embodied in numerous laws, stories, and wisdom material, set the tone for the development of Christianity.[23]

True to their Jewish heritage, the early Christians viewed God as male, primarily as father (see, for example, Matthew 6:9; John 16:25–28; Philippians 2:11), and as one who sent a male Messiah, Jesus, to save the world. The warlike nature of God as king receded to the background, but battle language continued to show up in some early Christian hymns (see Luke 1:51–52; Revelation 11:18) and teachings, as exampled in the New Testament teaching which admonishes Christians to "Put on the whole armor of God" (Ephesians 6:11).

While social structures and attitudes toward women remained essentially patriarchal, there is evidence in the earliest Christian period of a slight rehabilitation of woman's role in that some women apparently took leadership positions in the new sect (such as Phoebe and Priscilla in Romans 16:1–5; Euodia and Syntyche in Philippians 4:2–3; and possibly

Chloe in 1 Corinthians 1:11 and Junia in Romans 16:7). Such a shift, however, was neither widespread nor permanent.[24]

Old notions persisted, and new images and ideas began to evolve, as Christianity expanded its sphere of influence and moved into its first few centuries. God continued to be understood and worshipped through the lens of masculine imagery and men still dominated the power centers of the church. The early fathers, such as Jerome and Augustine, are well known for their fierce attacks on sex.

Jerome's Letter 22 ("To Eustochium: The Virgin's Profession") has been called "the greatest slander of women since Juvenal's sixth satire.[25] "I praise virgins," Jerome says, "but it is because they produce me virgins."[26] Taking a position that became influential in the Roman Catholic Church, Augustine argued that the only good purpose of sexual relations is procreation.

> The union, then, of male and female for the purpose of procreation is the natural good of marriage. But he makes a bad use of this good who uses it bestially, so that his intention is on the gratification of lust, instead of the desire of offspring.[27]

A major new role for women, in addition to that of wife and mother, surfaced during this patristic period—that of virgin. Virginity, that is, overcoming the body and living the angelic life according to the spirit, was considered the superior life and was, in fact, the only socially and sexually acceptable option for women outside the conventional family. The Virgin Mary, played off against evil Eve who made man fall in the Garden of Eden, was held up as the model for women to emulate; those who could not conform to this model were expected to be wives and mothers.[28]

Compared to other periods, little has been written about women in the Middle Ages. However, it is clear that a woman's socially acceptable options were wife/mother in the traditional family or virgin nun in the increasingly institutionalized convent. The nun wore a veil and lived under the vow of obedience, ultimately to the male deity. The Roman Catholic cult of the Virgin Mary is a complex phenomenon and has been interpreted as evidence for a latent feminist spirit. While there may be some truth to this position, it does not negate the fact that Mary, primarily a creation of male ascetic monks, was for women an example of obedience, humbleness, and service.[29]

The most influential writer of the Middle Ages was the thirteenth-century scholar and theologian St. Thomas Aquinas. While Aquinas expressed ideas that could have been worked into a positive view of women,[30] for the most part he developed traditional lines of thinking. Absent here is the misogynist element that is so blatant in some of the earlier writers; yet the thought of Aquinas is thoroughly androcentric. In an adaptation of Aristotle, Aquinas saw woman as naturally subordinate to the male.[31] Additionally, echoing earlier thinking, the woman is useful as a partner in reproduction, but also embodies sensuality and as such threatens the male mind and spirit.[32]

The crusades of the eleventh through fifteenth centuries illustrate the warlike nature that Christianity could exhibit. While their causes and outcomes are complex, they are a clear militant expression of Christianity. By the thirteenth century the term crusade was broadened to include all wars against the enemies of the church.

With respect to male violence against women, the killing of women which occurred in the witch hunts from 1500–1700 cry out for analysis. Estimates of people (overwhelmingly female) killed as witches range from 50,000 to over one million. Witches were believed to have special sexual and reproductive powers, including the ability to inhibit male virility. Such notions were disseminated in the 1486–1487 *Malleus Maleficarum,* the "Hammer Against Witches." This popular handbook was used by inquisitors in witchcraft investigations and persecutions.[33] Several theories have been offered to explain this holocaust, and it is clear that the sexuality of women played a role and some scholars suggest a major role. One contention is that the witch hunts were rooted in male anxiety about women's sexual powers and constitute, therefore, a form of sexual aggression against women.[34] Interestingly, studies of rapists have shown that in the high-risk individual "a sense of worthlessness and low self-esteem combine with deep-seated feelings of personal insecurity and inadequacy to result in a negative self-image."[35]

The Protestant Reformation of the sixteenth century brought changes but not necessarily in the direction of liberation. The reformers rejected the monastic life and its supporting theology. Sexuality was seen as fundamentally good. From one perspective, though, this change was a setback for women in that they no longer had the option of community monastic life allowing for the development of sisterhood. The reformers all taught that women should be subject to their husbands. Luther, the leading reformer, followed earlier thinking in viewing women as sexual "medicine" or "antidote" to quell men's sexual desires.[36] Although not explicit, the implication was that a woman was to submit sexually to a man when he needed (desired) for her to do so.

While there are important and interesting exceptions,[37] especially in the Protestant wing of Christendom in part because of the splintering nature of Protestantism, in the modern period the male and warlike images of God have continued to reign in the mainline and traditional expressions of the religion in all countries. Likewise, in Roman Catholicism and most Protestant denominations, women generally have continued to play subordinate roles to men, and sexuality is often viewed with suspicion.

While the ideas about God surveyed above show up in all expressions of traditional Christianity, fundamentalist Protestant Christianity illustrates them in particularly striking fashion.[38] Admittedly, fundamentalists also celebrate the softer attributes of God (such as, Jesus as a compassionate friend), but that does not necessarily negate the infiltration of harsher male warrior God notions into the larger cultural fabric.

No attempt is being made to suggest that fundamentalist Christians are more likely to be sexual aggressors against women than liberal Christians, non-Christians, or members of other religious groups. In fact, it can be demonstrated that the Christian (including fundamentalist) emphases on love, service, grace, and justice have been important factors in fostering the context for various liberation and social justice movements. The point here is that fundamentalist Christianity is a place where one can easily observe the male warrior God that is a part of the cultural ideology and possibly providing the context for male sexual violence against women.

Royal and military metaphors, which permeated fundamentalist writings in the 1920s when the movement began, have continued to be prevalent in fundamentalist language about God and the Christian life. A review of hymns popular in fundamentalist churches includes the following titles: "Come, Thou Almighty King," "O Worship the King," "All Hail the Power of Jesus' Name," "Onward, Christian Soldiers," and "Lead On, O King Eternal." Lyrics from the above titles include "Come, thou incarnate word, gird on thy mighty sword," "His chariots of wrath the deep thunderclouds form," "Onward Christian soldiers, marching as to war . . . Christ, the royal master, leads against the foe," and "The day of march has come, henceforth in fields of conquest thy tents shall be our home . . . the crown awaits the conquest, lead on, O God of might." Titles of books, magazines, and pamphlets popular among fundamentalist Christians at various points in their history also reflect a fighting spirit and include *Sword of the Lord, The King's Business, Capturing a Town for Christ* (Jerry Falwell), and *Combat Faith* (Hal Lindsey). One of the more popular and effective evangelical college organizations is Campus Crusade for Christ and Billy Graham's revival meetings were called "crusades."

Power and might, the theological ground for the image of God as warrior, are clearly associated with maleness in fundamentalist thought.[39] True to the predominant biblical language about deity, God is understood in male images of father, king, and Lord. Fundamentalists reject any attempt to think of the deity in female or androgynous imagery or to use nongendered language.

Consistent with the above view of God, it is males who are the "mighty men of God" and who take the lead in all arenas of power, including politics, business, religion, and family, and women who are to be subordinate to men in these areas.[40] The "traditional family," in which the father and husband is the authority and the wife is the "helper," is the model for all areas of life.[41] The doctrine of God serves to support and legitimate the sociopolitical order espoused by fundamentalists.[42] While that order does not advocate overt violence against women, it is a part of the cultural and ideological context for that violence and could serve, perhaps unconsciously and in a warped fashion, to legitimate that violence.

While studies of rapists and abusers sometimes note religious preference,[43] I am unaware of any study that delves into the particular concepts of religion, much less the view of God, of the aggressor. Yet, while it might prove interesting, a study which simply queried the aggressor's formal or conscious religious preference and view of God would probably prove woefully inadequate. Rather than there being a direct connection between theology and violence, the view of God as male warrior probably acts more as a justification at the unconscious level, in what has been termed "nonconscious ideology."[44] More indirectly, during gender role socialization the male warrior God encourages and supports the development of "normal" male traits like competition, aggression, and tenaciousness and "normal" female traits like obedience, passivity, and affection. These traits in turn help create an environment that can lead to sexual violence against women.

There are several particular aspects of the historical legacy and fundamentalist expression of Christianity that can be seen as consistent with an unconscious, and perhaps sometimes conscious, ideology that directly or indirectly creates the environment for male sexual violence against women.

First, and fundamentally, God is male, the Savior figure is male, and both head up a male-dominated world. Power, control, and choice lay in the hands of men in a fashion similar to the way it lay in the hands of the absolute monarch in the ancient Near East. Second, the deity is often viewed as a warrior king who leads men into holy war against the spiritual enemies of Christ. This holy violence is usually symbolic, but it can take actual forms as exampled in the crusades and witch hunts. "Male plus warrior" is a formula for male aggression. It is generally agreed that rape, whatever else it may be, is an act of aggression by men against women. Indeed, forcible rape, as opposed to statutory rape, is, by legal definition, violent. While I am suggesting a correspondence in society between the male warrior God and actual, physical sexual violence against women, some suggest that rape be understood in a broader context. Griffin[45] and Daly[46] move beyond the physical act of rape and draw a connection between the mentality that produces rape and the phenomenon of war.[47] The disposition of some conquering soldiers to commit rape, though not carefully studied, is often noted[48] and may serve to clarify the connection.

A third theme embedded in the above surveys, one which is implied in the formula "male plus warrior," is that women are controlled by men. The idea is expressed in the Old Testament to the degree that women are viewed as property of their fathers and husbands. It is found throughout the whole tradition in terms of men having authority over women who, because of divine command or the natural order of things, are to be obedient to men as to Christ. In the family, this obedience is to the husband or father, and in the church it is directed to the pastor, elders, or supervising male monks. Certainly, in many cases rape has to do with issues of hostility and control rather than passion.[49] Brownmiller[50] argues that the meaning of rape is to be understood in terms of property. Both Daly[51] and Brownmiller see rape as a form of male control and domination of women.

Finally, the Christian tradition, as a whole, is ambivalent about human, and especially female, sexuality. One idea that periodically surfaces, although not stated quite this explicitly, is that a woman's sexuality is her man's and he can do with it what he wants when he wants to do it. Sex is sometimes depersonalized and, correspondingly, the wife is viewed as a masturbatory outlet, an antidote (Luther's term), when the husband falls to fleshly lusts. He controls sexual expression; she is to be there, passively, for him.

On the other hand, the tradition suggests that men can be very insecure, even fearful, with respect to females and sexuality. The purpose of sex, especially in Roman Catholicism prior to the twentieth century,[52] is procreation. In the New Testament and early church fathers (that is, leaders of the church in the early centuries) women are admonished to dress modestly in order that men will not be tempted. Implied in the admonitions to dress modestly and the images of woman as temptress is the notion that women are responsible for the discrimination "due" them, an idea that echoes victim provocation theories in the literature on rape and spouse abuse. The witch hunt is perhaps the most visible example of violence that can be evoked when men feel threatened by woman's sexuality. These various notions about sexuality that are woven throughout the tradition are particularly disturbing when set in the "male plus warrior" context.

Originated in the ancient Jewish scriptures (admittedly, reflecting the surrounding cultures), the idea of a male warrior God and related gendered notions of women, men, and sexuality find expression in and gain momentum in the first few centuries of Christianity. The theology (such as that of Aquinas), practice (as in the cult of the Virgin Mary), and institutions (for example, convents) of the medieval church reinforced these ideas. The church-sanctioned witch hunts of 1500–1700 are an unfortunate confirmation of the violent direction the tradition could take. The Protestant reformers brought innovations in theology and institutions, but with regard to our concerns, they did not effect any fundamental changes.

Fundamentalist Christianity is a modern expression of religion where we can see the male warrior God and the related notions of women, men, and sexuality exhibited in a clear fashion. These various ideas can be seen as providing society with a justification—albeit unconsciously and indirectly—for male sexual violence against women.

With the historical and theological framework in place, we now turn to a psychological analysis of the typical fundamentalist.

PART THREE

A Psychological Profile

CHAPTER 10

The Psychological Model

COGNITIVE THERAPY

As soon as Frankie sat down in my office, I knew there was something weighing heavily on his mind. He squinted his eyes and spoke with a nervous intensity. "The Bible says God brought 600,000 men out of Egypt in the exodus. But you said in class last Thursday that this number couldn't be accurate," he began. I nodded. "You're saying the Bible isn't true?" he continued, looking intently at me as if seeking an answer different from that given in class. At this point I briefly reviewed our class discussion about the nature of the Bible and the different kinds of truth (namely, historical and spiritual). He was not satisfied. "This number has to be right, doesn't it?" he asked. I briefly recounted the reasons why the number 600,000 in Exodus 12:37 is problematic. "But if the Bible is wrong here, it's wrong everywhere," he said, with an anxious look on his face. "It cannot be wrong here." After some discussion, I asked him, "Frankie, I know you do not think the number is incorrect, but what if it were? What would that mean to you?" He thought for a moment. "It would mean that the Bible cannot be trusted and that it's wrong about God. It would mean that we wouldn't know how to be saved." Over the course of the semester, Frankie sat down in my office a half dozen times. Every conversation was some version of this one. He was a bright student and actually performed well in the class. However, he resisted the possibility that there was any kind of error in the Bible; entertaining the very idea left him troubled and uncomfortable. It was as if his logical mind saw the reasoning, but his anxiety about being saved overwhelmed any rational processes.[1]

To communicate with fundamentalists, it is necessary to have some basic understanding of their belief system, especially with regard to the

Bible. However, it is also important to keep in mind that the particulars of the theological system are relatively unimportant, compared to the historical and cultural forces that have shaped fundamentalism's basic worldview and to the psychological forces that drive the individual fundamentalist believer. We now turn to this important psychological story.

Cognitive therapy, originated by Aaron Beck, offers a theory of personality and pathology, and a therapeutic program, that can be useful in understanding the fundamentalist. The basic idea in the cognitive model is that our core cognitions (assumptions, attitudes, beliefs) determine how we interpret events, and our interpretation of events in turn produces our emotions and behaviors. When our core cognitions are distorted and illogical, then our patterns of thinking lead to distressing emotional states and dysfunctional behavior. The cognitive therapist helps clients change their maladaptive thinking. Events, then, in themselves do not produce particular emotions and behavior. Rather, it is the meaning that we attach to events that determines emotional and behavioral outcomes. This basic notion explains why the same event can evoke different responses in different people. My main orientation is derived from Beck's model; to a lesser degree, I will also draw upon the rational-emotive therapy (RET) of Albert Ellis. It is similar to cognitive therapy and will also provide useful insights into the general personality type of fundamentalists.

The cognitive model, which places the emphasis on our thinking patterns, is in contrast to two other influential models of psychology. The Freudian psychoanalytic model is built on the assumption that we are governed by a whole array of unconscious motives and impulses. Beck agrees that the core thoughts that drive us are buried in the unconscious and in this sense he shares an appreciation of the unconscious with the Freudian model. A third major mode, behaviorism, assumes we are driven by external events.

To attempt a substantial psychological interpretation of the fundamentalist is no small task. Before I proceed with that task, I wish to be clear with my reader about three things. First, I am not saying, nor implying, that anyone, by virtue of being a fundamentalist, meets criteria for mental illness. I am simply using the cognitive model as a general guide for understanding the fundamentalist mind. I need to emphasize this point because I will look specifically at pathological profiles and compare those to the fundamentalist profile I will construct. Drawing these comparisons does not mean I am suggesting mental illness in the fundamentalist. Rather, analyzing pathology can provide insight into the psychological structure of healthy individuals, because the pathological profiles exaggerate tendencies, and, therefore, bring to light proclivities that exist in healthy persons. For example, I know myself well enough to know that I have a definite bent toward obsessive and compulsive behavior. One could say I have an obsessive style. My tendencies, fortunately, are not to a degree sufficient to fit the mental illness diagnosis of obsessive-compulsive disorder (OCD). However, I can certainly better understand myself and my propensities by looking at a full-blown obsessive-compulsive disorder profile. When this book is published, I am sure I will be accused of saying that fundamentalism is pathological. I have just said, as plainly as I can, otherwise. But I will say it yet another way.

In the mental health field in this country, the accepted standard for diagnosing mental illness is the *Diagnostic and Statistical Manual of Mental Disorder*, produced by the American Psychiatric Association. It is difficult to arrive at an operational definition of mental disorder that covers all situations and conditions. However, the basic idea of mental disorder, used by the American Psychiatric Association, is a behavioral or psychological syndrome or pattern in an individual that is associated with present distress, disability (such as, impairment in some important area of functioning), or some significantly increased risk of suffering death, pain, disability, or an important loss of freedom. Additionally, the syndrome or pattern must not be merely the expected response to some "normal" event, such as the death of a family member. Political, religious, or sexual deviant behavior is not a mental disorder unless the deviance fits the above description. Fundamentalism is not listed in the manual as a mental disorder and I certainly do not see it as one.

Having distinguished fundamentalism and mental illness, and acknowledged that one does not necessarily produce the other, it is appropriate to note some possible connections between the two. In general, religious faith and mental illness may be related in several ways, two of which are relevant for our discussion. First, particular religious attitudes and behaviors can be manifestations of mental disorders. I will give an example related to my own mental proclivity. "Scrupulosity" is the recognized religious expression of obsessive-compulsive disorder. Obsessive-compulsive disorder is an anxiety disorder characterized by obsessions or compulsions. Obsession, in this sense, means recurrent and persistent thoughts, impulses, or images that are distressful. Compulsions are repetitive behaviors that one feels obligated to perform in order to prevent or reduce distress. The fear of sin and irresistible doubt are associated with scrupulosity. The person cannot feel clean and accepted by God because they see themselves as bad and they see God as intolerable of any deviation from an extreme and impractical standard of behavior their mind has constructed.[2] A second way religion and mental health can relate is that religion can sometimes be harmful for mental well-being. While there is now a solid body of literature showing that under certain conditions religion can be therapeutic, there is also some suggestion that some forms of religiosity can at times be a hazard to mental health. With regard to the latter, admittedly, the empirical research is limited.

However, some studies propose that absolutist attitudes and strict models for life that are characteristic of fundamentalism may hinder normal adjustment to life and thereby may pose a danger to mental health.[3] So, despite the overlap between symptoms of mental illness and some form of religiosity, the first thing I want to clarify, again, is that I am not saying or even suggesting that fundamentalism equates to mental illness.

The second thing I want to emphasize is that I see my observations as applying to what I think is a typical fundamentalist psychological profile. The "typical" fundamentalist may not hold to fundamentalist doctrine as classically formulated in the fundamentalist movement, but I have no interest in constructing a psychological profile of some abstract fundamentalist. My interest is in understanding real fundamentalists who are players in our country's political, cultural, and religious life, and who are our neighbors and family members. This typical profile, as an initial working hypothesis, is based in part on my experience of fundamentalists, primarily in the academic setting, and secondarily, in the therapy room. I have factored in the fact that fundamentalists who show up for therapy constitute an atypical sample with respect to mental illness. As noted in the introduction, my knowledge and experience of fundamentalists did not start when I embarked on my professions as educator and therapist. I have known fundamentalists all my life and today count fundamentalists among my friends and family members.

Finally, I want the reader to know that the model of the fundamentalist personality I present will not apply to all fundamentalists. I claim that cognitive theory is a model that can be useful in understanding the intersection of fundamentalist theology with psychological development. How useful it is in understanding any individual fundamentalist will depend on that fundamentalist's particular psychological story. With those caveats in mind, I now turn to the model.

Cognitive therapy is a highly effective therapeutic modality; some argue it is the most important and most scientifically validated therapeutic approach currently being used by the mental health profession.[4] It seems especially useful for my purposes for at least four reasons. First, while it does not consider issues relating to the client's family of origin to be unimportant, cognitive therapy does not require extensive exploration into childhood material. I believe the cognitive modality can also yield benefit for understanding and encountering fundamentalists, without requiring the layperson untrained in psychology to engage in lengthy inquiry into complicated childhood issues. Second, unlike many other psychotherapy models, the cognitive therapist is active, viewed as a collaborator in the therapeutic process. A collaborative model is more serviceable for my goal of promoting dialogue than, for example, the traditional Freudian doctor-patient model in which the doctor treats the sick patient. Third, while cognitive therapy pays attention to the client's emotion, it primarily addresses thinking patterns, and this makes it amenable to the kind of encounter with fundamentalists I hope to foster, that is, an encounter that is based on a rational and free exchange of ideas. Finally, cognitive therapy is a proven treatment for depression and anxiety/panic. The modality emerged out of Beck's work with depression and treating depression is still its showcase. While it has been effectively used to address a wide variety of other disorders, its most striking success beyond depression has been with anxiety and panic. In my analysis, I will suggest that anxiety can be a key emotion fueling the fundamentalist's staunch defense of his or her position. I will suggest that, at a deeper level, the fundamentalist may be striving to ward off depression.

Beck was trained in Freudian psychoanalysis and had been practicing it for many years when he "discovered" what he calls "automatic thoughts," one of the building blocks of the cognitive therapy system.[5] According to his account,[6] he was working with depressed clients when he noticed that his clients were having certain streams of thought. These thoughts did not validate the Freudian psychoanalytic theory of depression as anger turned on the self. By directing the client to focus on these streams of thought, it became apparent to Beck that this internal communication consisted primarily of a negative bias in thinking, was usually there in all interpersonal relations, and played a dominant role in the client's depression. As it turned out, Albert Ellis, the founder of RET and also trained in the psychoanalytic method, independently had made similar observations.[7]

With the psychoanalytic model now seriously compromised in Beck's mind, he continued his investigation of the thinking of depressed clients, in time uncovering an array of cognitive errors. Meanwhile, he began to develop strategies to address those patterns of faulty thinking. The cognitive therapy approach to treating depression has been refined and the model is increasingly applied to a wide variety of other disorders, although the literature suggests that cognitive therapy is most successful with depression, anxiety, and panic.

Much of the early work in developing cognitive therapy was done by Beck and associates at the University of Pennsylvania. His Center for Cognitive Therapy was administered through the School of Medicine's Department of Psychiatry. In 1994 the Beck Institute for Cognitive Therapy and Research was founded as a natural outgrowth of Beck's earlier associations. Theoretical treatments, clinical manuals, and empirical studies have been published at an increasing rate since the late 1960s. Centers for Cognitive Therapy, established by persons who studied at the Beck institutes, have been established all over the world and train increasing numbers of clinicians in the cognitive model. One year after Beck's *magnum opus* on depression appeared in 1979, David Burns published a best seller, *Feeling Good: The New Mood Therapy,* which helped popularize, in the best sense of the word, cognitive therapy in the form of self-help techniques. Donald Meichenbaum's writings on cognitive-behavior modification also run along the same lines. Along with RET and Meichenbaum's work, Beck's cognitive therapy has played a major role in the "cognitive revolution" in psychology and has taken its place as a viable and popular option in the arena of psychotherapy. The model I am using to understand the typical fundamentalist is not on the fringe; it is in the mainstream of what cutting-edge psychology considers as an important way to understand human beings.

COGNITIVE SCHEMAS

In the cognitive model the personality is dependent on the way data are processed by the client's various layers or levels of cognition. Not coincidentally, the early development of cognitive therapy occurred in the days when computer technology was emerging. Beck, himself, has used the analogy of a computer program to introduce the idea that each neurotic disorder has its own specific "program" that determines the "kind of data admitted."[8] Although cognitive therapists use various terms for the layers or levels of cognition, the first, and from the perspective of achieving therapeutic change the least important level, can be called voluntary thoughts. Voluntary thoughts are thoughts that we consciously and deliberately form in our active thinking process. Voluntary thinking can proceed according to sound principles of logic if the "thinker" is intellectually capable of logical thought and has been exposed to the basic principles of logic, and if sound thinking is not thwarted by deeper levels of cognition. It is these deeper levels of cognition that I am most concerned about here.

Before turning to these deeper and more important levels of cognition, a second "surface" level is usually called the automatic thought level. These cognitive products are called "automatic" thoughts because they occur spontaneously and without effort. They are involuntary and, as with a reflex, they arise without prior reasoning. They seem plausible to the client, and they are close restatements of underlying beliefs. The client is usually unaware of them, hence Beck's Zen-like phrase "thoughtless thinking."[9] They are triggered by circumstances and accompanied by emotions. Such thoughts are usually never challenged by the client.

A still deeper level of cognition generates the automatic thoughts. At this deeper level, the level important for our purposes, personality is shaped by a cognitive structure called schemas, also called assumptions, attitudes, beliefs, thought patterns, and underlying mechanisms. Cognitive schemas are the elementary, relatively stable, central structures of thinking that are formed early in life as a result of experience and identification with significant others. These schemas can be detected as themes running through automatic thoughts. The schemas act as an unconscious grid to mold data from the outside world into automatic cognitions that more directly impact behavior and affect.

Schemas are usually in a "contractual" form: "If I do X, then Y will occur." They are also often expressed in "childish" terminology that are self-depreciating (as in, I'm stupid, dumb). Additionally, because fundamental rules can have a positive payoff, schemas can sometimes be discerned by questioning the client about something he or she is particularly happy about. Finally, the way a client interprets the behavior of others often expresses his or her basic rules about life.[10] The overall focus of cognitive therapy is to modify these deeper dysfunctional cognitions that maintain the pathology. Utilizing an array of techniques, the therapist works with the client to uncover, test, and, where appropriate, shift the client's thought process to patterns that are adaptive, functional, logical, and reality based. In the process clients will learn to recognize the way they construe the world and the connection between this construction of the world and their affect and behavior. It is often necessary, because of time constraints or extensiveness of the client's symptoms, for the therapist and client to identify specific cognitive targets among several alternatives. A distinction can be made between peripheral cognitive processes and core cognitive processes, the latter being more important to change. Schemas are a part of the core cognitive processes—and usually are related in some way to the client's understanding of self, predict the client's emotional and behavioral responses in a wide array of situations, and evoke more anxiety than peripheral cognitions when challenged.[11]

Here are some examples of maladaptive cognitive schemas, along with the mental/emotional state that can accompany them:

1. Unless I do everything perfectly, I am a failure. (depression)
2. If I'm nice, bad things won't happen to me. (depression, sadness, anger)
3. If I make a mistake, it means I am bad. (depression, sadness)
4. If someone disagrees with me, it means he or she doesn't like me. (depression, sadness)
5. If I do or believe "x," I will be safe. (compulsion, anxiety)
6. If I'm not careful, something terrible will happen. (panic)
7. Others are out to get me. (paranoid)
8. I am in danger. (panic)

There are several themes running through these common schemas. Depression and various types of anxiety are common. Numbers 1, 2, 3, 5, and 6 have to do with behaving in a certain way and numbers 4, 5, 7, and 8 have to do with thinking in a certain way. So, the themes in the common schemas above include depression, anxiety, thinking, behaving.

Given these themes, the common maladaptive cognitive schemas can be seen as supporting, or maybe even symbiotically related to, fundamentalist theology. As pointed out, depression was the first disorder with which Beck began his work, and it is still the showcase for cognitive therapy. Early in his work Beck identified the now well-known cognitive triad found in depressed clients. First, the depressed person exhibits a pattern of thinking that involves a negative view of the self, the world, and their future.[12] The self is seen as inadequate, defective, deprived, and/or worthless. The client believes distress is their own fault. The negative view of self, identified by cognitive therapists in depressed clients, is consistent with fundamentalist doctrine that emphasizes the unworthiness of the human being and also places responsibility for that condition on the human sinner.

Second, the depressed client sees the world as being without pleasure or gratification, that is, the client sees his or her ongoing life experiences negatively. This outlook also fits snugly with fundamentalist doctrine. Religious orientations can be classified on a continuum from an otherworldly focus (such as, heaven, hell, God) to a this-worldly focus (such as, peace on earth). Fundamentalists are on the extreme otherworldly part of the continuum. This world is evil and to be avoided. The goal is to live "in" but not "of" the world, focusing instead on the afterlife.

Finally, the client has a pessimistic view of the future, which can evolve into hopelessness and suicidal ideation. This aspect of the depressive triad does not fit the fundamentalist profile, at least in the sense of the long-term future. The otherworldly fundamentalist is quite hopeful and optimistic about the long-term future, which involves eternal life in heaven with God. However, it does fit the fundamentalist short-term expectation that non-Christians are in for a terrible tribulation period.

While the depression profile is oriented around negativity, anxiety arises because of a perception of danger. When anxiety is pathological (that is, not appropriate to the real situation), one of the following errors is common: (1) overestimating the probability or severity of the feared event, or (2) underestimating the coping resources or rescue factors (what others can do to help you). While the same basic strategies used to treat depression are used for anxiety, the anxious client presents in some ways a more difficult case. Identifying the negative thoughts is more difficult because we find that anxious clients are often not anxious when in the clinic. Clients avoid anxious thoughts more than depressed thoughts and thoughts and images that trigger anxiety are often of a fleeting nature.[13]

The anxiety that fundamentalists feel is probably related to their moral code, a strict code of personal morality. These "dos and don'ts" recall the strong behavior theme that ran through many of the maladaptive schemas given earlier. The fundamentalist moral code is absolutist, legalistic, and has an impact that potentially lasts forever. By absolutist, I mean that the rules cannot vary. Fundamentalists will have none of the cultural relativism that allows for different norms in different societal contexts. They are not postmodernists. As I use the term, legalism refers to the adherence of a rule because of the existence of the rule (given by God), not because the rule reflects some underlying moral principle.

Finally, the personal moral code that rules the fundamentalist's life can produce consequences for the fundamentalist that are eternal. Behavior that is not in accord with the "dos and don'ts" of the moral code is sinful. These sinful actions would, without the salvation afforded by Jesus Christ, send the fundamentalist to hell in the first place. In classical fundamentalist doctrine, there is allowance for the Christian's sinful behavior to be covered by the grace of Christ. However, in my experience, most fundamentalists carry significant anxiety about engaging in sinful behavior. My suspicion is that at an unconscious level they are anxious that their sinful behavior means that they were never genuinely "saved" by Christ in the first place, and so the sinful behavior will, indeed, result in their eternal damnation. If I am correct, this dynamic would provide one reason that fundamentalists are adamant and inflexible when it comes to issues (for example, sexual immorality, abortion, drinking alcohol) that they perceive as relating to their moral code.

Another theme running through the schemas has to do with thinking (believing) in a certain way in order to avoid the same damnable consequences that attach to sinful behavior. Fundamentalists believe that significant deviation from their fixed doctrinal system puts them at risk. Underlying both behavior and belief is a deep-seated anxiety. Danger is lurking out there in the "world" of malevolent forces. Suspicion and resistance is the appropriate stance in the face of these dangers.

In the cognitive model of psychopathology, schemas and automatic thoughts that are associated with distress usually involve errors in the cognitive process of thinking.[14] Some of the common ones identified in the cognitive therapy model are useful in our consideration of fundamentalists because these errors will often surface in conversations with fundamentalists. These common errors include the following:

ARBITRARY INFERENCE or JUMPING TO CONCLUSIONS: Unwarranted conclusion, that is, without relevant evidence or contrary to the evidence. Fundamentalists are especially susceptible to logical fallacies of this type. One of the more challenging aspects of communicating with fundamentalists is their refusal to think clearly about issues, retreating instead to illogical and unexamined assertions learned from their fundamentalist families and churches.

ALL-OR-NOTHING or DICHOTOMOUS THINKING: Seeing things in black and white, absolutist categories. Word clues to this distortion include always, never, completely, totally, perfectly. In raising a concern about dichotomous thinking, I am not here advocating relativism with regard to metaphysical truth. For the fundamentalist, however, his or her metaphysical absolutism bleeds over into absolutism about a whole host of issues related to biblical interpretation, politics, and morality. When the fundamentalist takes absolutist positions, it makes dialogue extremely difficult.

SHOULD STATEMENTS: Shoulds, shouldn'ts, musts, and oughts and so on "should" be used rarely, if ever, and always cautiously. They are often a mechanism of dichotomous thinking. They usually come packaged with guilt when directed at oneself, and with anger, frustration, and resentment when directed at others. Should statements do not always include the word "should": for example, "Why didn't my son call me on Mother's Day?"

OVERGENERALIZATION: Drawing an unwarranted conclusion from one or more pieces of evidence or from one or more isolated experiences. If it is true in one case, it will be true in any case which is even slightly similar. For example, one of my clients once said, "My father's a SOB; all men are alike," and one of my fundamentalist students once said, "My minister said they found Noah's ark, so this proves the Bible is true and can always be trusted."

LABELING AND MISLABELING: An extreme form of overgeneralization via the use of labels that are usually emotionally charged and counterproductive. Examples include, "I'm a loser," "She's a bitch." The favorite fundamentalist labels include "liberal," "secular," "humanist," and "modernist." These labels stereotype and serve to cut off communication.

MENTAL FILTER or SELECTIVE ABSTRACTION: Ignoring the positive. Picking out a single negative detail and dwelling on it exclusively so that one's vision of all reality is so colored. I heard a fundamentalist preacher deliver a sermon in which he told a story about a gay man taking sexual advantage of a young boy. This alleged incident was the basis for his sermon on "The Evil of Homosexuality."

MAGNIFICATION or CATASTROPHIC THINKING: Exaggerating, making too much of something.

MINIMIZATION: Making too little of something. Fundamentalists are prone to discount hard evidence, if that evidence calls into question their fundamentalist belief.

EMOTIONAL REASONING: Making inference about the self, the world, or the future on the basis of an emotional experience. For example, "I feel incompetent, therefore I must be incompetent." For fundamentalists, their religious experience is of paramount importance in fueling their beliefs and perspectives. Religious experience should not always be discounted; in certain domains and in certain ways, it can provide useful evidence. However, to base one's total view of the world on what one experiences at the emotional level, without attention to evidence that appeals to reason, will lead to a skewed view of things.

So, with the structure of automatic thoughts and schemas in place, along with certain patterns of thinking, let us examine a particular example of a cognitive subsystem given by Beck.[15] As a therapist I have seen this pattern many, many times.

- Affect: depression or anger
- Automatic thought: I caused my husband to behave badly.
- Schema: If I'm nice, bad things won't happen to me.

Looked at in the reverse, this person, early in life, generated the schema, "If I'm nice, bad things won't happen to me." This schema, as all schemas, is not reasonable, that is, it includes errors in thinking. In this case thinking errors include arbitrary inference and all-or-nothing thinking. With a little imagination, one can see how a little child, fearful, might emerge from some anxious situation with this conclusion. The schema gets embedded at a deep level in their psyche. As an adult, when something bad happens in her life, the easy tendency is to explain it with the schema. The result is depression.

One of my clients was an accountant who came in with a severe anxiety disorder. When we uncovered the underlying schema, it explained not only his anxiety, but also his chosen profession. The client's parents had loud verbal arguments when the client was growing up. Sometimes, after the argument, the father stormed into the room and scolded the boy. On one of these occasions, at around four years old, the young boy heard his parents arguing in the next room. Anxious and afraid that he would be scolded, he looked at the curtain in his room and began counting the designs on the curtain. As he remembers it, his parents stopped arguing and on this particular occasion the father did not scold him. The child generated the rule, "If I count correctly, I will be safe." The child learned to do well in math, became an accountant, and because of the schema unconsciously felt that he was at risk if he did not perform his calculations correctly.

CHAPTER 11

Profile of the Typical Fundamentalist

CONSCIOUS BELIEFS

With the cognitive model in place, I now want to suggest a psychological profile of the typical fundamentalist. I have constructed this profile from my work with clients and students who exhibit the "habits of mind" discussed in the Introduction and profess the general theological positions detailed in Part Two. These clients and students are Christians who also characterize themselves as fundamentalist and participate in churches that claim to be fundamentalist. In this psychological profile, I am highlighting certain fundamentalist beliefs that are important for understanding the fundamentalist psyche. Also, as I have already stated, I am not suggesting that the psychological profile I provide is true of every fundamentalist. Clearly, each fundamentalist has a different family of origin, developmental story, and emotional makeup. This is a profile encountered in many, perhaps most, fundamentalist Christians.

First, Protestant fundamentalists believe the truth of the universe is contained in the Bible (or the church tradition for fundamentalist Catholics, or the *Qur'an* and hadiths for the fundamentalist Muslim). The Protestant fundamentalist says that biblical truth includes scientific and historical truth. This extreme belief of fundamentalists can be traced in a milder form back to the Protestant Reformation where Protestants distinguished themselves from Roman Catholics in several ways, one being the Protestant principle of "*sola scriptura,*" that is, theology is based solely on the Bible. The early Protestants were not fundamentalists in the modern sense, but their emphasis on the Bible finds later expression in the fundamentalist obsession with the Bible as the truth about everything, including science and history.

The second piece of the profile is that the fundamentalist believes in a literal heaven and hell and that the status of the fundamentalist with respect to being "saved," or being a Christian, entirely determines where they will spend eternity. To say it differently, the fundamentalist is convinced that his or her religious belief determines eternal destiny. In order to communicate with fundamentalists, it is necessary to appreciate the centrality of this belief.

Thus far we have discussed conscious beliefs. The third aspect of the profile is usually unconscious. Fundamentalists operate out of a schema that if any one part of their fundamentalist belief system is in error, it challenges their entire system (absolutist, all-or-nothing thinking) and, to a significant degree, the basis on which they have built their identity (or, in the case of adolescents, the basis on which they are building their identity). So the structure of this schema is very similar to the common anxiety/panic/depression schema structure I described earlier. Fundamentalist identity is intertwined with and based on the fundamentalist religious belief.

There is, indeed, in the fundamentalist mind a slippery slope. If, for example, it were to turn out that their literal reading of the creation account in the biblical book of Genesis is not accurate, then they unconsciously fear that they would slip perilously towards disaster, as might be exemplified in the following scenario.

> If I believe "X" (where "X" is some idea contrary to fundamentalist belief), then the Bible is wrong about it; if the Bible is wrong about that, then it is wrong about God, God doesn't exist, I'm not saved, and I will go to hell.

The same basic schema can entail variations. For example, the conclusion could be that "my life plan is in error" or "I'm not who I thought I was."

In the therapy room cognitive schemas, when they emerge, usually do so after several versions have been explored. When they become conscious, it is often with an "Ah ha" type of response from the client. Therapists using the cognitive therapy model dig for the cognitive schema, which, when uncovered, yields some version of the following statement: "Ah ha, I see now, that's it. That's what's been driving me." It is a potent and special moment in the therapy room when the client distinguishes some foundational, always irrational, principle, generated early in life, and around which they have organized much of their life, often in a destructive way. It often turns out that the new revelation underlies the very issues that caused them to enter therapy in the first place.

In my therapy practice I addressed issues related to religious belief only if treating them was called for by the diagnosis and the generally accepted treatment plan for that diagnosis. However, I was one of the therapists in town with a reputation for dealing with religious issues as a specialization. Over the course of several years I had the opportunity to work with numerous fundamentalists; some in the process of exiting the movement, and some former fundamentalists. Of course, the schema of a fundamentalist that leads to depression can be the same or similar to the schema of the depressed atheist or the depressed liberal. My concern is not with the particular schema that leads the fundamentalist to diagnosable mental illness. Rather, I am here interested in distinguishing what I believe I have found to be a general schema held by the typical fundamentalist, whether they are healthy or mentally ill. Remember that schemas are unconscious and they are primitively formulated at an early age.

THE UNCONSCIOUS FUNDAMENTALIST SCHEMA

In the clinical setting, and in working with students in the classroom and professor's office, and in my various associations and services in the church, I have found that the cognitive schema of the fundamentalist Christian is something very close to, if not exactly, the following:

If I don't get it right, I am not a Christian, and I will go to hell.

As this schema is a core assertion of my psychological analysis, it is appropriate that I carefully unpack it.

Let us first consider the basic assertion in the schema, "If I don't get it right, I am not a Christian, and I will go to hell." "It" refers to the religious beliefs of the fundamentalist. This statement is not even accurate in terms of classic fundamentalist doctrine. What I call "classic fundamentalism" is to be distinguished from the fundamentalist beliefs espoused by many laypersons ignorant of the historical context and theological issues. Classic fundamentalism does not teach that a Christian has to be accurate in every single religious belief. However, I think this is how the typical fundamentalist feels and, at the level of cognition schema, thinks. So, with regard to the schema, "If I don't get it (i.e., my belief system) right, I am not a Christian, and I will go to hell," there is a flaw in this "thinking," just as there are flaws in all maladaptive cognitive schemas. To repeat for emphasis a qualification I made earlier, when talking about fundamentalists, I am not asserting that their maladaptiveness leads to mental illness. Rather, the fundamentalists have a particular type of maladaptive schema that prevents them from being willing and/or able to seriously entertain any view that challenges their own cherished conceptions.

I want to call attention to the absolutism implied in the schema. In the fundamentalist mind there is no room for a single error. This absolutist position locks the fundamentalist into a tight spot, generating considerable emotional distress. The fundamentalist doctrine of the inspiration of the Bible means that there cannot be a single error in the Bible. Any discrepancy, however minor to a liberal Christian or a critical scholar, is dangerous for the fundamentalist because it means that God the Holy Spirit, which authored the very words of the Bible, was in error, a situation that cannot be explained by the fundamentalist and is, therefore, intolerable. Thus, a single unexplained discrepancy anywhere means that the whole system comes tumbling down. That theological position, when linked with the psychological threat, requires the fundamentalist to be ever vigilant about making a costly error. This causes them to be perpetually anxious since personal disaster is just one mistake away.

Notice what is absent from this schema. There is no mention of improper behavior that would have negative consequences. Considering fundamentalism's strict moral code, and its long history of fighting what it perceives to be moral evils (such as alcohol and sexual sins), one would expect that the fundamentalist schema would include a concern about improper behavior. Indeed, I have worked with fundamentalists who had some version of the following schema:

If I do one wrong thing, I am not a Christian, and I will go to hell.

Many years ago now, actually in my first year of teaching, an older student walked purposefully into my office. After a few pleasantries, and without much of a transition, he launched into reports of his experiences in the Vietnam war. Therapists know that what clients start talking about initially is often not at all what they are really there to address. Through the years I have learned that this is sometimes the case with students as well. This young man's accounts of his experiences in Vietnam quickly exhibited a theme—his sexual indiscretions while off duty. For a few minutes I was taken aback as he recounted numerous sexual encounters in the Siagon red light district. As it turned out, the young man grew up in a fundamentalist family and church in Louisiana. I will never forget his comment near the end of the conversation, a comment that revealed the true purpose of his visit. "I thought that telling you, a minister (which I was not, but as a professor of religion, I am often seen as a minister), about my affairs, would make me feel clean. But it doesn't help that much, because I know that I will probably go to hell for my sins."

I could give more examples of fundamentalist obsession with moral behavior. However, I have not found this emphasis on behavior to be as prevalent in fundamentalist schemas as the emphasis on belief, which may be universal among fundamentalists. While Christianity in general, and fundamentalism in particular, certainly give much weight to the "dos and don'ts" of a moral code, a distinguishing feature of Christianity is the attention it gives to right belief or right thinking. Judaism, for example, out of which early Christianity emerged, places emphasis on behavior. This point is illustrated by the old story of a group of rabbis, each one having different beliefs about God, but all agreeing on the practice of keeping kosher. Other religions, as well, seem to place more emphasis on right action. Christianity, however, has a long history of fine-tuning right thinking. In the Sermon on the Mount, even Jesus is depicted as saying,

> You have heard that it was said, "You shall not commit adultery." But I say to you that everyone who looks at a woman with lust has already committed adultery with her in his heart.
>
> (Matthew 5:27–28)

This saying on adultery is in a collection of antithetical sayings all utilizing the formula, "You have heard that it was said . . . but I say to you." In each case the emphasis is shifted from outward behavior to inner motivation and intention (thinking). Scholars call attention to this difference between belief and practice with the words "orthodoxy" (right belief) and "orthopraxy" (right practice).

So, deep in the fundamentalist mind, the end point of wrong belief (meaning, wrong thinking) is that one's identity as a Christian is demolished. For the fundamentalist, Christianity is at the core of their identity. They have constructed their identity in a way that cannot tolerate deviation in one belief. The end point is a place that is intolerable. In one way of looking at things, our identity is all we have. To poke around in a way that seems to challenge that identity, and therefore our existence, can create enormous, even intolerable, distress. The perceived threat of annihilation should not be underestimated. Most fundamentalists are not psychologically sophisticated enough and/or psychologically trained to understand the underlying etiology of the distress that lives just below the surface when they are having seemingly simple conversations about the subject matter of their religious belief. The person who sees these cognitive schemas and the mechanisms that activate the fundamentalist's anxiety is much better prepared to understand the fundamentalist and, if desired, to enter into a productive conversation with them. And I do think productive conversations are achievable and needed.

Very few attempts have been made to understand the psychology of fundamentalist Christians. One exception is an excellent recent psychological study that argues fundamentalism is a meaning system. Here is the thesis:

> We believe that the meaning fundamentalists derive from their religious beliefs is what allows them to persevere in an inhospitable culture: It creates a way for them to interpret the world, as well as themselves in relation to the world. This meaning system encompasses all of life and is strongly felt, for it deals with issues of eternal

importance. It also provides a framework for motivation, and in the process helps meet several personal needs for meaning, such as purpose, value, efficacy, and self-worth. Meaning, for fundamentalists, is found wholly within the pages of the sacred text.[1]

I am not suggesting that the authors of this thesis agree with my psychological model of fundamentalists. I do think, however, that their extended treatment of fundamentalism as a meaning system supports my thesis about the seriousness of the threat of the loss of that meaning for the fundamentalist Christian.

While the loss of meaning and threat of non-being is serious enough, the fundamentalist worries also about an active punishment that perhaps is as psychologically intolerable for them to imagine as is nonexistence. The symbolic language of the Bible depicts hell using evocative language that plays upon some of the deepest human fears. The anxiety elicited by traditional Christianity's severe descriptions of hellfire and eternal punishment can be profound, and especially so when they are conveyed to children whose experience and view of the world is so limited. Fundamentalist preachers often use the fires of hell as a way of motivating sinners to convert and urging Christians to live the holy life. Fundamentalists cannot really consider a whole host of scientific, moral, and religious questions that emerge in contemporary life, if at some level they believe that accepting any single concession will send them to this literal and eternal hell. Other religions have their severe threats (such as, the "wheel of sharp weapons" in Buddhism), but I dare say Christianity wins the prize on this point.

The psychological paradigm of cognitive therapy, which I draw upon to understand the fundamentalist, is organized around thinking, but this does not mean that emotion is relegated to the sideline. There is an interaction that occurs between emotion, behavior, and thought, especially when addressing issues that relate to identity. In the cognitive therapy model, the term "hot cognition" refers to the idea that change in thinking often is facilitated when strong emotions are triggered in the process. Some schemas may lie dormant until activated by a particular, usually stressful, situation. Encounters with fundamentalists do not usually entail the kind of intense emotional dynamic that one gets in the therapy room. However, a significant level of emotion can be provoked, even if not always visibly displayed, when a person's basic beliefs are called into question. This is particularly the case when such people feel their worldview and identity have also been undermined. The fundamentalist, understandably, needs to defend against what they consciously and unconsciously perceive as threats against their identity and future well-being.

So, the encounter with the fundamentalist can be, for the non-fundamentalist, a frustrating exercise in dealing with a highly defensive person who resorts readily to cognitive errors in thinking. If, however, the dynamics are understood and taken into account, it is possible to take advantage of a "teachable moment." To put it in cognitive therapy terms, a "teachable moment" can be a time when maladaptive cognitions can be altered. Once again, in this context I use the term "maladaptive" to refer to patterns of thinking that effectively block the fundamentalist from genuinely engaging in a give-and-take conversation where important questions are seriously considered.

Finally, there are legions of persons who think of themselves as former fundamentalists. My own clinical experience in working with former fundamentalists, or those trying to leave the fold, echoes that of others who have worked with this population. Ex-fundamentalists usually go through a period when they feel they are heretics and sinners. Leaving fundamentalism can be destabilizing and can lead to guilt, confusion, depression, anxiety, and loneliness. Sometimes the clinical disorder is severe and takes years to effectively address.[2]

My client Jim is a good example of someone who left fundamentalism. He grew up a Baptist fundamentalist and his exit from the movement started when he fell in love with a mainstream Roman Catholic woman. Even though he was very bright and understood the flawed logic and questionable theology of his fundamentalist background, Jim suffered panic attacks that we finally related directly to irrational anxiety about going to hell because he was a heretic. Jim came from a close-knit family and his family's pressure on him—albeit subtle and framed in a supposedly loving way—to conform to his fundamentalist upbringing took its toll. Although it took three years to do so, Jim finally forged an authentic path for himself that allowed him to be true to his new religious orientation and maintain contact with his family, although that relationship continued to be strained as long as I worked with him.

ROUNDING OUT THE PROFILE

As we work to understand fundamentalism, insights gained from cognitive therapy can be supplemented with other research. There is a body of literature on authoritarianism that is useful in understanding the fundamentalist profile. Given the significance of the fascist and Nazi movements in the middle of the twentieth century, authoritarianism has been studied extensively since the 1950s. Admittedly, some of the old claims that identify fundamentalism with an authoritarian personality may have been based on poorly constructed studies and perhaps motivated by prejudice of social scientists against fundamentalists.[3] The most recent effort to study authoritarianism and fundamentalism is by Bob Altemeyer, utilizing social learning theory. Authoritarianism here is understood as encompassing three attitudinal clusters: (1) authoritarian submission to established authorities,

(2) authoritarian aggression perceived to be sanctioned by established authorities, and (3) conventionalism, that is, a high degree of adherence to the social conventions perceived to be endorsed by society and its established authorities. Clearly, not all fundamentalists fall neatly into the category of authoritarian. However, fundamentalists appear to be more authoritarian than those with other religious orientations.[4]

By "submission to established authority," Altemeyer means a general acceptance of the statements and actions of authorities and a general willingness to comply with instructions, all of which are derived from the belief that authorities should be trusted, obeyed, and respected. The fundamentalist pastor fosters this kind of submission through his demands for loyalty and unquestioning support. The fundamentalist does not stand alone. The fundamentalist exists in and is supported by a social network that usually includes a religious community and, often, a biological family as well. The church or campus group that serves as the primary social group for the fundamentalist provides not only social interaction and support, but also ideological training. The leaders of the group are viewed as authoritative in their pronouncements on the Bible and other matters. There is a definite reluctance on the part of fundamentalists to criticize their leaders, because in effect one is finding fault with God's servants.

For most fundamentalists, the most important leader for them is their pastor. The pastor of a fundamentalist church wields enormous authority among the members. Normally, he delivers a sermon to the congregation three times a week—Sunday morning, Sunday evening, and Wednesday night "prayer meeting." In smaller churches, the pastor will also teach a Sunday School class, usually the adult class. Fundamentalists go to church to "hear the pastor"; his preferences in books, magazines, and parachurch organizations are communicated to the members.

The second of Altemeyer's attitudinal clusters, "authoritarian aggression," refers to a predisposition to cause physical, psychological, financial, or other harm to someone when the aggressor believes that such harm is approved by the authorities or will help maintain social conventions. The targets of the aggression are usually people considered unconventional by the fundamentalist (for example, homosexuals, liberals).[5]

Finally, the third attitudinal cluster, "conventionalism," fits the fundamentalist who adheres to the conventions endorsed by their society (the fundamentalist church) and established authority (the fundamentalist pastor).

In conclusion, and in Altemeyer's words, the three attitudinal clusters covary because

> Highly submissive, conventional persons seem unusually fearful that the world is personally dangerous and the society is collapsing into lawlessness. This fear, along with other factors, instigates aggressive impulses.[6]

The positive correlation between Protestant fundamentalists—and others with "tightly wound religious ideologies"[7]—and authoritarianism is understandable in light of basic fundamentalist teaching.[8] Fundamentalists have highly organized religious ideologies and teach that one's loyalty is to a supernatural authority and, relatedly, to earthly authority that acts in its name (parents, church leaders, and perhaps political leaders). Put in this context, it is understandable why deviation from moral values, defined by the authorities, can be a source of great stress. "The greater the intolerance, the certainty, and the lists of 'dos and don'ts,' the greater the likely conventionalism."[9] One can also understand the sometimes aggressive impulse of the fundamentalist, whose resistant and even hostile stance may be the verbal expression of significant psychological forces.

Other research that is relevant here includes several findings. First, people need a measure of consistency and certainty in their lives. Cognitive consistence theorists postulate a need for consistency (sometimes called "uncertainty reduction") as a major mechanism for closure strivings, or what in layman's terminology is usually called "closed-mindedness." The need for consistency shows up as closed-mindedness and is aroused by a situational encounter with a cognitive inconsistency. Research findings on authoritarianism show that the characteristic shares common features with and coheres with closed-mindedness, as evidenced in a significant body of research devoted to understanding persons who are closed minded and crave clear-cut knowledge of their social realities.[10] Next, people with a low tolerance for ambiguity tend to "seek certainty by clinging to the familiar, by distorting the meaning of information, and by imposing on it simplistic clichés and stereotypes."[11] Profiles of conservatives indicate that conservatives have a variety of traits that have been discussed above: conformity, dogmatism, intolerance of ambiguity, authoritarianism, and the need for closure.[12] Finally, the "dogmatic individual" exhibits traits such as the denial of contradictions, a strong orientation toward authority, and closed-mindedness.[13]

I want to be careful about the use of the word "cult" in any book about fundamentalism, mainly because the scholarly literature on cults cannot justly be used to characterize fundamentalist groups. Fundamentalists simply do not meet the criteria generally used for defining cults. This is also a delicate issue because the word "cult" has pejorative connotations that are nearly as negative as "terrorist" has come to have in the popular mind. With these cautions and qualifications, however, the large body of research on cults may help to illuminate some of the features of fundamentalist groups.[14]

In my survey of the literature, two specific areas of research may be helpful. First, one of the generally accepted marks of a cult is that it is organized around a central, authoritative, charismatic leader. I am using "charismatic" here to refer to someone with an engaging personality who is able to sway people. I am using it in its secular meaning, not as referring to the religious practice of speaking in tongues that I discussed in Part One. So, in the typical cult we find a person who has the ability to move and motivate and, to use a stronger word, control the group. The cult leader demands loyalty and unquestioning support. The People's Temple had Jim Jones, the Moonies have Rev. Sun Myung Moon, and so on. This aspect of cults does not apply exactly to fundamentalism, because fundamentalism is a movement that crosses over the boundaries between various groups, whereas cults usually lack prior solid ties with religious bodies and emerge afresh behind the cult leader. However, it is true that most fundamentalists are members of a church, sometimes with hundreds of active members. These churches are usually led by a preacher who is granted much authority by the church members.

The second area of cult research that seems relevant for understanding the fundamentalist has to do with our knowledge of brainwashing, a term for various loosely defined techniques of coercive persuasion used by cults and cult leaders.[15] Techniques used by cults include

- total control and isolation,
- confusion and uncertainty,
- guilt and humiliation,
- release and resolution, and
- physical debilitation and exhaustion.

The first three of the above techniques are worthy of examination in light of fundamentalism and can shed light on fundamentalism, but I hasten to add that fundamentalist groups do not use any of them to the extent they are used by *bona fide* cults. First, with regard to "total control and isolation," many fundamentalist churches seek to isolate their members from worldly influences. As we have seen, "be ye separate" is the motto reaching back to the origins of the fundamentalist movement. Organizationally and institutionally, separatist tendencies have resulted in the development of a fundamentalist infrastructure consisting of church, primary and secondary education, publishing ventures, television stations, and dating networks. Ideally, the fundamentalist Christian can live his or her life inside a protected cocoon constructed in a form consistent with fundamentalist ideology. The fact that total separation is only an ideal and that fundamentalists do not as a rule go off to the mountains and live communally apart from society is one thing that distinguishes fundamentalism from cults that take this radical approach. Also, some fundamentalists have more of a separatist orientation than others.

In the list cited above, "confusion and uncertainty" refer to the cult practice of challenging the convert's belief system and ideological orientation that is derived from "the world." The cult, of course, addresses the tension resulting from the uncertainty with a clear and uncompromising new system of thought. I have shown how fundamentalism has developed what is regarded by adherents as a clear, absolutist, and infallible doctrinal system. The fundamentalist is taught and pressured to accept this tight system in its entirety, rather than the "secular, humanistic" teachings of the world.

Finally, fundamentalists are as good as anyone at using and manipulating "guilt and humiliation," and especially guilt. In the cult, the convert is made to feel unworthy if he or she continues with their prior beliefs and commitments. In a similar fashion, fundamentalism has an effective arsenal of guilt-producing ideas and tactics. The traditional notion of sin is effectively deployed into the fundamentalist member's psyche via preaching, hymns, and "counseling."

The array of empirical data I have reviewed paints a consistent psychological picture of the fundamentalist mind and its orientation to the world. All of the findings make even better sense when interpreted in light of the underlying cognitive schema that I suggest is driving the fundamentalist psyche. That underlying schema driving the entire profile, as stated earlier, is

If I don't get it right, I am not a Christian, and I will go to hell.

In order to avoid the intolerable condition of spending eternity in hell, the fundamentalist is psychologically desperate for the true beliefs and is eager to look to experts in their fundamentalist network to obtain and solidify those true beliefs. With the true beliefs in hand, the fundamentalist, intolerant of ambiguity, must defend the beliefs at all costs, even if they are contrary to evidence and otherwise unreasonable. This pattern has been called a "sacrifice of intellect."[16] This defense of true beliefs at all costs is a formula for closed-mindedness, irrational argumentation, and perhaps aggressive impulses. For the fundamentalist, only a successful defense of the true beliefs will maintain one's identity as a Christian and save the soul from a burning hell.

Given the serious psychological issues at stake, as described in the previous section, it is not surprising that the fundamentalist extensively uses an array of conscious and unconscious tactics to defend their position. The old psychoanalytic category of defense mechanisms can be useful in understanding fundamentalist patterns and in shedding light on how to communicate with the fundamentalist.

Confronting new ideas for the fundamentalist can be problematic if those ideas are incongruent with the fundamentalist's existing worldview. Incorporating this new information can cause anxiety because the new information threatens the existing worldview. Anxiety is unpleasant and so we try to avoid or eliminate it through the use of defense mechanisms—devices we use to defend against anxiety, even if it means distorting reality. The term and concept of defense mechanism originated with Sigmund Freud, whose program of psychoanalysis is no longer dominant; yet, most therapists believe that the concept is useful as a description of how people cope with anxiety. The following summary of some of the defense mechanisms attempts to capture how they are generally thought of today.

The defense mechanism of "denial" is simply denying that some external, unpleasant reality exists. I vividly remember a situation in which a young Muslim man had occasion to come into the home of a fundamentalist Christian family during a large extended family gathering. The fundamentalist Christian belief is that the Muslim is going to burn in hell for eternity because the Muslim does not accept Jesus Christ as savior. However, perhaps for the first time, many of these fundamentalists were confronted directly (as opposed to the often distorted images of television) with the human face of a Muslim. This young man, like most Muslims around the world, was moral, kind, courteous, and generous. Also, he believed in God and because he used general moral and religious language when speaking (such as, God, God's will, doing the right thing), it did not immediately clash with the language and perspective of the fundamentalist Christians. The fundamentalists accepted this young man and included him as one of their own. When I privately pointed out to one of the family members that according to her theological belief this young man would go to hell, she simply replied, "But he believes in God," and quickly shifted the conversation away from the subject. I was amazed at the family members' denial of the unpleasant reality, according to their official doctrine, that this young man was going to burn in hell for eternity. The defense mechanism of denial is an amazingly powerful and effective defense against an anxiety producing idea.

"Rationalization" does not mean to act rationally. Rather, it is a psychological move that allows something to seem rational when, in reality, it is not. Most of my students, when they get to know me, like me. The fundamentalist students like to believe that I am one of their own. Of course, I am not a fundamentalist. In the conduct of my Bible classes, I draw upon the scholarly consensus, which usually challenges fundamentalist claims. Fundamentalist students often make comments to me to the effect that they know I must teach certain things in class because of the constraints I have on me by virtue of working in a public university. Their comments suggest that they know that in my heart I do not believe what I teach, and over the years a few fundamentalist students have said this explicitly. My fundamentalist students like me, see me as a good and moral person, and cannot entertain the idea that, according to their doctrine, I will burn for eternity in hell. In effect, they are using the defense mechanism of rationalization to conclude that I am required to teach things I do not believe and am, therefore, a fundamentalist like them.

People are often driven to counter unwanted feelings by giving strong expression to an opposite feeling, a cognitive strategy referred to as "reaction formation." The classic examples of this are the fundamentalist's strong objections to homosexuality and pornography. I certainly do not think it is true in all, or perhaps even most, cases, but I am clear that homophobia, for example, can be a defense mechanism covering up latent homosexual tendencies, for fundamentalist and non-fundamentalist homophobics.

I now offer my own contribution to the lexicon of defense mechanisms, inspired by what I have observed in fundamentalists. A common fundamentalist defense mechanism, which can be viewed as a type of rationalism, is "prooftexting." I did not invent the word, of course. My contribution is the suggestion that prooftexting is a common fundamentalist mechanism used to defend against the particular brand of anxiety built on the fundamentalist schema. The prooftexting defense is one of the more frustrating fundamentalist tactics and it is hard to figure out how to get around it. When confronted with some idea or situation they cannot handle, fundamentalists simply quote the Bible. Sometimes the Bible is actually misquoted. If quoting the words correctly, it does not matter if the quotation from the Bible is taken out of context or is contradicted by other things in the Bible or is irrelevant to the issue at hand. It certainly does not matter if the way the fundamentalist uses the quotation is unsupported by any reasonable method of interpretation. Whatever point the fundamentalist wants to make is "proven" by a Bible "text" and that, in their mind, settles the matter. Because of the role of the Bible in fundamentalist churches, most fundamentalists have a pocketful of verses they can readily quote to get them out of tight spots. When confronted with something they cannot explain, especially regarding scientific matters, a common response is "But with God all things are possible" (Matthew 19:26). Another common prooftext used by fundamentalists as a defense against anxiety is "God's ways are not our ways" or "God works in mysterious ways." While these lines are not in the Bible in exactly this form, the fundamentalist is probably referring to Isaiah 55:8–9, which reads,

> For my thoughts are not your thoughts, neither are your ways my ways, saith the Lord. For as the heavens are higher than the earth, so are my ways higher than your ways, and my thoughts than your thoughts.

I have a colleague who told me that he once had a student who genuinely seemed to want to discuss issues raised in the New Testament course in which the student was enrolled. Often the student followed my colleague to his office after class to inquire about something raised in class. However, whenever the student was confronted with something too uncomfortable, the student made this statement, "I cannot accept that because the Bible says there will be false teachers among you," and walked away. He was quoting a part of 2 Peter 2:1.

Understanding the psychology of the fundamentalist will go a long way toward mitigating the use of the prooftexting defense mechanism tactic. Later in the book, I will give specific strategies for dialogue that can be used to respond to a fundamentalist when they resort to prooftexting.

The fundamentalist profile and the cognitive thinking pattern that underlies it become clearer when we relate them to the various theories of religious development that have emerged within developmental psychology. Most such theories of religious development are derived to one degree or another from the influential work of developmental psychologist Jean Piaget. James W. Fowler, based on extensive interviewing, has suggested that individual religious faith develops in a sequence of stages.[17] Fowler couches his developmental program in terms of faith and posits the following stages:

Stage 1: Primal faith (infancy). Emotional trust based on body contact. Development of play routines.

Stage 2: Intuitive/projective faith (early childhood). Imagination combines with perception and feelings to create faith images.

Stage 3: Mythical/literal faith (elementary). Can distinguish between fantasy and the real world, but religious beliefs and symbols are accepted literally.

Stage 4: Synthetic/conventional faith (early adolescence). Hunger for a more personal relationship with God.

Stage 5: Individuative/reflective faith (late adolescence, young adult). Critical examination of values and belief. Sense of authority moves from that which is external to the self. Capacity for empathy.

Stage 6: Conjunctive faith (midlife or beyond). Integration of opposites. Capacity to appreciate multiple perspectives.

Stage 7: Universalizing faith (unspecified age). Emphasis on oneness with God. Rare for people to reach this stage.

For our purposes, the most important stages begin with "mythical/literal faith" (stage 3, usually in the elementary school years) and end with "individuative/reflective faith" (stage 5, usually in late adolescence or young adulthood). In "mythical/literal faith" the child can distinguish the real world, but has not developed an appreciation for the symbolic and metaphorical nature of much religious language. By the "individuative/reflective faith" stage, the individual has moved to a critical examination of values and beliefs, including, significantly, a shift from reliance on external authorities to authority within one's self. Also, the developing youth is increasingly able to adopt a third-person perspective.

Fundamentalists tend to be stuck at the earlier mythical/literal faith stage because their overall cognitive structure requires that they take their religious narrative at face value. In their insistence on the literal reading of the Bible, they have not yet learned to understand and appreciate the nature and role of religious symbols. Also, their willing submission to authority places them in the earlier stages of development in which the reliance on external authorities is natural.

The value of locating fundamentalists in this developmental theory of faith depends, of course, on the credence one gives to Fowler's system. In all fairness, I should point out that Fowler is longtime professor in the moderate Methodist Candler School of Theology at Emory University. He and his associates at the Center for Research on Faith and Moral Development obviously construct their theories based on their judgment about what kind of faith is more mature and valuable. Certainly, one could assert, as fundamentalists likely would, that reading the Bible literally and respecting external authority reflects a "higher" form of religious faith. The fundamentalist assertion can be placed in the context of a more general critique challenging the value judgments entailed in Fowler's system. Two responses can be made to this critique of Fowler.

First, as pointed out earlier, Fowler's system is rooted in the influential work of developmental psychologist Jean Piaget. If the fundamentalist is going to argue that Fowler's stage theory is incorrect, at least let it be acknowledged that what is being challenged is not just some professor in a theological school, but, rather, one of the major theorists in the discipline of psychology. Now, of course, Piaget could be all wrong in the way he has outlined the normal human developmental process, but taking on Piaget is a huge task. If their critique is to be successful, fundamentalists will have to show how Piaget has misconceived that process.

Second, it is generally understood that literalness and the reliance on external authorities are attributes that characterize people in their adolescent and earlier years during the formative phase. Fowler did not formulate his stages based on pure theoretical speculation. He and his associates had interviewed hundreds (perhaps thousands) of people as the stage theory was formulated and refined.

Lawrence Kohlberg's influential work on moral development, also based on Piaget's developmental psychology, follows the same general profile set forth by Fowler. In Kohlberg's framework, the sense of what is right during early childhood, which he calls "the pre-conventional level of moral development," focuses on punishment, obedience, and the instrumental satisfaction of one's own needs. The conventional level of moral development in late childhood and early adolescence gives great emphasis to law and social rules as valuable in their own right. It is only at the postconventional level, which may develop from late adolescence on, that people address morality as an abstract principle and are able to distinguish the moral values of a group from their own identification with that group. As in Fowler's stage theory, the fundamentalist outlook corresponds to Kohlberg's earlier levels. Appreciating morality as an abstract principle and distinguishing one's self apart from the group are more mature developments that occur in late adolescence and later; these patterns are not evident in the fundamentalist profile we are developing.

It reaches back in time a bit, but it was Eric Erikson who suggested the importance of the adolescent's struggle to establish an identity. Adolescents quest for who they are and what they will become. In the early years, their values and morals derive largely from their parents. As they move through high school and college years, wider influences from peers, teachers, and other adults come into play. Usually this involves experimentation where the student tries on various commitments and identities in the areas of vocation, social relationships, and religion. Role confusion and anxiety occur when the parental views and values differ significantly from the new influences. In complex, modern societies this process of developing individual identity can continue through the college years. In these terms, the fundamentalist fails to manifest this aspect of the maturation process, namely, establishing an identity separate from the authoritative fundamentalist group.

Two things stand out here. First, the establishment of a healthy identity apart from the group can entail considerable anxiety. In the normal process of development, this anxiety is tolerable and tolerated. As pointed out earlier, however, the fundamentalist is anxious about something much more dreadful than most individuals have to face. For most adolescents, the anxiety includes taking positions contrary to, for example, one's parents; adolescents fear suffering the negative consequences of parental disfavor. For the fundamentalist, however, the anxiety is rooted in the belief that they may lose the identity they have as a Christian and burn in hell forever. This anxiety is nearly intolerable.

Second, the development of a healthy identity entails opening oneself up to influences beyond those of the family of origin and experimenting with new commitments and identities. Fundamentalists tend to avoid new experiences by remaining isolated in their fundamentalist networks, thereby avoiding the various novel influences that flow into an emerging identity. Even college students can avoid many non-fundamentalist influences by barricading themselves inside a fundamentalist/evangelical church or religious group. When they do inadvertently come into contact with other people or ideas that threaten the cohesion of their worldview, other defense mechanisms are deployed in order to maintain their identity.

Before leaving the world of empirical study, I want to mention one other theme that will enable us to understand the fundamentalist profile. There is a small but interesting body of empirical research on religious doubting. Thus far, the data suggests that people who score high on a fundamentalism scale do not typically report doubt about God or religion.

> Any divergence (e.g., active questioning of God or religion) seems to be resolved by interpreting information as consistent with one's beliefs, or at least by accepting the religious explanation for the doubt or concern.[18]

This finding fits with the fundamentalist cognitive schema I found in my clinic and classroom. That is the bad news—"bad" in the sense that some willingness to question one's views can facilitate genuine dialogue that would permit the person to move beyond the delivery of prooftexts or the unthinking embrace of dogmatic positions. The good news is that there is some evidence that highly authoritarian people like fundamentalists often do have doubts about their faith. Of course, these doubts are taboo to express, and therefore people are unwilling to confront them in normal circumstances because of the strong anxiety such expression would entail.

An interesting study, using a creative survey instrument that assures anonymity, actually found that about one-third of these people said they had "secret" doubts, doubts that had been kept private.[19] This study was done on a general population of students. Fundamentalists who have "secret" doubts and are willing to engage in vigorous dialogue may be on the attack as a way of firming up their beliefs. However, perhaps they have more "secret" doubts than most fundamentalists and are willing to express those doubts. The second case offers the possibility of genuine give-and-take dialogue. Finally, there are those who are unable even to confess doubts to themselves for fear of falling apart. Unfortunately, these fundamentalists will never engage non-fundamentalists in dialogue about religious issues. Religious doubting is a fruitful area for further study. The importance of this line of research for our purposes is that it increases the likelihood that the fundamentalist resistance to learning will be overcome by thoughtful strategies, and thoughtful strategies are my concern in the Part Four of the book.

CHAPTER 12

The Threat from Rapid Cultural Change

As noted earlier, some of the more striking successes of cognitive therapy have been in working with anxiety issues. The perception of danger produces anxiety. When anxiety is pathological, that is, not appropriate to the real situation, one of the common errors is overestimating the probability and severity of the feared event. Clients avoid anxious thoughts more than depressed thoughts, and thoughts and images that trigger anxiety are often of a fleeting nature.

The above profile, which gives attention to the natural anxiety resulting from a perceived challenge to identity, corresponds with a widespread view about fundamentalism. Many analysts suggest that fear and insecurity are at the root of the fundamentalist psychological profile, prompting the fundamentalist search for something absolute and infallible to anchor the self.

Thus far, I have concentrated on the individual fundamentalist and his or her internal dynamic. As individuals, however, we live in context, in an environment that must be taken into account, if we are to fully understand the individual. Anxiety in the face of threat to one's identity can be fueled by a deep concern about change that is occurring in one's environment. Fundamentalism addresses our basic human desire for security and stability in the midst of the great and increasingly rapid culture change. *The Fundamentalism Project* of Marty and Appleby, which I discussed earlier, makes this point quite clear. The nature of the changes can be as disturbing as the rate of change. Modern culture, with its ever-improving technologies of communication, is becoming as impersonal as it is fast. I think many people in the Western industrialized world yearn for a slower and more personal existence. Most fundamentalists have no particular problem with cell phones and, in fact, use them and other technologies quite effectively. Markedly increased cell phone use, however, is a visible example of changes occurring in many other realms. When those changes call into question traditional values and practices, a fundamentalist reaction is almost certain.

My own awareness of this general issue is informed by the response to The Monastic Project, an optional class assignment I invented for a couple of my university courses and which has now been adopted or adapted by a number of professors around the country. The ambitious goal of The Monastic Project is to provide students with a structure where they can experience and gain empathy for the monastic life in general and, specifically, contemplative and ascetic disciplines, and to do this in the setting of an educational institution that is certainly not monastic. Broadly conceived, the goal is to experience in some small measure the discipline, purification, and concentration often facilitated by monasteries. The Project guidelines call for four weeks of lifestyle changes and daily practices that push hard against the drift of our culture. Students who choose to participate in the optional Monastic Project commit to follow a set of strict guidelines, which include eating food in its natural state without preservatives or chemical additions; eliminating sugar, white flour, fried foods, and salt additions from their diet; abstinence from alcohol, tobacco, and sexual activity; silence on Mondays; truth-telling; limited television, cell phone, and computer use; acts of kindness; and 65 minutes each day of contemplative and meditative exercises.

The modern higher education setting can be a quite alien environment in which to cultivate the monastic lifestyle, and so I initially had modest expectations about how much interest students would have in the Project and how much interested students could achieve. I have found the preliminary results astounding; they go beyond my most optimistic expectations. The Monastic Project has evolved into the one thing I do that I believe makes the most significant positive lifelong contribution to my students. Interest from other professors around the country prompted me to write an Instructor's Manual to assist them in producing the Project in their schools.

Along with other faculty members who have used the Project, I have speculated about why the Project, which requires such a strong commitment to severe guidelines, is an attractive option for many students. The same question can be asked about the fundamentalist, because the fundamentalist theological and moral system is very demanding. I am convinced that the strong student and educator interest in The Monastic Project derives from the same yearnings that also fuel fundamentalism. I think both the Project and fundamentalism speaks to a deep yearning among many in our culture for substantive experience, religious or otherwise, that goes deeper, offers more, and—yes—requires more than the easy, quick, sensual froth offered up by much contemporary culture. While The Monastic Project and fundamentalism are in many ways quite different programs, they both provide an outlet for those seeking something substantial.

Christian Smith, a sociologist from the University of North Carolina at Chapel Hill, led a team of researchers in a $3.9 million grant from the Lily Endowment to study the religious lives of American youth. His recent book suggests that a new, *de facto,* inter-religious faith is spreading in American culture. He calls it "Moralistic Therapeutic Deism." This gutted religious "faith" is one that makes few demands and offers its adherents a deity that is mostly interested in fostering easy piety and solving personal problems. While it serves the felt needs generated by popular culture, it leaves many young people feeling unfulfilled. Fundamentalism and The Monastic Project are both programs that challenge the prevailing cultural drift that is evident by the spread of "Moralistic Therapeutic Deism."

Like The Monastic Project, fundamentalism has something to say that is worth hearing. It is a valuable diagnostic tool, pointing out the inauthenticity and irrelevance of much of our culture. That critique is valuable and needed. Also like The Monastic Project, fundamentalism offers echoes of traditional values and approaches that can be relevant in today's world. It is the extremism of fundamentalism, as with its biblical inerrancy and premillennial dispensationalism, that I think caves in on itself and becomes destructive.

As noted earlier, I am primarily concerned with shedding light on the individual fundamentalist Christian, and so I have used psychological models in an effort to create a plausible profile of such a person. However, a related sociological model seems relevant at this point in the discussion of fundamentalism and culture. The sociologist Christian Smith observes that tension, conflict, and engagement between evangelicals and other groups positively strengthen evangelical identity, solidarity, resources mobilization, and membership retention. For Smith, this confrontational relationship explains the strength and vitality of contemporary American evangelicalism. So evangelicals actually capitalize on their culturally pluralistic environment to foster engagement and tension. From this perspective, old line fundamentalism, which separates from the world, and liberal Christianity, which compromises with the world, both fail to gain the vital energy from the conflict and tension that energizes evangelicalism. Translated psychologically, it means that the fundamentalist identity is fortified and maintained by the adversarial attitude that characterizes fundamentalists. The point here, of course, is that conflict is actually natural for fundamentalists and so may show up as resistance and hostility in conversations with them.

Giving an account of the psychology of a typical person in any social grouping is a challenge fraught with pitfalls. I certainly do not presume to have accurately described every aspect of the psychology of the fundamentalist. However, I am confident that there is a general psychological profile that is important for understanding many fundamentalists, and I believe one way to access that profile is via the schema concept from cognitive therapy. Fundamentalists are driven by a core, influential schema, which I have distinguished as

If I don't get it right, I am not a Christian, and I will go to hell.

Positing this schema explains much about the thinking and behavior of fundamentalists. The schema is a way of explaining the at-risk identity that Marty and Appleby call attention to in their definition of fundamentalism.[1] The schema approach to the psychology of the fundamentalist is also consistent with other empirical research on authoritarianism, closed-mindedness, intolerance of ambiguity, dogmatism, and cults. It also conforms well with the literature on the stages of religious development. Fundamentalism can be understood in a larger context as responding to superficiality, rapid change, and other aspects of the modern world.

On Saturdays sometimes my wife Susan and I explore the rural areas outside the busy university town where I work. On this particular Saturday, our goal was to visit a "country store" and our visit to the Lowland's Country Store gave me a deeper insight into conservatism's reaction to rapid cultural change.

Most readers who grew up outside the South will need explanation about this increasingly rare Southern institution. Up until three or four decades ago, the country store was, could we say, the male cultural center of southern farm communities, rivaled perhaps by the barbershop in town. Following a big hunt or a day's work, the country store was the place to gather after supper and talk it all over. In the old days the country store stayed open until ten or eleven o'clock every night, which was notoriously late. It sold a few staple grocery items—gasoline, kerosene, oil, snacks, and sodas. An old potbelly wood heater—later oil—usually stood prominently in the middle of the store. The men gathered around on soda crates, old beat up chairs, and split log benches telling crazy stories, speculating about the weather, cursing the government, complaining about the school system, and in general tending to everybody's business but their own and having a grand time doing it. The store reflected the moral tenor of the community and served to socialize the younger men as to what views and behavior were acceptable. The country story started declining about the mid-fifties. That was when televisions began to arrive in southern communities. As more and more folk purchased televisions, the country stores started closing earlier and earlier. Now, with Wal-Marts and cell phones everywhere, the country store as a central institution is only a memory.

There are still a few around, however, and Lowland's was open on this particular Saturday. I'm sitting, drinking Coke from a bottle, with a half dozen old men, crusty characters with stories as rich and textured as the hard lines on their faces. On the wall are cartoons and signs making fun of Bill Clinton and advocating "Love America or Leave It!" These men routinely take conservative political and religious positions on any issue that comes along. Why? Is it because they carefully examine the facts of the matter, critically weighing pros and cons of an argument, to arrive at a sound position? No. The clear insight I had, sitting with these men, is that at some deep level they feel threatened because they sense their way of life slipping from them. These men are old enough to have sat in the country store when it was the central institution in this farm community. Now threatened by the fast, impersonal, technological world of McDonald's and computers, these men will gravitate to any political or religious organization that they perceive as preserving the old ways. Certainly, there are conservative intellectuals who articulate careful political and religious arguments. However, many Americans lean conservative out of a visceral reaction to rapid, scary cultural change.

I began this part of the book with a story about Frankie, the student whose reading of the Bible was influenced by his anxiety about being saved. Deeply embedded in the structure of his mind, Frankie believed that if the Bible is wrong about anything, or if he stumbled onto one wrong belief, his salvation would be lost and he would go to hell. I never heard from Frankie again and have often wondered how he is doing. If I do ever get an opportunity to talk to Frankie, I will likely use some of the "strategies for dialogue" that have emerged in my years of working with fundamentalist clients and students. We now turn to those strategies.

PART FOUR

Strategies for Dialogue

CHAPTER 13

Talking Theology

"BUT THE BIBLE SAYS . . ."

Even if you never have the occasion to talk to fundamentalists, and even if you have no desire to ever do so, this section of the book will help you understand them better. I write this part as if you were going to engage fundamentalists in conversation.

Perhaps you have had an encounter with someone that was some version of the following conversation? You make some point and they say, "But the Bible says that . . . ." The final noun clause contains some statement that challenges something you just said. You reply, or at least begin to reply, by referring to the evidence for whatever point you made. Your fundamentalist conversation partner, fairly quickly, takes a defensive posture by indicating that the Bible is the word of God and, therefore, what you just said cannot be true. Your attempt to have them understand the issue, apart from what the Bible says, is futile. Often, the result is that both of you simply withdraw into your respective ideological and psychological worlds and the issue is ignored. If you have not had such an encounter, then you probably have not talked to many fundamentalists about significant religious, moral, and social issues.

Versions of the above encounter occur, for example, in classrooms throughout this land where the subject matter being taught is perceived by the student to contradict fundamentalist Christian theology and/or biblical teachings as interpreted by fundamentalists. Those encounters are duplicated wherever fundamentalists and non-fundamentalists, even non-fundamentalist Christians, talk science, social policy, or religion. In my own classroom, my intention is not necessarily to change the student with regard to theology or Bible interpretation. As a teacher my immediate goal is to free students from the anxiety and resistance to learning (not necessarily believing) the material of the course.

Teachers who love teaching live for teachable moments. A teachable moment is a moment when teacher and student are ready and available for teaching and learning to occur in an exceptionally significant, deep, and lasting way. Teachable moments are intrinsically rewarding and deeply satisfying for both teacher and student. Such moments, all too rare to begin with, are also elusive. They usually seem to present spontaneously; at least they are difficult (though not always impossible) to predict. I think many encounters between fundamentalists and non-fundamentalists offer potential teachable moments that slide by without ever being mined for the rich possibilities they offer.

Currently, our country is seriously divided along political, cultural, and religious lines that can roughly be characterized as rightest and moderate/leftest. As a strong believer in the free exchange of ideas, I believe the path forward, whatever shape it takes, will be a better one if we can understand each other and have honest, clear conversations.

From my psychological perspective, there are several categories of fundamentalists. Some fundamentalists have the cognitive schema, "If I don't get it right, I am not a Christian, and I will go to hell." It is deeply embedded and for a few fundamentalists it will not be dislodged. For many other fundamentalists, however, the schema can be dislodged. Logic and accurate information about the Bible and Christianity will make a huge difference in their thinking. So, my hope is that uninformed fundamentalists will shift their theological position when they are introduced to good information about the Bible and Christianity. Mentally ill fundamentalists, along with mentally ill liberals, will be successfully treated in therapy. A few fundamentalists will be left who have thoughtfully decided for the ideology of fundamentalism, but their percentage of the population will not be large enough to sway public opinion or political trends.

In this book my desire is not to equip you with strategies for changing people at any cost. Rather, my first goal is to help you understand fundamentalist Christians. Being familiar with strategies for talking with fundamentalists will help you understand them, whether or not you ever use the strategies. I am aware that many people have no desire to actually talk to fundamentalists. However, should you desire to talk with them and have the occasion, I will make some suggestions that will provide you with background knowledge and thoughtful strategies that will assist you in having conversations with fundamentalists that are productive moments of dialogue, rather than unproductive and potentially time-wasting encounters. I have friends who are quite conservative—some religiously, some politically, and some in every way—and I want to be open to learning from them, just as I want them to understand me and hear me out. I will admit to a tinge of agnosticism—humbleness, to use a good biblical word. While I have figured out a few things for myself and I think thoughtful minds have arrived at some truths about reality, I am mindful of how the "assured results" of one scholarly generation can, in retrospect, quickly fade into the "assured results" of the next. Even a cursory knowledge of the history of ideas prompts me to caution. So, while I want fundamentalists to be open to critical inquiry, I have no desire whatsoever to repeat the religious indoctrination I see occurring in many fundamentalist so-called educational institutions.

In one sense the main goal of this book is to facilitate sound thinking by fundamentalists, via conversations with persons informed by the materials in this book. My theological and psychological commentary is designed to facilitate logical thought. The sometimes complete or near complete lack of rationality, when addressing issues related to their faith, is perhaps the most frustrating aspect of working with fundamentalists.

My reflections are targeted to understanding fundamentalist Protestant Christians, because this is the version of religious fundamentalism most prevalent in the United States. What I say, however, can be useful for and adapted to working with Roman Catholic fundamentalists as well as fundamentalists of other religions.

I now provide some strategies, many of them conversational suggestions, that may be helpful in engaging fundamentalists in dialogue. As an educator I have a special interest in facilitating teachers of all levels and disciplines as they work with fundamentalist students in the office and classroom. Fortunately, strategies that teachers might find helpful can be easily adapted to many nonacademic encounters with fundamentalists.

None of the strategies presumes anything with regard to your faith commitment or lack thereof. To utilize some of these strategies, you will need to have some elementary understanding of fundamentalist Christian beliefs, and I either have already provided those in this book or will provide what you need. In each case I give more information than you necessarily need to bring into the conversation. The point is to use what you need to prompt the fundamentalist to reflect on core beliefs they hold in a way that opens the possibility for them to freely consider the points you want to make. Beyond the first strategy, "A Helpful Metaphor," this list is not prioritized. You may find one or another strategy useful, depending on the situation and drift of the conversation at hand.

The strategies do work, at least for me, as they all emerge from numerous successful conversations I have had with fundamentalists through the years. The reason they work is that, in general, they are designed to get the fundamentalist to think. There are, as I have pointed out, thoughtful fundamentalists. However, in my experience most fundamentalists, for reason of anxiety or because they have never been challenged, have never really thought much or carefully about their core fundamentalist ideas.

Many fundamentalists, when they are successfully prompted to engage the issues rationally, will alter their positions. In Appendix 1, I provide, with permission, some letters from former fundamentalist students that illustrate this point. Certainly not all of my encounters with fundamentalist students have a happy outcome, but I have had more happy outcomes than unhappy ones.

Finally, before proceeding to the strategies, I will make five important and somewhat related suggestions. First, in your conversations there will be many instances where you can state the same point in positive language or negative language. To minimize a defensive posture on the part of the fundamentalist, I recommend as much as possible that you state things positively. You can make almost the same or similar point and are less likely to elicit a defensive reaction. For example, rather than saying, "The Bible is not always historically accurate," you can say, "The Bible's accuracy does not necessarily extend to matters of history," or, to put it in positive terms, "Have you considered that the Bible's role is to provide guidance in matters of faith and practice?"

Second, as much as possible, following the model of the cognitive therapist who works in collaboration with the client, meet fundamentalists where they are. That may mean working within their theological and hermeneutical framework, as a way of neutralizing the threat of anxiety and moving them to a point where they can at least be open to consider what you are saying. In fact, the most interesting and effective conversations are ones where the fundamentalists, with prompting questions from you, find their own way to a place where they give themselves permission to consider alternative viewpoints, even when such viewpoints contradict their fundamentalist outlook. I am not suggesting you deceive them; I am suggesting that for the sake of discussion, you explore *with* them and *within* the framework they bring to the conversation. And you can tell them what you are doing; that is just fine, even advisable. You will see what I mean when I give examples later.

Third, the fundamentalist absolutist thinking means that in many cases finding one exception to some belief they have about something will work wonders in terms of opening up possibilities for them. Finding exceptions to some perceived absolutist schema is a useful technique used often by the cognitive therapist. This approach is akin to the claim of solution-focused brief therapy that exceptions to every problem can be created, which can then be used to build solutions. Often, small changes lead to large changes.

The next point perhaps goes without saying, but it is so important that I will note it for the record. While the issues should, I think, be decided on the merits of the data and reasoning, you will find that empathy, willingness to listen and understand, and respecting the fundamentalist as a person, will do as much as anything to make for the possibility of a rational discussion of issues. Most people are not professionally trained, nor perhaps personally inclined, to address in depth complicated emotional issues. However, it is naïve to completely ignore that there can sometimes be a significant emotional dimension to encounters with fundamentalists. Given the sensitive identity issues, it is useful to bring to the encounter with a fundamentalist a measure of warmth and empathy in an attempt to foster trust and rapport and keep the dialogue going. Nothing is accomplished, and the dialogical moment is lost, if conversation is terminated. Non-fundamentalists also need to be aware of their own emotional issues so they do not interfere with the integrity of the conversation. Certainly, you should not show up to the fundamentalist in some version of the anecdote I presented in the preface, trashing the Bible and other fundamentalist sacred symbols at every chance. Communicating explicitly, or with subtle, implicit language, that the fundamentalist is stupid or misguided is not going to forward the process. The cognitive therapy model has a "humanistic" bent in that the client is respected as an individual person and a worthy partner in the therapeutic relationship. Beck uses the phrase "collaborative empiricism" to describe the way the therapist and client join together to understand and explore, to "investigate," the client's inner life. Therapy proceeds out of a learning model, where the therapist teaches, in large part through the use of questions.

The overall focus of cognitive therapy is to modify dysfunctional cognitions that maintain the client's pathology. Utilizing an array of techniques, the therapist works with the client to uncover, test, and, where appropriate, shift the client's thought processes to patterns that are adaptive, functional, logical, and reality based. In the process clients will learn to recognize the way they construe the world and the connection between this construction of the world and their affect and behavior. Change usually occurs a step at a time. So, I am suggesting that an encounter with the fundamentalist is more likely to be productive if (1) you are aware of what is at stake, psychologically, for the fundamentalist, and (2) you use techniques that allow anxiety to be neutralized. I will elaborate on various techniques later.

Finally, I do recommend that you be open to what you can learn from the fundamentalist. You may not agree with much in the fundamentalist system. However, true dialogue involves a genuine willingness to consider what is being presented. As I pointed out at the beginning of the book, I do think the fundamentalist brings some ideas and perspectives that are worth considering.

A HELPFUL METAPHOR

There is one specific strategy I use routinely in my university courses that I think contains elements that can provide an approach and perspective useful for any encounter with fundamentalists. I will provide it exactly as I use it in my courses and then discuss how it can be useful for anyone in dialogue with a fundamentalist.

In my religion courses, early in the semester, I give students a recommendation about how they personally choose to relate to the course material. The recommendation includes a metaphor. Over the years scores of students, including fundamentalist students, have told me this simple ten-minute lecture segment early in the course was one of the most valuable things I said in the course, and that it allowed them to learn the course material where they had shut out the material from so many other courses when the material contradicted their beliefs. This metaphor is the single most effective standard thing I do. I should add that, while I cannot recall the specific details, I trace my metaphor back to my undergraduate days at the University of North Carolina at Chapel Hill where my venerable Bible professor and early mentor, Dr. Bernard Boyd, used some such helpful metaphor.

The talk has a number of details and contains little twists and features, such as humor, that I have included for various reasons, as I have refined and revised it over time to accomplish the goals of reducing anxiety and having students heed my advice. It is as follows:

Now, before we move on, I want to say something that could be very important for some of you. Some of you may become bored by what I say and see it as totally irrelevant for you; for others, this may be the most important thing I say all term. Many students tell me after the course that this was the most important thing I said all semester. So, for what it's worth, here it is. By the way, this is free; you don't have to take notes. Consider this as friendly advice from your teacher.

You may be reading the textbook or listening to me lecture and you may get a sick feeling in the pit of your stomach. Now, it may be that you ate too much pepperoni pizza for lunch. Or, it may be a physical manifestation of what I call a crisis of faith. What is a crisis of faith? Well, all of you come into the course with a preunderstanding about a lot of things, and some of you have a preunderstanding derived from your religious faith. You have a belief system that derives from your family of origin, maybe your church teaching, and/or personal reflection and experience. Now, in this course you'll get new information and ideas on issues about which you already have answers that come from your religious belief. So you will be introduced to lots of information, data, and theories about the subject matter. It is likely, well, actually I think inevitable, that you will encounter some information or idea that is contrary to your preunderstanding derived from your religious faith. Now, when that happens, it can create dissonance, discord, and anxiety. There's upset. While I was being a bit dramatic with the notion of a sick feeling in the pit of your stomach, the discord can sometimes take a dramatic and even physical form. You see, for many of you, your belief in God and the Bible is at the core of your understanding of who you are, your purpose and goals, your identity. And so to question something that your religion teaches, well, this can be quite threatening to your identity and upsetting to you generally.

Oh, by the way, with my talk of "crisis" and "upset" I bet some of you are thinking that I'm saying a crisis of faith is something that you should avoid. Actually, that's not what I'm saying at all. In fact, I recommend you have a crisis of faith this semester, even several, and maybe a big one. But that's up to you. My point is that it may happen. And crises of faith can come in various sizes and forms. Now, if you have a crisis of faith, I have three recommendations to make. First, keep in mind that you will not die. A crisis of faith is not fatal. No one has ever died from a crisis of faith. I suppose this may be the first year someone dies in one of my classes from a crisis of faith, and then in future years I'll have to report that. But I doubt it. A crisis of faith may make you feel bad, mad, and upset, but you will not die. So relax. Second, talk to someone about it. Communication is a wonderful thing. Talk to someone who will listen. Not everyone is a good listener. You know how sometimes you begin to speak to someone and, pretty soon, usually within a minute or two, they are talking, usually about themselves. That's not a good listener. Find someone who will really listen to you. It may be a friend, family member, or pastor. And I'm a pretty good listener. You are welcome to speak to me. I have considered it a great privilege through the years to listen as students work through their crises of faith.

Also, you are welcome to raise your hand in class and share your upset. If you're so inclined, raise your hand, and say, "stop the train, I'm having a big upset right now over what you just said." If you're comfortable doing that, it's fine with me. You'll have to trust me to conduct the class in an appropriate manner. What we won't do is hold hands and pray for you. That may be appropriate in other contexts. In class, if you're bold enough to lay your upset out before us, then we can look at it critically, just like we consider all the course material. We might take a few minutes to explore it and ask specifically what are your physical and emotional reactions. We might explore how your crisis of faith is similar to or different from crises of faith that occur in other parts of the country or world. Do Roman Catholics have crises of faith over the same issues that upset Protestants? On and on. You see, we could discuss it historically, culturally, psychologically. But my main point is: don't sit on your upset. Communicate about it with someone who will listen.

Finally, my advice to you is to treat the course like a cafeteria. In a cafeteria you go through the line and take on your plate what works for you. You go through and say, peas, I want some. Hold the cabbage. Ah, mashed potatoes, yes, that works for me. I'll take some carrots, hold the squash. In a cafeteria you look at everything on the line, but you take onto your plate only what works for you. Treat this course like a cafeteria. In this course you will be introduced to much data, many ideas, new theories. I recommend that you thoroughly understand everything. You have to do that to pass the tests. However, I recommend that you take into your belief system only what makes sense to you, only what works for you. Don't believe it even if it makes rational sense, if it feels bad in your gut. Please do not understand me as trying to get you to believe anything. There are times when my voice will grow loud and I'll become intense as I'm explaining something. You may think, "he's trying to get me to believe what he's saying.'" Actually, that's not true. I'm trying to get you to thoroughly understand what I'm saying. And I can get quite intense about that, but don't mistake my excitement and intensity. For this class, it is unimportant what you believe; I only want you to understand. Once you genuinely understand something, I trust that you'll choose appropriately what to believe. When you take the test, you must show me that you thoroughly understand the material, but whether you accept it into your own belief system is your choice. In fact, on the test you can give me excellent essays explaining the material thoroughly. Then, at the end of the test, you can write "By the way, Dr. Mercer, I don't believe a thing I've written. I think it is all heresy and I also think if you believe it that you are going to hell." Now, if you write out a perfect essay showing you understand the material, and then write that statement, what grade will you get? An "A." Correct. I don't care what you believe; I am very committed to your understanding the material. So treat the course like a cafeteria and relax. OK, any questions about that?

There are two main parts to the speech. First, I distinguish a "crisis of faith" which I explain is some kind of upset that occurs when students read or hear something that does not fit their belief system. This in a nutshell is what my psychological analysis of the typical fundamentalist is all about. The crisis of faith that students experience in a university religion class is no different from what any fundamentalist experiences when they encounter information inconsistent with the belief system on which their identity is based.

Second, I use the metaphor of a cafeteria line as a way of saying they will encounter much data and many ideas in the course. I advise them to put on their theological plate what works for them and fits with their belief system and leave on the cafeteria line what does not feel good, even if they do not know why and even if it does not make rational sense.

As I give this little speech, I always see a number of the bodies in the room visibly relax. The speech allows students to move from the perception that I am trying to make them wrong and change their beliefs in some way that will result in a shipwreck of their faith. It takes the pressure off and allows them to give themselves, internally, permission to learn the material of the course because they do not have to believe it and, therefore, their faith and eternal destiny are not at risk.

As we have seen, the fundamentalist need for cognitive closure can prematurely result in maladaptive closed-mindedness. The metaphor allows the student to consider rival alternatives to their inherited belief system without the severe anxiety that can attach to the consideration. It is analogous to the technique used in Altemeyer's secret doubt study I referred to earlier where creative measures had to be used to uncover "secret" doubt. Altemeyer asked students:

> Suppose there is a Hidden Observer in you, which knows your every thought and deed, but which only speaks when it is safe to do so, and when directly spoken to. This question is for your Hidden Observer: does this person (that is, you) have doubts that (s)he was created by an Almighty God who will judge each person and take some into heaven for eternity while casting others into hell forever?[1]

The metaphor can be understood as my implementation of one of the central strategies of cognitive therapists, that of examining options and alternatives. The speech to my students has been effective in disarming their anxiety mechanisms, and positioning them to engage the course material. The various strategies I now discuss are, in effect, ways of accomplishing with fundamentalists anywhere what I do more explicitly with the metaphor in class.

TALKING ABOUT JESUS

I have studied classical fundamentalist Christian doctrine formulated, for example, by the Princeton professors referred to in the history of the movement. Fundamentalist scholars and thoughtful, informed fundamentalist laypersons are aware of problematic issues surrounding critical study of the Bible, philosophy of religion, and Christian faith and modernity. I am not convinced by the fundamentalist view of the world and religion. I acknowledge, however, that there are fundamentalist writers who have thought through these issues. They are almost never the ones you see on television or hear on the radio. For sure, the vast majority of fundamentalists you encounter will not be knowledgeable about or skilled at handling these issues. So while your dialogue with the fundamentalist will probably be at an introductory level, it is possible to address some rather significant theological questions.

What I want to suggest, first, is not so much a clear strategy as it is a general theological perspective that is helpful to keep in mind. A "fundamental" doctrine of the Christian religion is the incarnation, the notion that Jesus Christ was both fully divine and fully human. Fundamentalists will naïvely believe that this doctrine is clearly found in the New Testament. Perhaps the raw material for the development of this doctrine is contained in the New Testament, but it actually took the church centuries to hammer out the doctrine's fine details. It will not be helpful to get into an argument with the fundamentalist about whether or not the New Testament teaches this. That is an interesting historical question, but it will not serve the purpose of engaging the fundamentalist in dialogue. However, it can be very helpful to note to the fundamentalist that it is your understanding that this is a central teaching of mainline Christianity. The fundamentalist will readily agree and you have established some common ground of a sort.

It can also be helpful to point out to the fundamentalist that there have been heresies around this doctrine, that is, sometimes Christians have gone overboard on one side or the other. Emphasizing the divinity and minimizing the humanity of Jesus is sometimes called docetism (from the Greek word, meaning "to seem like"). Docetists taught that Jesus "seemed like" he was human, but really was only divine. Docetism was judged heretical by the church. Most fundamentalists will not be aware of the docetic movements in the early centuries of the church, but they will affirm that, yes, this is not true biblical teaching. Emphasizing the humanity and minimizing the divinity of Jesus is sometimes called Arianism. This belief, too, was judged to be heretical and fundamentalists will, for sure, affirm that Jesus was God and that any teaching minimizing Christ's divinity is wrong.

With it established that the incarnation means that Jesus was fully divine and fully human, you can then proceed to prompt the fundamentalist to reflect on a possible implication of this teaching. Fundamentalists will likely relate well to the idea that God became human and fully understood and felt the human realm. The incarnation, with the attendant teaching that Jesus was fully human, can be understood as meaning that the world is at the least worthy of attention and understanding. To say it another way, which gets the fundamentalist's attention, you can suggest that by refusing to understand God's world (and, of course, science and history can help us in this regard), the fundamentalist is perhaps in danger of falling into a docetic heresy. They are emphasizing the divinity of Jesus, but not working out the full theological implications of Jesus's humanity. Any suggestion that the fundamentalist is in danger of heresy will get their attention.

An attendant idea, with which the fundamentalist will agree, is that God created the world in the beginning of the Bible and was incarnated into the world through Christ at the beginning of the New Testament. This seems to suggest that the world is important to God, worth attending to, and worth understanding. The objection the fundamentalist may make is that the world is in a sinful, fallen state. In the interest of continuing the discussion, you can grant this point and simply attempt to gain the point that science and history can, at least to some degree, help us understand the glory of God's created order.

CHAPTER 14

Talking About the Bible

LITERAL VERSUS SYMBOLIC

As you will quickly discover, fundamentalist Christians turn to the Bible, interpreted in a very specific manner, to support all their assertions. Conversing with fundamentalists about the Bible to at least some degree is probably going to be important in having dialogue. In Appendix 2, I have provided an elementary guide to critically interpreting the Bible, in order to provide some detailed account of how scholars proceed in their investigations. "Hermeneutics" refers to the study of principles one uses in interpreting a text. While it is likely impractical and undesirable to enter into involved hermeneutical discussions with the fundamentalist, it can be helpful to at least raise some questions and possibilities with them. I will make several suggestions, some of which are strategies that implement the cognitive therapy practice of dislodging tightly held cognitive schema systems by finding at least one exception to the rule.

First, at an elementary level, sometimes it can be useful to initiate a discussion about the term "literal." Fundamentalists will sometimes claim that the Bible should be understood literally. They really do not understand what they are saying, that is, they seem not to understand the meaning of the word literal. I know of no fundamentalist who really believes in taking the Bible literally everywhere, once they understand what that means. When Jesus says "I am the door" (John 10:7), no one goes looking for a literal door. Jesus said if your right eye causes you to sin, pluck it out and throw it away (Matthew 5:29) and if your right hand causes you to sin, cut it off and throw it away (Matthew 5:30). I know of no Christian, and your fundamentalist friend will not either, who takes these words literally, or at least obeys them literally.

Along this line, another example fundamentalists can relate to is parable. Parables constitute the distinctive teaching method of the historical Jesus. I know of no fundamentalist teacher, preacher, or layperson who claims that the parables of Jesus are to be taken literally. Everyone, appropriately, understands them in some general sense to be stories Jesus told to make a point. Another example, but not the best one to use, unless the fundamentalist insists, is the last book of the Bible, Revelation, which is full of symbols. Fundamentalist interpreters of this book do indeed view the various creatures and events in the book as symbolic. In fact, that is at the heart of fundamentalist interpretation of this book.

When fundamentalists say they take the Bible *literally,* what they mean is that they take the Bible *seriously.* To take the Bible seriously everywhere does not mean to take it literally. The point, and usually the fundamentalist can be brought to this view, is to interpret the Bible seriously everywhere which means to interpret it literally where it was meant to be taken literally and symbolically where it was meant to be taken symbolically. Once you can establish, sometimes with only one example, that taking the Bible seriously does not necessarily mean taking it literally, you have gained great ground. The fundamentalist view of the Bible is so tight that if you can provide one exception the fundamentalist agrees to, then it can open up broader possibilities for understanding the Bible and other issues. At least it becomes a legitimate question as to which (literal or symbolic) is the proper way to interpret a particular passage. This kind of wiggle room, just the possibility of reading some Bible passage differently than in the standard fundamentalist way, generates significant openings for the fundamentalist to see other points of view.

While taking the Bible seriously is certainly a concern, I suspect that what is also at issue, when they insist on taking the Bible literally, is that the Bible be interpreted in a fashion such that there is no admission of error in the Bible. What actually occurs quite often is that fundamentalists, without realizing they are not always following a literal interpretation, use literal and non-literal readings, depending on which serves their purpose. For example, at the beginning of the Bible fundamentalists interpret the mythological story of Adam and Eve literally, because it fits their anti-science, anti-evolution agenda. At the end of the Bible, they interpret the apocalyptic book of Revelation as containing symbols of things that are occurring in the world today, because that fits their obsession with end-time scenarios.

READING IN CONTEXT

You often hear people, sometimes out of frustration, claim that anyone can prove anything they want to from the Bible. It is true that isogesis (reading into a text what is not there) is rampant, and that, in fact, people do go to the Bible and focus on those parts that support their preconceived view, and interpret passages to fit their opinion. It is not true, however, that there are no reasonable principles for interpretation that, in principle, most thoughtful persons, including fundamentalists, will agree to.

A basic principle is that words should be read in context. You can get your fundamentalist partner to readily agree that it is a misreading of the Bible to take the following parts of three verses from three different sections of the Bible, put them together, and view it as God's divinely inspired will for one's life now:

> He went and hanged himself.
>
> (Matthew 27:5b)
>
> Go and do likewise.
>
> (Luke 10:37)
>
> Do quickly what you are going to do.
>
> (John 13:27)

My favorite story about taking things out of context was told to me by one of my students about a sermon he heard many years ago. The ladies in this rural church were wearing their hair in "top knots," a hair style that was influencing female members of the church. The pastor opposed this new hair style on the part of his female members. He chose a biblical text from Mark 13:15, which in the King James Version reads,

> And let him that is on the housetop not go down into the house, neither enter therein, to take anything out of his house.

The pastor took for his sermon text only part of this sentence, and, in fact, part of a word. He preached a sermon entitled "Top Not Go Down!" and admonished his female parishioners to separate themselves from the evil hair styles.

The basic principle here, of course, is that words should be read and interpreted in the context of the sentence in which they are found. Extending that principle to taking into account the context of the paragraph and book in which things are found should not be that hard to accomplish with the fundamentalist. They will likely also agree that things should be taken in context of the whole Bible. In fact, the fundamentalist will understand this idea when you point out that fundamentalists interpret the Old Testament in light of the New Testament. The next related step is more difficult to accomplish but is worth the effort because the dividends are enormous.

CULTURALLY CONDITIONED STATEMENTS VERSUS ETERNAL TRUTHS

Reading things in context can be extended to reading the Bible in the context of the culture of its day. Invite the fundamentalist to consider that it is important to distinguish between what in the Bible is there because it is one of God's eternal truths and what is there because it is culturally conditioned, that is, God put it there because of the particular time and place of writing of the Bible.

There are some things in the Bible that are obviously there because of where and when the Bible was written. Examples include that the Old Testament was written (mostly) in Hebrew and the New Testament was written in Greek. The Bible was written in these languages because these are the languages that the Israelites and early Christians used in that day. Jesus rode donkeys because that was the means of transportation in his day. Jesus did not use a cellular phone because that was not a part of the culture of his day. I think fundamentalists will agree with such examples. There are teachings in the Bible that the fundamentalist will agree are what I am calling eternal truths. Some that the fundamentalist will agree to are love, forgiveness, and the existence of God. So there should be easy agreement on some culturally conditioned items (language, donkeys as means of transportation) and some eternal truths (love, forgiveness).

The controversy, of course, has to do with teachings where there is disagreement about their category. An obvious example is the Bible's subordination of women in family, church, and society. Once you get the fundamentalist to agree on the principle, namely, the need to make a distinction between eternal truth and a peculiarity of the culture, you have opened the door for discussion and possible shifts in one's position.

To continue a bit with the gender issue example, here is something you can ask the fundamentalist that will likely get them thinking. In the New Testament book of Colossians (3:22) we have this admonition, "Slaves, obey your masters." No fundamentalist I know today advocates slavery, yet this admonition for slaves to obey their masters is found in the same general passage as this admonition, "Wives, obey your husband" (Colossians 3:18). The second verse is one of a number of texts in the Bible used by fundamentalists to support the subordinate status of women. Ask the fundamentalists if they take the second passage as God's eternal truth for humanity, why they do not take slavery as God's eternal truth for humanity. This question has them grapple with the principle at hand. Again, once you obtain agreement on just one example that illustrates the principle, you have cracked open the possibility that they can reconsider other teachings they have before considered eternal truths.

With the slavery verses, you are not taking verses out of context in order to beat the fundamentalist at his or her own "prooftexting" game. Both the Old and New Testaments regard slavery as normal and nowhere is the system fundamentally condemned. In fact, the slavery practice in ancient Israel included using female slaves and female captives as sexual objects, concubines, or involuntary wives (see 2 Samuel 5:13, Judges 19–21, and Numbers 31:18). American slave owners used these very verses to justify similar practices at an earlier point in our country's history. Preachers proclaimed from Southern pulpits that slavery was God's will and used a variety of verses from the Bible to support their position.

In addition to slavery, there are many other issues that highlight inconsistencies by fundamentalists. The Old Testament law forbids sexual intercourse during a woman's menstrual period (Leviticus 18:19, 15:19–24). Violators are to be "extirpated" or "cut off from their people." The term used is *kareth,* which in Leviticus 15:24 refers to execution by stoning, burning, or strangling or to flogging or expulsion. Fundamentalists have no program to resurrect this old legal practice. Having many wives (polygamy) and living with a man to whom the woman is not married (concubinage) were regularly practiced in ancient Israel. Except for the questionable texts of 1 Timothy 3:2, 12 and Titus 1:6, these two practices were not condemned by the New Testament. Fundamentalists certainly do not advocate polygamy and concubinage. An interesting old practice among the Jews was levirate marriage, whereby when a married man died childless, his widow was commanded to have intercourse with the man's eldest brother. Jesus refers to this practice, but certainly does not condemn it (Mark 12:18–27). These and many other biblical practices are not advocated by fundamentalists. Clearly, they pick and choose biblical injunctions.

Most fundamentalists will pick and choose the Old Testament laws they think should be obeyed. They dismiss many of the Old Testament laws on the basis that the New Testament has made them irrelevant. Fundamentalists are usually vague about the criteria they use to choose which laws to discard. However, occasionally a fundamentalist will claim that all Old Testament laws should be obeyed and, of course, they do not realize the implications of this claim. All you have to do is point out some of the ancient Israelite laws and the fundamentalist will begin to backpeddle on this point. Here are some interesting ones: do not touch the skin of a dead pig (Leviticus 11:8); for seven days following a women's menstrual discharge, do not touch the woman or any chair or bed she has used (Leviticus 15:19, 20–21); fathers are permitted to sell their youngest daughters as slaves (Exodus 21:7); and do not lend money for interest (Exodus 22:25). The first one I listed would prohibit the playing of football and the last one would wreck havoc on the financial markets. Observing these two alone would grind life in America to a halt.[1]

THE WORD OF GOD IN THE WORDS OF MEN

Related to the previous points about the Bible is the notion that the words in the Bible, even if considered the inspired words of God, are found in the words of men (as far as we know no females wrote any book in the Bible). The Bible, as pointed out earlier, was written in the languages (Hebrew, Aramaic, Greek) used by people of that day. The writers also have their distinctive styles, although it is probably not helpful to press this particular point.

The notion that God chose to put the divine word into words used by historical men in a particular time and place is consistent with the incarnational theology I discussed earlier. If you have had a discussion about the incarnation, you can make that point. If you have not, you can briefly point out that the Bible, just like Jesus, is the divine, inerrant (the fundamentalist will not give this up, so you may as well work within that framework) word that is placed in the form of words and language that real people used to speak and write. If you can get the fundamentalist to this point, then the payoff should come.

Because the "divine, inerrant" Bible is found in the words and language of men in history, to understand and fully appreciate God's divine message, it can be helpful to study those words and that history. This can mean learning the languages of the Bible, the meaning of words, and so on. The fundamentalist's pastor likely has in his personal library all kinds of books that help explain the meaning of the Hebrew and Greek words in the Bible. The fundamentalist will likely have heard sermons where this kind of information is used. What the fundamentalist agrees to, however, perhaps without realizing the full implications, is the fundamental principle that it can be helpful, and consistent with fundamentalist theology, to study the Bible historically, that is, in terms of the meaning of the words in the context of their culture.

FAITH AND PRACTICE VERSUS SCIENCE AND HISTORY

This may be a tough one, and perhaps not worth addressing head on. In any case, one way some (not necessarily fundamentalist) Christians understand the Bible is that it is authoritative where it speaks on matters of faith and practice, but not where it speaks on matters of science and history. Some Christians see that the Bible is a devotional book, designed to give persons of faith guidance in their spiritual lives. It is not intended to be a science or history book. While this will be a difficult issue to press head on with fundamentalists, the payoff for a successful conversation can be significant.

This idea of faith and practice versus science and history is easily related to the incarnation and various points I have made about biblical interpretation. To state it using terms I have already introduced, God's eternal will for human beings was made known in a particular time and place, in the Bible and in the person of Jesus Christ. The human writers of the Bible books intended for people to gain an understanding of how Christians are to know God and live spiritual lives. They did not intend for their words to be read like a science book or history book.

To use history, as the example, there are a couple of reasons why the Bible should not be read as a modern history book. First, history writing as we know it today did not exist in the ancient period. The ancient period had historians (for example, Herodotus), yes, but history writing as we know it today is, of course, a long, complex, refined process that involves acquiring requisite technical skills in graduate study, careful research, presenting one's research before peers at professional meetings, submitting finished articles for peer review, and, finally, possibly, hopefully, publication. All this technical, scholarly work occurs even before someone surveys the field and writes a U.S. history textbook for students. History writing is significantly a product of modern developments such as the Enlightenment.

A second reason, and one perhaps more useful to present to the fundamentalist, is that the authors of the Bible did not intend, or at least did not always intend, for their words to be read as science and history. A good example is the New Testament book of John. Here is what this author says at the end of his book, in 20:30–31:

> Now Jesus did many other signs in the presence of his disciples, which are not written in this book. But these are written so that you may come to believe that Jesus is the Messiah, the Son of God, and that through believing you may have life in his name.

I am sure at some point in his life Jesus ate a grape. I have been many times to the land where Jesus grew up. That land produces luscious grapes. For sure there was a particular point in time and a place on the map when the historical Jesus ate his first grape. However, there is no record in the gospels about Jesus eating his first grape. That is an event that surely occurred in history, but it is not recorded in the Gospel of John because the author is not interested in the brute facts of history. The author has a devotional agenda; he is interested in sharing with the reader the good news of Jesus and encouraging the reader to believe in order to have abundant life. This devotional agenda is quite different from the agenda of the modern historian or scientist.

The point is really a quite simple one: to read the Bible the way it was meant to be read. Fundamentalists can understand that there are different genres of writing. A stop sign, letter from the IRS, love letter, and comic strip are all quite different kinds of texts, easily identifiable by their context and features, and each written for a particular reason and properly interpreted in different ways. One does not read the Bible the way one reads a comic strip. This is clear. The distinction between reading the Bible as devotional literature and reading it as a scientific or historical document is not always as clear to fundamentalists.

We should not be too quick to judge fundamentalists on this point. Our public school system does a fairly good job, at least in principle, teaching students to read history and science books. Someone in authority, at a fairly early grade level, puts a book in front of the student. The book says George Washington did this and then did that and said so and so. The student, appropriately, is taught that this is a history book and is an accurate record of past events. Of course, knowledgeable persons know that historiography is not this simple, but that is at least the general intention of the author of the U.S. history book. Then, one day someone puts another book (the Bible) in front of the student and it says Abraham did this and then did that and said so and so. The student, quite naturally, assumes this is a history book and is providing an accurate record of past events. We can gain knowledge of historical events from the Bible (and we earnestly strive to do so because we are culturally conditioned to think this matters!), but to interpret the Bible as fundamentally history writing along the order of the research university-produced U.S. history book is a vast misstep.

BIBLICAL MODELS

A final, perhaps relatively minor, point is that the Bible offers models that can fruitfully be used to help fundamentalists be willing to question and investigate. I point this out because it is common, usually at some early point in a conversation with a fundamentalist about a controversial issue, to hear them say that one should not question God or the Bible. One should only believe. If not countered effectively, this positional attitude obviously can terminate any type of dialogue.

Several biblical examples come to mind. The person of Job, in the Old Testament, is presented as struggling mightily with deep questions about God and justice. On one hand, Job feels God is against him and Job can even speak of God as a monster, a beast of prey (see for example 6:4, 7:11–21, 9:13–24, 10:16–17). Job honestly pursued these questions until, eventually, his faith was stronger in the end, and more mature. If he had not questioned God, he likely would not have struggled with and strengthened his faith.

Jeremiah is a Hebrew prophet who was brutally honest in his communication with God. The so-called "confessions" of Jeremiah (for example, in 11:18–12:6, 15:10–21, 20:15–18) give us insight into the inner conflict and pain he felt about his calling and the plight of his people. This prophet was given a message to deliver to the people that he did not want to deliver and he felt pressured and deceived by God. In 20:7 Jeremiah prays, "O Lord, thou hast deceived me and I was deceived." In plain language, he is calling God a liar.

BEING "BORN AGAIN"

Here I make a suggestion about a delicate question that can be quite useful. Ask the fundamentalist on what is their faith based. It's a very direct and personal question and I have found time and again that it presses to the heart of the matter, provides needed perspective, and opens possibilities for the fundamentalist.

Classic fundamentalism teaches that salvation is by grace through faith. That is, God offers salvation to human beings in the person and work of Jesus Christ. The particular way salvation is effected can be understood in different ways, but that is a subtlety not needed for the conversation I am here suggesting. The point is that salvation occurs when a person believes in or has faith in (synonymous terms) Jesus Christ. Fundamentalist Christians are usually adamant that one cannot "work" one's way to salvation, one cannot "earn" salvation. It is a gift, freely given by God, which is the meaning of grace, that is, unmerited favor. In fact, Christian fundamentalists often assail other religions and Catholics on this basis. Fundamentalists generally do not like to call Christianity a religion; they save the term religion for those traditions where "they think you can work your way up to God." Jews keep the law, Catholics repeat their "Hail Mary's," and Hindus protect the cow. Fundamentalists give these and other examples, often reflecting a misunderstanding of various traditions.

Now, for purposes of this book I am going a little beyond what fundamentalists say, but basing it clearly on their understanding of salvation. Fundamentalists are making a distinction between what is required for salvation and what is not. Faith in Jesus Christ is required. Believing other particular doctrines is presumably not required for salvation. Believing a particular interpretation of a particular passage of the Bible is presumably not required for salvation.

Within this context it can be useful to ask the fundamentalist to tell you about their conversion experience. Conversion stories can be richly revealing in what they tell you about the person of any religious tradition.[2] For our specific purposes here, the point is that the fundamentalist's conversion story will likely involve a heartfelt experience of God where they had faith in Jesus. It may have occurred when they were quite young. This conversion moment will not include assent to a whole host of biblical, theological, moral, and (un)scientific notions that the person may now hold to as a fundamentalist Christian. The fundamentalist, then, must conclude that his or her salvation, his or her status as a Christian, is not dependent on adherence to any of those things. Asking them what is their faith based on and asking them to describe their conversion experience, in my experience, makes crystal clear to them that they can still be a Christian, even if they give up some of the beliefs they have been holding tightly and come to hold beliefs different from those to which they have been committed.

The exercise does help the fundamentalist see that the issue they may find problematic (such as, evolution, women's roles, homosexuality, miracles, using scientific and historical methods) is an issue that is open for discussion and possible disagreement among *Christians.* What one concludes about these issues may be important in terms of having good doctrine or proper Christian ethics, but the conclusions have nothing to do with salvation. So, presumably, there can be a roomful of Christians, all of whom have faith in Jesus Christ for salvation, but who disagree on many other points of doctrine and practice. Just as Christians can disagree on whether baptism involves sprinkling (Methodists) or immersion (Baptists), so perhaps it is acceptable for Christians to have different positions on the controversial moral and scientific issues of our day.

A related biblical concept that works with fundamentalists is the Bible's admonition that Christians "grow in the grace and knowledge of the Lord Jesus Christ" (2 Peter 3:18). Ask fundamentalists when they were converted. Often their conversion occurred when they were much younger. In any case, it will likely have occurred long enough ago that the next question can be useful. Ask them if they hold the same exact views about things that they held when they were converted. Almost all fundamentalists will respond that their views have changed, more or less. You can then help them interpret these changes as illustrative of their "growing in the grace and knowledge of the Lord Jesus Christ." Pointing out that they have changed in their views, and yet continue to remain Christian, supports the possibility of their continuing to question, investigate, grow, and possibly change.

You may be thinking that you don't have the time or inclination to chew away at all the fundamentalist beliefs. And I'm sure you don't want to do therapy with fundamentalists. You don't have to do either of these. What cognitive therapists find is that often when some maladaptive schema is successfully challenged by finding one exception to the schema rule, and the schema is revised in a more healthy direction, the dam of resistance begins to break. Successfully calling into question one cognitive pattern can break things open in ways that genuine learning begins to occur across the board, and this has been my experience with fundamentalists. Teachers should keep in mind, as well, that usually you are dealing with adolescent or late adolescent students who are perhaps still trying to sort things out with regard to their identity. These techniques would not be as successful with an older fundamentalist whose identity is likely set.

Concluding Reflections

My primary goal has been to provide a new theoretical perspective that helps us understand the mind and world of the fundamentalist. A secondary, related goal is that this perspective empowers nonfundamentalists who so wish to effectively engage fundamentalists in productive conversation that benefits both parties. There is no simple formula for understanding fundamentalists. There can be no cookbook with easy recipes for successful conversations with fundamentalist Christians, and I have made no attempt to create one. Fundamentalist Christians are human beings with a particular take on the world and often with a psychological structure that gives rise to their worldview. Understanding fundamentalists takes some effort. Successful, empowering conversations with fundamentalists occur the same general way such conversations occur with anyone holding a radically different worldview—by speaking clearly, respectfully, and sensitively. I have, however, provided strategies that can be useful in such conversations with fundamentalists.

While engrossed in writing this book, a friend asked me, "What are you so concerned about that you would expend such effort on a study of fundamentalism?" Actually, on any given day I am concerned about one of two scenarios. Sometimes I am concerned that fundamentalists are going to implode. Fundamentalism is such an extreme position, so at odds with the modern world (unnecessarily I think), that I fear it will become so isolated and sectarian that generations of people caught in fundamentalism are sure to be lost in terms of having any real place in society and the Christian religion. While it may sound like an idealistic and lofty goal, I suppose I could put it another way. I would like to save fundamentalist Christians for Christianity. Those are my pessimistic days.

On other days, when I am even more pessimistic, I fear the opposite scenario. In 1922, smack in the middle of the emergence of Christian fundamentalism, the great liberal minister, Harry Emerson Fosdick (1878–1969), preached from his New York pulpit a sermon entitled, "Shall Fundamentalists Win?" On a bad day, and when I take stock of much of the mood and direction of the country, churches, and world, I fear the answer to Fosdick's question will be "yes." I shudder to think of what life will be like if the fundamentalist mind that I described in Part Three, structured by the theological system I described in Part Two, has its way with our secular and religious institutions, and with our children. I want to do my part with integrity, grace, and reason, but I will do my part to avoid that disaster, to effect a negative answer to Dr. Fosdick's pertinent question.

Some readers of earlier drafts insisted that I had unfairly placed all conservative Christians in a box and labeled them fundamentalists. In this final draft of the book I have tried to distinguish evangelicals and fundamentalists and suggest that fundamentalists are not all the same theologically. Some give more weight to biblical inerrancy; others are obsessed with the imminent rapture of Christians from the earth. I am also most willing to admit that not all Christians who are theological fundamentalists fit the psychological profile I have presented. However, if we are going to meaningfully explore any group, we have to focus on those aspects and patterns that group members generally have in common. In my effort to generalize, and paint a psychological picture of the typical fundamentalist, perhaps I have failed to say with sufficient clarity that not all fundamentalists are the same. I will try again with a concrete example.

I recently visited Roman Catholic friends in Buffalo, New York. They took me to a Christian ministry they support in a poor, predominately African-American, rundown section of the city. I was introduced to Rev. Otis C. Tillman and Geraldine "Gerri" Tillman. Rev. Otis, as he is affectionately called by his friends, and Gerri are 88 and 86 years old, respectively. If every Christian on the planet had one-tenth the love for kids, and the dedication to putting that love into practice, that this husband and wife team have, every social problem on this planet would be solved in a generation.

Gerri and Rev. Otis are fundamentalist Christians. Both tell stories of when they were converted at a young age. "I was 16 years old when the Lord Jesus saved me," Gerri said. "In October I was baptized in a creek and I've lived for the Lord since that time long ago," she explained. Rev. Otis grew up in one of the Baptist denominations. He believes the Bible is the inerrant word of God, that Jesus Christ is literally coming back soon, and all the other fundamentalist doctrines. This fundamentalist couple, however, does not fit the typical psychological profile of fundamentalists that I have provided in this book. In my conversations with them, I get no sense that they are inflexible, authoritarian, or that their identity is at risk when encountering those of a different theological persuasion. For example, they are good friends with my Roman Catholic friends who introduced us. While Gerri and Rev. Otis technically espouse all the fundamentalist theological points, their obsession is with serving needy children in the ghetto.

Many years ago this humble African-American couple started inviting poor neighborhood kids into their home during long, empty summer days when the kids were out of school and likely to fall into trouble in the rough neighborhood. The need was great and the hearts of Gerri and Otis were big. In my visit to their home/church/summer camp, I saw about 60 kids of all ages playing basketball and other games in the extended backyard of the Tillman's. Gerri and Rev. Otis play, love, feed, discipline, and care for these children who are always one wrong move away from chemical abuse, crime, and dropping out of school.

Gerri and Rev. Otis are extraordinary people with fascinating stories. Gerri's father used to beat her mother. At seven years old, when her father was beating her mother soon after the mother had given birth to Gerri's baby brother, Gerri put a gun to her father's head and told him she would kill him if he ever beat her mom again. The father left home. Later, a stepfather repeatedly beat Gerri because she would not submit to his sexual advances. She overcame the cruelty she received as a child and became a loving and caring woman for all these children. She gives Jesus the credit for saving her from a life of abuse and misery. This incredible women, every day, through the long summer months, cooks two full meals for 60 or so kids. Don't forget. She is 86 years old. "I cannot stand to see children dirty, hungry, and without decent clothes," she said.

Kids running playfully up to Rev. Otis constantly interrupted my conversation with him. And why wouldn't kids be attracted to this loving, grandfatherly man. At 88 years old, he has active plans to raise money and build a gymnasium next to his home so he can serve more children better. "No child should be without love and joy in their life," he said. "Children are the joy of the Lord. They shouldn't have to put up with broken down houses, dope, and sex abuse." Rev. Otis tells the story of one of his ghetto kids who is now a child psychiatrist, another who is a minister, and another who serves proudly in the Navy. "All of them, I know their stories. They so easily could have ended up wasted lives," he said.

In my visit, and subsequent conversations with Gerri and Rev. Otis, we did not talk a lot of explicit theology. When I asked about doctrine, they would answer, but within a sentence or two they were again talking about children and their plans to serve more of the poor kids in their neighborhood.

My point is, I would prefer to have Gerri and Rev. Otis as my neighbors, rather than an arrogant liberal who interprets the Bible like I do. I would prefer my children to be mentored by Gerri and Rev. Otis, rather than by a selfish liberal who thinks like I do about God. All fundamentalists are not the same, as all liberals are not either. Both fundamentalists and non-fundamentalists have incredibly loving, generous, contributing members of society. While I acknowledge that, I do not back away from my basic thesis. I think, on balance, fundamentalist Christianity is biblically unsound, theologically suspect, and psychologically dangerous, and it is a threat to the common good when it influences public policy and political processes.

I am not sure the conservative members of my family will be pleased with the final version of this book. I am sure they love me all the same, and I am sure that on family visits to mom's house our late, late night discussions of things religious and political will continue. If this book generates a small measure of the relatedness and open communication I have with the conservative members of my family, then the future is bright indeed. If this book in some small way cuts through the pretense and arrogance of false religion, and somehow fosters the authentic expression of the divine as exhibited by Gerri and Rev. Otis, I will be humbly pleased.

APPENDIX 1

Letters from Former Fundamentalist Students

(Email dated December 24, 2004, from Brian Henson, school teacher—used with permission.)

Dr. Mercer,

I hope you remember me. My name is Brian Henson, I graduated from ECU with a Religious Studies major in 1999, I went to Italy with you that summer (Harmon was there), I wrote a long thesis paper on the Messiah, I had long hair, and I took every class you taught at ECU. You filled out a recommendation form for my application to Wheaton College. I also asked you to be a reference for a job that I interviewed for about 3 and a half years ago. Remember?

Anyway, I just wanted to write to you and let you know what an incredible influence you have had in my life. I learned a lot in grad school at Wheaton and in Israel (I went to school there for 6 months at Jerusalem University College); however, your classes and teaching style are the most memorable to me. I am now living in Charlotte, NC, teaching Theology, New Testament, and World Religions at Charlotte Christian High School. It is my fourth year teaching, and I find myself copying your teaching style before my students. I hope you don't mind, but I have picked up your idea of redrawing the maps of the biblical period to learn geography. I have students draw the maps for map quizzes and I add to them every month so they have 40 sites memorized by the end of the semester. Also, with regard to the timelines that you put on the board, I have students memorize those and draw them out for quizzes. And, as I teach world religions, I tell your story of visiting the Zen Buddhist temple and day dreaming about running away if the head monk proceeded to hit you with the stick. And about the time you could not eat all of the food placed before you.

In Old and New Testament class, you always took the "critical" perspective when studying what I believe to be inspired scripture. I must admit, it hurt my faith at first, but you taught me to know what I believe and why I believe it. You taught me to analyze everything from the perspective of what is true, instead of from what my culture or traditions taught me. Now I understand why you always gave the "hairstyle" assignments. We only tend to notice what we are told to notice and we filter out everything else. You taught us to look at the big picture and to notice everything from a different perspective. I would still consider myself a conservative Christian; however, I have learned to be skeptical and critical and to seek for what is true. I do not simply believe something because I am told to, but I investigate to make sure it is true, and I do not disregard all other possibilities and interpretations to phenomena without investigating them. I am not claiming to have all the answers, but I do believe that God used your classes to make me a better Christian. Sometimes I feel more comfortable dialoguing with atheists and agnostics than with closed-minded, legalistic, ultra-conservative Christians.

I remember most of the facts you taught us in Old Testament, New Testament, and World Religions. In fact, I use my class notes to aid me in the classes I teach. But more than that, I have become a better thinker because of you and I have been teaching teenagers the same skills you taught me.

I hope this letter has been encouraging to you. Keep up the good work, I am sure there are hundreds of students out there that feel the way I do but have not expressed it to you.

I hope you have a great Christmas, and as I go, remember, think hairstyle.

Brian Henson

(Email dated January 5, 2005, from Brian Henson, school teacher—used with permission.)

Dr. Mercer,

Of course you may use my letter. I saw that you wrote an article on "Teaching Fundamentalist Christian Students," and I must say, I think you do a fine job when educating fundamentalists. I would say I was a "fundamentalist" when I took your Old and New Testament courses. Many of the things you said bothered me but the way you presented the material was extraordinarily professional. At the time I was frustrated at the difficulties you brought up with the biblical text, but I did not discard everything you taught in class. I still pull from many of the great lessons you taught. I now realize that I did indeed treat your class like you told us to, "like a cafeteria line." I took what I liked and left what was not as appetizing.

I would say I shifted toward the evangelical camp during my last couple years at ECU. I would still classify myself as an evangelical and looking back I would say you had a brilliant way of diffusing volatile situations with fundamentalists. Christians need to learn to enjoy your class and look at all the great lessons you do teach. Instead of directing anger at you, I sought alternate explanations for the challenges you brought up and I did have to make some changes in my theology. But, I believe the changes have been for the better. I do see the Bible as a divinely inspired document, but I must also see it as a human document that God works through to speak to mankind. It is a beautiful piece of literature with a story that reaches the heart of humanity.

I admire the way you dealt with students that disagreed with you. You always let their voice be heard and considered it as a possible interpretation to truth. I would say I felt most comfortable participating in your class than any other. Keep up the good work.

Brian Henson

(Excerpts shared with me from a letter by Christopher Skinner, a pastor who has a Ph.D. in biblical studies—used with permission. The letter was to an awards committee, dated December 15, 2005.)

My relationship with Dr. Mercer goes back to 1992 when I was an undergraduate student at East Carolina University. It was in Dr. Mercer's "Introduction to the Old Testament" course where I was first introduced to the critical study of the Bible. I remember being a young, naïve, uncritical Christian student who was hoping for a more "devotionally" oriented approach to the Bible. Boy, was I wrong! In fact, during that first class session, Dr. Mercer carefully explained that there was a big difference between the *critical* study and the *devotional* study of the Jewish and Christian Scriptures. I must admit that I was—initially—quite scandalized by what Dr. Mercer had to say.

I would describe my mentality as being that of a "fighting fundamentalist." Dr. Mercer's words were not only a challenge to my faith but to my whole view of reality. Needless to day, I didn't particularly care for that . . . at first. I remember coming to class every week ready for a "battle" over "truth." As I listened to his lectures on the history of Biblical scholarship, watched his slide shows from trips to various portions of the Middle East and mulled over the audacious claims he seemed to make, I began to realize (over a period of a few years) that there was a world of "truth" about which I had no idea and to which I had little, if any, exposure. Over time I came to appreciate many of the perspectives Dr. Mercer was offering in his well-crafted courses and have since integrated some of them into the driving passions of my vocational life. (As an aside, I believe effective pedagogy is less about *disseminating information* and more about *causing the uncritical student to think critically.* Dr. Mercer consistently accomplishes the latter in his classes.)

I have been particularly impacted by Dr. Mercer's presentation of different critical approaches to the Biblical text and their relationship within the context of their historical development. As he lectured on the interrelationships of historical criticism, source criticism, redaction criticism and literary critical approaches, I found myself drawn into reading the Bible in a totally different manner—and truly learning.

Christopher Skinner

APPENDIX 2

An Elementary Guide to Exegeting the Bible

The noun "exegesis" is derived from the Greek verb, *exegeomai,* which can be translated to make known, reveal, or explain (see John 1:18). As I am using the term for the purposes of this guide, to do exegesis of a biblical text means to discover the original meaning(s) of the text—to determine what the text meant when it was first written. Exegesis is asking the question, "What *did* the text mean then?" It is, in a sense, taking a trip from Greenville to Jerusalem. To do this well requires a commitment to critical study as you attempt to understand the text in the context of its own time and place. It may involve research into the meaning of words, context of passages, ancient geography, ancient culture, and so on in order to, as much as is possible, place yourself in the historical context of the text.

The goal of exegesis is to approach an objective reading of the text rather than a subjective reading where you make the text say what you want it to say, where you force an unnatural or unintended meaning on the text. The latter is sometimes called *eis*egesis or reading incorrect meaning into a text as opposed to *ex*egesis or reading correct meaning out of a text. (The Greek prefix *eis* is a preposition meaning "into" while the prefix *ex* is a form of a preposition meaning "out of.") What follows is the assignment given to my students for completing their exegesis.

The following are steps in doing your exegesis:

CHOOSE THE TEXT (passage) that will be the focus of your work. You will be looking for several verses or, depending on the text, maybe just one, that you are interested in studying for whatever reason. Your choice of text must be approved by me and I will be looking for a selection that constitutes a unit. Be thoughtful about your definition of the limits of the passage. Why do you set them where you do? A change in setting? Characters? Theme? Topic? Issue?

TRANSLATE. Ideally, you attempt your own translation of the text from the Hebrew or Greek and then compare with standard English translations. However, if you are unable to use the languages, you should read the text over and over and over again in three different modern translations. It is amazing how valuable this exercise can be in enabling you to grasp the thrust of the passage as well as the different shades of meaning that characterize many Hebrew and Greek words and phrases, and how word choice and order can influence meaning. Write out in your paper the three translations, being sure to provide the name of the translation. Do not use the *Living Bible* or any version or edition of it; it is a paraphrase, not a translation.

TEXTUAL ANALYSIS. We do not have, of course, any of the autographs (original manuscripts) of any of the books of the Bible. What we have are copies and fragments of copies—and they're all different—which in most cases are to be dated hundreds of years and many manuscript generations later than the original. The task here, then, is to establish the text to be interpreted and to take note of any significant variations in the manuscripts. If you happen to use Hebrew or Greek, there are several excellent resources available. For those who do not use the languages, the process will need to be more elementary. You may see in footnotes of English translations comments like this: "Other ancient authorities delete verse 47," or "Some manuscripts read 'he.'" If you find no textual variants provided in the English translations, continue with the next step. You will be exposed to the important textual problems in later steps as you consult the best critical commentaries.

PONDER THE TEXT. Now that you have the translations of a passage before you, it is crucial for you to spend time with the text alone. What does it seem to say? What comes to mind as you sit with the text? Work very hard not to impose your particular belief system onto the text; rather, read it as if you had never read the Bible or heard of the Christian religion before. Do not be afraid at this point to venture out and entertain images and ideas that you may never have associated with the text. Writing them down on scratch paper can be helpful. You can always revise your thoughts after further study if you discover they are inconsistent with what your research indicates. To end interpretation at this step can lead to *eis*egesis, to misinterpretation. However, to leave this step out is to rob yourself of what can be one of the most rewarding experiences in exegeting a text.

The next series of steps can be called literary and historical analysis. It is an important and multifaceted process that, in essence, involves asking any question of the text that will enable you better to understand its original meaning. At this point you are using the best concordances, commentaries, Bible dictionaries, and other resources available to you. A Bible commentary is a book in which the author has commented, usually verse by verse, on the text of some book of the Bible. Good libraries will have a number of critical commentaries. Many (I should probably say most) of the specific answers to the questions you will ask are disputed by various scholars, but this will not keep you from arriving at the essential meaning of most texts. Diligently working through these questions with the aid of competent guides will help to minimize reading incorrect meaning (from your own experience and cultural situation) into the text. Throughout the process try never to force the text to say what you want it to say. This is extremely difficult—in actuality I think impossible—but to strive for impartiality is a helpful exercise. Your analysis should include at least the following steps and questions.

AUTHORSHIP. Who wrote the passage or the book in which the passage is found? When, where, to whom, and why was it written? Your introductions to the Old and New Testaments are helpful here and you should definitely read what they have to say about your Bible book.

KEY WORDS—CONCORDANCE. Identify key words in your passage. A concordance will give you the other locations in the Bible where key words in your text are found. An online concordance is available at www.gospelcom.net. Read other texts where the key words are found.

KEY WORDS—DICTIONARY. What do the key words mean in the context of your passage? Do they have different meanings in other passages of your book, in other books in the Bible, or even in nonbiblical books from that culture? How do these writings themselves (not Webster's dictionary or your pastor) define the words? Bible dictionaries are helpful here. Look up the key words in either *The Anchor Bible Dictionary* or *The Interpreter's Dictionary of the Bible* (with supplementary volume). These are the best dictionaries of the Bible in the English language. If you can reduce a question you have about the text to a word or phrase and there is an entry in these resources under that word or phrase, you will likely find a wealth of information. You might also consult the multivolume *Theological Dictionary of the Old Testament* or the *Theological Dictionary of the New Testament*. While these works assume you know Hebrew or Greek, you might be able to glean some useful information from these resources, even without the language skills.

COMMENTARIES. Read three critical (not purely devotional) commentaries on your text. By the way, the Matthew Henry commentary is a wonderful old commentary, but it is devotional, so do not use it for the exegesis. The commentaries should help answer questions such as the following:

- What is the context of the passage in the book and how does this impact on its meaning?
- How might you best categorize the text in terms of genre? Is it poetry, prose, preaching, teaching, riddle, parable, myth, prophesy, apocalyptic, or something else?
- What sources did the author use in composing the text? How are these sources used and what does that say about the intention of the author?
- If you are exegeting a text in the gospels, does it have a context in the life of the historical Jesus and, if so, what is it?
- What is the context of the passage in the life of the author and/or the author's community? What was the author trying to say to the audience and why?
- What is the relationship of your text to the same kind of thought found elsewhere at or before the date of your text? For example, how do the ideas in your text relate to the rabbis, Hellenism, or Gnosticism?
- For studies in the gospels, you will want to pay careful and close attention to how the other gospel writers treat your passage (do they leave it out or include it and, if so, how is it different). What does this mean for what your author is up to? To help here, use Burton H. Throckmorton, *Gospel Parallels: A Comparison of the Synoptic Gospels, New Revised Standard Version,* 5th ed. (Nashville: Thomas Nelson, 1992).

These are only representative of some of the issues that might need to be raised with your text. Some of the above questions will be more important for arriving at the original meaning of your text than others. Each text has its own unique set of issues and the nature of your exegesis should be, to a great degree, controlled by the text. Also, again, keep in mind that as you get into the best scholarly works you will find that there is sometimes much disagreement among these "experts" about the issues. Do not be overwhelmed by this. Do not be afraid to come to you own conclusion about an issue, but be sure to do it only after careful consideration of the various scholarly interpretations. When you write your paper make sure you give the various interpretations so I will know that you know what they are.

For some reason at this point I am reminded of one Elector Frederick of Saxony who, in 1521 CE,

> *wished to be enlightened as to the meaning of Scripture, and appointed a committee. But the committee could not agree.*
>
> —Recorded in Roland H. Bainton,
> *Here I Stand: A Life of Martin Luther*
> (New York: Abingdon-Cokesbury Press, 1950), 203.

Notes

INTRODUCTION

1. Martin E. Marty and R. Scott Appleby, eds., *The Fundamentalism Project*, 5 vols., vol. 3, *Fundamentalisms and the State: Remaking Polities, Economies, and Militance* (Chicago: University of Chicago Press, 1993), 3.

2. Bernard Spilka, Ralph Hood, Jr., Bruce Hunsberger, and Richard Gorsuch, *The Psychology of Religion: An Empirical Approach*, 3rd ed. (New York: Guilford Press, 2003), 389.

3. Marty and Appleby, eds., *The Fundamentalism Project*, vol. 1, *Fundamentalisms Observed* (Chicago: University of Chicago Press, 1991), 817–42.

4. Gabriel A. Almond, R. Scott Appleby, and Emmanuel Sivan, *Strong Religion: The Rise of Fundamentalisms Around the World* (Chicago: University of Chicago Press, 2003), 110.

5. George M. Marsden, *Understanding Fundamentalism and Evangelicalism* (Grand Rapids, MI: Eerdmans, 1991), 1.

6. James Barr, *Fundamentalism* (London: SCM, 1977). On the distinction between evangelicalism and fundamentalism, with special attention to the psychological dimension, see Mark A. Yarhouse and Stephen R. Russell, "Evangelicalism," in *The Psychologies of Religion: Working with the Religious Client*, eds. E. Thomas Dowd and Stevan Lars Nielsen.

7. Marty and Appleby, *Fundamentalisms Observed*, ix.

CHAPTER 1

1. Winthrop S. Hudson, *Religion in America* (New York: Charles Scribner's Sons, 1965), 137.

2. Peter Cartwright, *Autobiography of Peter Cartwright,* introduction, bibliography, and index by Charles Wallis (Nashville: Abingdon, 1956 [first published: New York: Carlton and Porter, 1856]), 12.

3. Ibid., 34.

4. Ibid., 43.

5. Ibid., 45.

6. Ibid., 46–47.

7. George C. Bedell, Leo Sandon, Jr., and Charles T. Wellborn, *Religion in America* (New York: Macmillan, 1975), 161.

8. Ibid., 172.

9. Marsden, *Understanding Fundamentalism and Evangelicalism,* 51.

10. Will Campbell, *Forty Acres and a Goat: A Memoir* (Lookout Mountain, TN: Jefferson, 2002), 6.

CHAPTER 2

1. Charles Hodge, *What Is Darwinism?* (Princeton: Scribner, Armstrong, 1874), 142.

2. George M. Marsden, ed., *The Fundamentals: A Testimony to Truth,* 4 vols. (New York: Garland, 1988).

3. George M. Marsden, *Fundamentalism and American Culture: The Shaping of Twentieth-Century Evangelicalism, 1879–1925* (New York: Oxford University, 1980), 119.

4. Marsden, *The Fundamentals: A Testimony to Truth,* 1.

5. Mark A. Noll, *The Scandal of the Evangelical Mind* (Grand Rapids, MI: Eerdmans, 1994), 3.

6. Ibid., 56–67.

7. Jerry Adler, "Doubting Darwin," *Newsweek* 165, no. 6 (February 7, 2005): 45–50.

8. Noll, *Scandal,* 192. For an example of Christian support for science and evolution, see The Clergy Letter Project at http://www.butler.edu/clergyproject (accessed January 25, 2009).

CHAPTER 3

1. Bob Jones University, www.bju.edu (accessed June 20, 2005).

2. Ibid.

3. Mark A. Noll, *American Evangelical Christianity: An Introduction* (Oxford: Blackwell, 2001), 44–55, for a recent, sympathetic evaluation of Graham.

4. Leslie R. Keylock, "Evangelical Scholars Remove Gundry for His Views on Matthew," *Christianity Today* 3 (February 1984): 36–38.

5. Quentin Schultze, "The Two Faces of Fundamentalist Higher Education," in *The Fundamentalism Project,* vol. 2, *Reclaiming the Sciences, the Family, and Education,* eds. Martin E. Marty and R. Scott Appleby (Chicago: University of Chicago Press, 1993): 490–535.

6. John R. Belcher gives an excellent overview of this trend in "Conservative Christianity: A New Emerging Culture," in *The Psychologies in Religion: Working*

with the Religious Client, eds. E. Thomas Dowd and Stevan Lars Nielsen (New York: Springer, 2006).

7. Adam Piore, "A Higher Frequency," *Mother Jones* 30, no. 7 (December 2005): 47–49.

8. Ralph Hood, Jr., Peter C. Hill, and W. Paul Williamson, *The Psychology of Religious Fundamentalism* (New York: Guilford, 2005), 115–32, provides an excellent discussion of serpent-handling sects.

9. Nancy Tatom Ammerman, *Bible Believers: Fundamentalists in the Modern World* (New Brunswick: Rutgers University, 1987), 49–54.

10. John Sugg, "A Nation Under God," *Mother Jones* 30, no. 7 (December 2005): 34. See also the discussion of David Barton and his dream of a "Christian America" in Kurt W. Peterson, "American Idol: David Barton's Dream of a Christian Nation," *Christian Century* 123, no. 22 (October 31, 2006): 20–23.

11. National Council on Bible Curriculum in Public Schools, www.bibleinschools.net (accessed June 26, 2008).

12. Mark A. Chancey, "The Bible in the Classroom: Lesson Plans," *Christian Century* 122, no. 17 (August 23, 2005): 18–21.

CHAPTER 4

1. Hood, Hill, and Williamson, *The Psychology of Religious Fundamentalism*, 183.
2. Marty and Appleby, eds., *Fundamentalisms and the State*, 3.
3. I have adapted these broad descriptions from Bedell, Sandon, and Welborn, *Religion in America*, 207–9.
4. Marty and Appleby, *Fundamentalisms and the State*, 3.
5. Barr, *Fundamentalism*, 293.
6. Ibid., 266.

CHAPTER 5

1. These kinds of lists are produced by many authors critical of fundamentalism. Many of the Old Testament examples in this list are taken from Barr, *Fundamentalism*, 309–10. I selected the New Testament examples.
2. Barr, *Fundamentalism*, 309.
3. Some of my discussion of the logistical issues presented by a literal worldwide flood is based on Bernard Ramm's, *The Christian View of Science and Scripture* (Grand Rapids, MI: Eerdmans, 1955).
4. Ramm, *The Christian View of Science and Scripture*, 139.
5. Noll, *American Evangelical Christianity*, 110.
6. My reflections on translation are taken largely from Calvin Mercer, "Contemporary Language and New Translations of the Bible: The Impact of Feminism," *Religion & Public Education* 17 (Winter 1990): 89–98.

CHAPTER 6

1. Barr, *Fundamentalism*, 239.

2. Hywel Jones, "Exodus," *The New Bible Commentary*, revised, eds. Donald Guthrie and J. A. Motyer (Grand Rapids, MI: Eerdmans, 1970), 115–39.

3. Ibid., 129.

4. Ibid., 181.

5. Bart Ehrman, *The New Testament: A Historical Introduction to the Early Christian Writings*, 4th ed. (New York: Oxford University, 2008), 20–22.

6. See Belcher, "Conservative Christianity: A New Emerging Culture," 135–37.

7. For a full discussion of each option, see Paul F. Knitter, *Introducing Theologies of Religion* (Maryknoll, NY: Orbis Books, 2002).

CHAPTER 7

1. Amy Frykholm, *Rapture Culture: Left Behind in Evangelical America* (New York: Oxford University, 2004) gives a thorough analysis of the *Left Behind* phenomenon, focusing on the readers of this series; and Barbara Rossing, *The Rapture Exposed: The Message of Hope in the Book of Revelation* (Boulder, CO: Westview, 2004) provides an excellent, recent critique of premillennial dispensationalism.

2. Bernard McGinn is a recognized authority on the Antichrist and apocalypticism. See the bibliography for some of his titles. For an excellent discussion of the American obsession with the Antichrist, see Robert C. Fuller, *Naming the Antichrist* (New York: Oxford University, 1995). On Barack Obama, see Lisa Miller, "Is Obama the Antichrist?" *Newsweek* 152, no. 21 (November 24, 2008), http://www.newsweek.com/id/169192 (accessed December 11, 2008).

3. James K. Elliott, "The Apocalypse of Peter," *The Apocryphal New Testament* (New York: Oxford University, 1993), sections 5, 7, 8, 11.

4. An example of Marcus Borg's work is *Jesus in Contemporary Scholarship* (Valley Forge, PA: Trinity, 1994).

5. Calvin Mercer, "Albert Schweitzer (1875–1965)," *Dictionary of Major Biblical Interpreters*, 2nd ed., ed. Donald K. McKim (Downers Grove, IL: InterVarsity Press, 2007 [1998]): 899–902.

6. Albert Schweitzer, *Von Reimarus zu Wrede: Eine Geschichte der Leben-Jesu Forschung* (Tubingen: J. C. B. Mohr, 1906). English translation, *The Quest of the Historical Jesus: A Critical Study of Its Progress from Reimarus to Wrede*, 2nd ed. (New York: Macmillan, 1968), 403.

7. I discuss this question of faith and history in some detail in Calvin Mercer, *Norman Perrin's Interpretation of the New Testament: From "Exegetical Method" to "Hermeneutical Process," Studies in American Biblical Hermeneutics 2* (Macon, GA: Mercer University, 1986).

CHAPTER 8

1. Paul Boyer, "The Growth of Fundamentalist Apocalyptic in the United States," in *The Continuum History of Apocalypticism*, eds. Bernard McGinn, John J. Collins, and Stephen J. Stein (New York: Continuum, 1998).

2. *Scofield Reference Bible* (New York: Oxford University, 2002 [1909]), ix.

3. Derek Maher and Calvin Mercer, *Religion and the Implications of Radical Life Extension* (New York: Palgrave Macmillan, 2009).

4. Boyer, "The Growth of Fundamentalist Apocalyptic in the United States," 540.
5. Nancy Gibbs, "Apocalypse Now," *Time*, July 1, 2002.
6. Frykholm, *Rapture Culture*, 18–20.
7. *Scofield Reference Bible*, 1187.
8. Boyer, "The Growth of Fundamentalist Apocalyptic in the United States," 534.
9. See also Yaakov Ariel, "An Unexpected Alliance: Christian Zionism and Its Historical Significance," *Modern Judaism* 26, no. 1 (2006): 82.
10. Ibid., 78.
11. Ibid., 79–80.
12. Ibid., 91–92.
13. Ibid., 93.
14. Rossing, *The Rapture Exposed*, 138–40.
15. Ibid., 139.
16. Boyer, "The Growth of Fundamentalist Apocalyptic in the United States," 518.
17. Ibid.

CHAPTER 9

1. *Notes of Debates in the Federal Convention of 1787 Reported by James Madison*, Bicentennial Edition (New York: Norton, 1987 [1966]).
2. Peter Marshall and David Manuel, with Anna Wilson Fishel, *From Sea to Shining Sea for Children* (Grand Rapids, MI: Fleming H. Revell, 1993), 18–19; and *The Light and the Glory for Children* (Tarrytown, NY: Fleming H. Revell, 1992), 156.
3. Noll, *American Evangelical Christianity*, 183–85, provides a fuller discussion of this "event."
4. Robert Bellah "Civil Religion in America," *Daudalus* 96, no. 1 (Winter 1967): 1–21.
5. Haig A. Bosmajian, *Freedom of Religion. The 1st Amendment in the Classroom Series* 2 (New York: Neal-Schuman, 1987), 7.
6. Ibid.
7. Ibid., 11.
8. Ibid., 17.
9. Ibid., 138.
10. Roland H. Bainton, *Christian Attitudes Toward War and Peace: A Historical Survey and Critical Re-evaluation* (New York: Abingdon, 1960).
11. Wallis discusses the evangelical manifesto in "An Evangelical Manifesto," *Sojourners* (July 2008): 5.
12. E. J. Dionne, Jr., "Message from a Megachurch," *Washington Post*, December 5, 2006. See also a similar comment about Obama's campaign in the summer of 2008 by Georgetown University professor Jacques Berlinerblau, a careful critic of religion in American politics, in "On Faith," an interactive conversation on religion moderated by *Newsweek* editor Jon Meacham and Sally Quinn of *The Washington Post*, http://newsweek.washingtonpost.com/onfaith/georgetown/2008/06/ dobson_hears_obamas_footsteps.html.

13. Much of this section is reprinted, with permission, from Calvin Mercer, "Sexual Violence and the Male Warrior God," *Lexington Theological Quarterly* 41 (Spring 2006): 23–37. Excellent studies of violence in various aspects of the Judaea-Christian tradition are found in the timely series edited by J. Harold Ellens, *The Destructive Power of Religion: Violence in Judaism, Christianity, and Islam,* 4 vols. (Westport, CT: Praeger, 2004). For the biblical period, see especially vol. 1: *Sacred Scriptures, Ideology, and Violence.*

14. Margaret L. Bendroth, "The Search for 'Women's Role' in American Evangelicalism, 1930–1980," in *Evangelicalism and Modern America,* ed. George Marsden (Grand Rapids, MI: Eerdmans, 1980), 127–28.

15. Clifford Geertz makes a strong case for this position in "Religion as a Cultural System," in *Reader in Comparative Religion,* 2nd ed., eds. William Lessa and Evon Vogt (New York: Harper & Row, 1966): 204–16.

16. Johann M. Vento, "Violence, Trauma, and Resistance: A Feminist Appraisal of Metz's Mysticism of Suffering Unto God," *Horizons: The Journal of the College Theology Society* 29, no. 1 (2002): 16; Mary Daly, *Beyond God the Father: Toward a Philosophy of Women's Liberation* (Boston: Beacon, 1973), 6–7, 13–14; Rosemary Radford Ruether, ed., *Religion and Sexism: Images of Woman in the Jewish and Christian Traditions* (New York: Simon & Schuster, 1974), 9–10; Charles Ess, "Reading Adam and Eve: Re-Visions of the Myth of Woman's Subordination to Man," in *Violence Against Women and Children: A Christian Theological Sourcebook,* eds. Carol J. Adams and Marie M. Fortune (New York: Continuum, 1995), 94; Elizabeth Clark and Herbert Richardson, eds., *Women and Religion: The Original Sourcebook of Women in Christian Thought* (New York: HarperSanFrancisco, 1996); Patricia Wilson-Kastner, *Faith, Feminism and the Christ* (Philadelphia: Fortress Press, 1983), vii; and Elizabeth Schussler Fiorenza, *Bread Not Stone: The Challenge of Feminist Biblical Interpretation* (Boston: Beacon Press, 1984), xi.

17. On this point, see Susan Brooks Thistlethwaite, "Every Two Minutes: Battered Women and Feminist Interpretation," in *Weaving the Visions: New Patterns in Feminist Spirituality,* eds. Judith Plaskow and Carol P. Christ (San Francisco: Harper & Row, 1989), 302–13.

18. Ess, "Reading Adam and Eve." Cf. Julia Watts, "With Memory of Violence: Toward A Restitching of Theological and Cultural Loopholes," *Journal of Women and Religion* 18 (2000): 60–74.

19. Naomi Goldenberg, *Changing of the Gods: Feminism and the End of Traditional Religions* (Boston: Beacon Press, 1979), 1–9.

20. Leona Stucky-Abbott, "The Impact of Male God Imagery on Female Identity Meaning," *The Journal of Pastoral Care* 47, no. 3 (Fall 1993); Clark and Richardson, *Women and Religion,* vii; Ruether, *Religion and Sexism,* 9, 13; and Denise L. Carmody, *Women & World Religions* (Nashville: Abingdon Press, 1979), 113–36.

21. John J. Scullon, "God in the OT," in *Anchor Bible Dictionary,* vol. 2, ed. David Noel Freedman (New York: Doubleday, 1992), 1047.

22. Phyllis Bird, "Images of Women in the Old Testament," in *Religion and Sexism: Images of Women in the Jewish and Christian Traditions* (New York: Simon and Schuster, 1974), 42, 49–50, 64–65.

23. Ibid., 41–88 provides an excellent summary.

24. Francine Cardman, "Women, Ministry, and Church Order in Early Christianity," in *Women and Christian Origins,* eds. Ross Shepard Kraemer and Mary

Rose D'Angelo (New York: Oxford University Press, 1999), 300–1; Elizabeth Schussler Fiorenza, *In Memory of Her: A Feminist Theological Reconstruction of Christian Origins* (New York: Crossroad, 1983), 105–59; Ross S. Kraemer, "Jewish Women and Christian Origins," in Kraemer and D'Angelo, *Women and Christian Origins,* 35–49; and Ross S. Kraemer, "Jewish Women and Women's Judaism(s) at the Beginning of Christianity," in Kraemer and D'Angelo, *Women and Christian Origins,* 50–79 take issue with the prevailing view that Judaism at the time of Christ was patriarchal and the Jesus movement rehabilitated the situation in an egalitarian direction.

25. David Wiesen, *Saint Jerome as a Satirist: A Study in Christian Latin Thought and Letters* (Ithaca: Cornell University Press, 1964), 119.

26. Jerome, Letter 22, "To Eustochium: The Virgin's Profession," in *Select Letters of St. Jerome,* trans. F. A. Wright (Cambridge, MA: Harvard University Press, Loeb Classical Library, 1933), 95.

27. Augustine, "On Marriage and Concupiscence," in *Augustine: Anti-Pelagian Writings, Nicene and Post-Nicene Fathers,* 1st series, vol. 5, ed. Philip Schaff (New York: Christian Literature Society, 1893), 265, which is book 1, chapter 5, number 4 of Augustine's work. See also book 1, chapter 17, number 15 where Augustine argues against birth control.

28. Barbara J. MacHaffie, *Her Story: Women in Church Tradition* (Philadelphia: Fortress Press, 1986), 36–39; and Elizabeth A. Clark, *Women in the Early Church* (Wilmington, DE: Michael Glazier, 1983), 15–25.

29. MacHaffie, *Her Story: Women in Church Tradition,* 51–54; and Anne M. Clifford, *Introducing Feminist Theology* (Maryknoll, NY: Orbis Books, 2001), 186–89.

30. For example, gender-neutral terminology for deity and the notion that woman was created in God's image.

31. Thomas Aquinas, *Summa Theologica,* ed. Fathers of the English Dominican Province, 3 vols. (London: Burns, Oates and Washbourne, Ltd., 1914), Part 1, question 92, articles 1 and 2, in a section entitled "The Production of Woman."

32. Eleanor Commo McLaughlin, "Equality of Souls, Inequality of Sexes: Woman in Medieval Theology," in Ruether, ed., *Religion and Sexism,* 213–66, especially 215–33, for an excellent summary of Aquinas with respect to his views on women.

33. Jacob Sprenger and Heinrich Kramer, *Malleus Maleficarum,* trans. Montague Summers (London: Pushlein, 1948).

34. Clark and Richardson, *Women and Religion,* 119–24 survey various explanations of this holocaust.

35. A. Nicholas Groth and William A. Hobson, "The Dynamics of Sexual Assault," in *Sexual Dynamics of Anti-Social Behavior,* eds. Louis B. Schlesinger and Eugene Revitch (Springfield, IL: Charles C. Thomas, 1983): 169.

36. Luther makes this point in his commentary on Genesis 2:8, found in his "Lectures on Genesis," in *Luther's Works,* vol. 1, ed. Jaroslov Pelikan (Saint Louis, MO: Concordia Publishing House, 1958).

37. For example, the Shaker female savior Ann Lee and the progressive notions of sex and marriage in the Oneida community.

38. Some of the material on fundamentalist Christianity is taken from Peter Phan, "Might or Mystery: The Fundamentalist Concept of God," in *The Struggle Over the Past: Fundamentalism in the Modern World,* College Theology Society

annual publication, vol. 35, ed. William Shea (Lanham, MD: University Press, 1993), 81–102.

39. Marsden, *Evangelicalism and Modern America,* 80.

40. For example, Jerry Falwell, *Listen, America!* (New York: Doubleday, 1980), 14.

41. For example, Larry Christenson, *The Christian Family* (Minneapolis: Bethany Fellowship, 1970); Dan Benson, *Becoming One* (Nashville: Thomas Nelson, n.d.); Don Meredith, *The Total Man* (Wheaton, IL: Tyndale House, 1981); and Dorothy Pape, *In Search of God's Ideal Woman* (Downers Grove, IL: InterVarsity Press, 1976).

42. Phan, "Might or Mystery."

43. For example, David Finkelhor and Kersti Yllo, *License to Rape: Sexual Abuse of Wives* (New York: The Free Press, 1985), 9, 207.

44. Sandra L. Bem and Daryl J. Bem, "Case Study of a Nonconscious Ideology: Training the Woman to Know Her Place," in *Beliefs, Attitudes, and Human Affairs,* ed. Daryl J. Bem (Belmont, CA: Brooks/Cole, 1970), 89–99.

45. Susan Griffin, *Rape: The Power of Consciousness* (New York: Harper & Row, 1979).

46. Daly, *Beyond God the Father,* 114–22.

47. Cf. Susan Brownmiller, *Against Our Will: Men, Women, and Rape* (New York: Simon and Schuster, 1975), 31–113.

48. For example, Donal E. MacNamara and Edward Sagarin, *Sex, Crime, and the Law* (New York: The Free Press, 1977), 33–34.

49. Lenore E. A. Walker, *The Battered Woman Syndrome,* 2nd ed. (New York: Springer, 2000), 236–37; Vento, "Violence, Trauma, and Resistance," 12.

50. Brownmiller, *Against Our Will,* 16–30.

51. Daly, *Beyond God the Father,* 114–22.

52. The Roman Catholic Church has issued various pronouncements, beginning around 1930, that moderated its views on birth control and on procreation as the only acceptable use of sex.

CHAPTER 10

1. Occasionally, I illustrate points with examples from my clinical experience as a therapist or my classroom experience as professor. As is common in discussing cases from one's own clinical practice, I have altered the details of these cases without compromising the substantive point so that no real person or situation can be identified.

2. George Mora, "The Scrupulosity Syndrome," in *Clinical Psychiatry and Religion,* ed. E. M. Pattison (Boston: Little Brown, 1969): 163–74; and W. M. Nolan, "Scrupulosity," in *Dictionary of Pastoral Care and Counseling,* eds. Rodney J. Hunter et al. (Nashville: Abingdon, 1990), 1120.

3. Spilka et al., *The Psychology of Religion,* 527–30, for a review of the literature.

4. Paul Salkovskis, ed. *Frontiers of Cognitive Therapy* (New York: Guilford, 1996), xiii.

5. Aaron T. Beck, *Cognitive Therapy and the Emotional Disorders* (New York: International Universities, 1976), 29.

6. Aaron T. Beck, "Cognitive Therapy: A 30-year Retrospective," *American Psychologist* 46 (1991): 368–75.

7. Albert Ellis, *Reason and Emotion in Psychotherapy* (New York: Lyle Stewart, 1962), 3–34.

8. Aaron T. Beck and Marjorie E. Weishaar, "Cognitive Therapy," in *Current Psychotherapies* (Itasca, IL: F. E. Peacock, 1989), 286.

9. Aaron T. Beck, Augustus J. Rush, Brian F. Shaw, and Gary Emery, *Cognitive Therapy of Depression* (New York: Guilford, 1979), 5.

10. Beck and Weishaar, "Cognitive Therapy," 304; and Jacqueline B. Persons, *Cognitive Therapy in Practice: A Case Formulation Approach* (New York: W. W. Norton, 1989), 51–57. One of the best discussions of what she prefers to call core beliefs is by Judith Beck, *Cognitive Therapy: Basics and Beyond* (New York: Guilford, 1995), 166–92.

11. Jeremy D. Safran, Michael T. Vallis, Zindel V. Segal, and Brian F. Shaw, "Assessment of Core Cognitive Processes in Cognitive Therapy," *Cognitive Therapy and Research* 10 (October 1986): 509–26.

12. Beck, "Cognitive Therapy," 372; Beck et al., *Cognitive Therapy of Depression,* 10–12, 209–243; Beck and Weishaar, "Cognitive Therapy," 296; cf. Albert Ellis, "A Sadly Neglected Cognitive Element in Depression," *Cognitive Therapy and Research* 11 (1987): 121–46.

13. David M. Clark, "Cognitive Therapy for Anxiety," *Behavioural Psychotherapy* 14 (1986): 283–94.

14. Beck et al., *Cognitive Therapy of Depression,* 14, 261; Beck and Weishar, "Cognitive Therapy," 295–96; David D. Burns, *Feeling Good: The New Mood Therapy* (New York: William Morrow, 1986), 40–41; and Persons, *Cognitive Therapy in Practice,* 106–15.

15. Beck et al., *Cognitive Therapy of Depression,* 250–51.

CHAPTER 11

1. Hood, Hill, and Williamson, *The Psychology of Religious Fundamentalism,* 5.

2. Sara Savage, "Fundamentalism," in *The Psychologies in Religion: Working with the Religious Client,* eds. E. Thomas Dowd and Stevan Lars Nielsen (New York: Springer, 2006), 160; R. Yao, *Fundamentalists Anonymous: There is a Way Out,* 4th ed. (New York: Luce, 1987).

3. Hood, Hill, and Williamson, *The Psychology of Religious Fundamentalism,* 3–4.

4. Bob Altemeyer, *Enemies of Freedom: Understanding Right-Wing Authoritarianism* (San Francisco: Jossey-Bass, 1988), 6, 11, 200–38. For a review of the literature see Sara Savage, "A Psychology of Fundamentalism: The Search for Inner Failings," in *Fundamentalism, Church, and Society,* eds. Martyn Percy and Ian Jones (London: SPCK, 2002).

5. Ibid., 3–5.

6. Ibid., 328.

7. Ibid., 230.

8. Ibid., 328.

9. Ibid., 203.

10. Arie W. Kruglanski, *The Psychology of Closed Mindedness* (New York: Psychology Press, 2004), 43–45.
11. Ibid., 46.
12. Ibid., 50.
13. Ibid., 51.
14. For a review of empirical research on cults, see Spilka et al., *The Psychology of Religion,* 375–415.
15. Ibid., 406–7.
16. Paul W. Pruyser, "The Seamy Side of Current Religious Beliefs," *Bulletin of the Menninger Clinic* 41 (1977): 332.
17. James W. Fowler, *Stages of Faith: The Psychology of Human Development and the Quest for Meaning* (San Francisco: Harper & Row, 1981). An excellent discussion of Fowler's model, in the context of religious conversion, is found in J. Harold Ellens, *Understanding Religious Experiences: What the Bible Says about Spirituality* (Westport, CT: Praeger, 2008), 116–43. The discussion of Fowler is on pages 120–22.
18. Alisat Hunsberger, S. M. Pancer, and M. Pratt, "Religious Fundamentalism and Religious Doubts: Content, Connections, and Complexity of Thinking," *International Journal for the Psychology of Religion* 6 (1966): 218.
19. Altemeyer, *Enemies of Freedom,* 328; and Spilka et al., *The Psychology of Religion,* 134–35.

CHAPTER 12

1. Marty and Appleby, *Fundamentalisms and Society,* 3.

CHAPTER 13

1. Altemeyer, *Enemies of Freedom,* 152–53.

CHAPTER 14

1. See Walter Wink, ed., *Homosexuality and Christian Faith: Questions of Conscience for the Churches* (Minneapolis: Fortress, 1999), 37–42, for more examples.
2. For an excellent survey of the empirical research on conversion, see Spilka et al., *The Psychology of Religion,* 341–74.

Bibliography

Adams, Carol J., and Marie M. Fortune, eds. *Violence against Women and Children: A Christian Theological Sourcebook.* New York: Continuum, 1995.

Adler, Jerry. "Doubting Darwin." *Newsweek* 145, no. 6 (February 7, 2005): 45–50.

Ali, Tariq. *The Clash of Fundamentalisms: Crusades, Jihads and Modernity.* London: Verso, 2002.

Allen, Brooke. *Moral Minority: Our Skeptical Founding Fathers.* Chicago: Ivan R. Dee, 2006.

Alley, Robert S. *School Prayer.* Amherst, NY: Prometheus Books, 1994.

Almond, Gabriel A., R. Scott Appleby, and Emmanuel Sivan. *Strong Religion: The Rise of Fundamentalisms Around the World.* Chicago: University of Chicago Press, 2003.

Altemeyer, Bob. *Enemies of Freedom: Understanding Right-Wing Authoritarianism.* San Francisco: Jossey-Bass, 1988.

Ammerman, Nancy Tatom. *Bible Believers: Fundamentalists in the Modern World.* New Brunswick: Rutgers University, 1987.

———. "North American Protestant Fundamentalism." In *The Fundamentalism Project.* 5 vols. Vol. 1: *Fundamentalisms Observed,* edited by Martin E. Marty and R. Scott Appleby. Chicago: University of Chicago Press, 1991.

Antoun, Richard T. *Understanding Fundamentalism: Christian, Islamic and Jewish Movements.* Walnut Creek, CA: Altamira, 2001.

Ariel, Yaakov. "An Unexpected Alliance: Christian Zionism and Its Historical Significance." *Modern Judaism* 26, no. 1 (2006): 74–100.

Armstrong, Karen. *The Battle for God.* New York: Alfred A. Knopf, 2000.

Ault, James M., Jr. *Spirit and Flesh: Life in a Fundamentalist Baptist Church.* New York: Knopf, 2004.

Babinski, Edward T. *Leaving the Fold: Testimonies of Former Fundamentalists.* Amherst, NY: Prometheus Books, 2003.

Bainton, Roland H. *Christian Attitudes Toward War and Peace: A Historical Survey and Critical Re-evaluation.* New York: Abingdon, 1960.

Baker, Hans Boersma. *Violence, Hospitality, and the Cross: Reappropriating the Atonement Tradition.* Grand Rapids, MI: Baker Academics, 2004.

Balmer, Randall. *Encyclopedia of Evangelicalism,* revised and expanded. Waco, TX: Baylor University, 2004.

———. *Mine Eyes Have Seen the Glory: A Journey into the Evangelical Subculture in America,* 3rd ed. New York: Oxford University Press, 2000 (1989).

———. *Thy Kingdom Come, An Evangelical's Lament: How the Religious Right Distorts the Faith and Threatens America.* New York: Basic, 2006.

Barker, Dan. *Losing Faith in Faith: From Preacher to Atheist.* Madison, WI: Freedom from Religion Foundation, 1992.

Barr, James. *Fundamentalism.* London: SCM, 1977.

———. *The Scope and Authority of the Bible.* Philadelphia: Westminster, 1980.

Bawer, Bruce. *Stealing Jesus: How Fundamentalism Betrays Christianity.* New York: Three Rivers, 1997.

Beck, Aaron T. "Cognitive Therapy: A 30-year Retrospective." *American Psychologist* 46 (1991): 368–75.

———. *Cognitive Therapy and the Emotional Disorders.* New York: International Universities, 1976.

———. *Prisoners of Hate: The Cognitive Basis of Anger, Hostility, and Violence.* New York: HarperCollins, 1999.

Beck, Aaron T., and Gary Emery. *Anxiety Disorders and Phobias: A Cognitive Perspective.* New York: Basic Books, 1985.

Beck, Aaron T., and Ruth L. Greenberg. *Coping with Depression.* New York: Institute for Rational Living, 1974.

Beck, Aaron T., Augustus J. Rush, Brian F. Shaw, and Gary Emery. *Cognitive Therapy of Depression.* New York: Guilford, 1979.

Beck, Aaron T., and Marjorie E. Weishaar. "Cognitive Therapy." In *Current Psychotherapies,* edited by R. J. Corsine and D. Wedding. Itasca, IL: F. W. Peacock, 1989.

Beck, Judith S. *Cognitive Therapy: Basics and Beyond.* New York: Guilford, 1995.

Beck, Martha. *Leaving the Saints: How I Lost the Mormons and Found My Faith.* New York: Crown, 2005.

Bedell, George C., Leo Sandon, Jr., and Charles T. Wellborn. *Religion in America.* New York: Macmillan, 1975.

Belcher, John R. "Conservative Christianity: A New Emerging Culture." In *The Psychologies in Religion: Working with the Religious Client,* edited by E. Thomas Dowd and Stevan Lars Nielsen. New York: Springer, 2006.

Bellah, Robert. "Civil Religion in America." *Daedalus* 96, no. 1 (Winter 1967): 1–21.

Bellis, Alice Ogden, and Terry L. Hufford. *Science, Scripture, and Homosexuality.* Cleveland: Pilgrim, 2002.

Belzen, Jacob A., ed. *Aspects in Contexts: Studies in the History of the Psychology of Religion.* Amsterdam: Rodopi, 2000.

Bem, Sandra L., and Daryl J. Bem. "Case Study of a Nonconscious Ideology: Training the Woman to Know Her Place." In *Beliefs, Attitudes, and Human Affairs,* edited by Daryl J. Bem. Belmont, CA: Brooks/Cole, 1970.

Bendroth, Margaret L. "The Search for 'Women's Role' in American Evangelicalism, 1930–1980." In *Evangelicalism and Modern America,* edited by George Marsden. Grand Rapids, MI: Eerdmans, 1980.

Benson, Dan. *Becoming One.* Nashville: Thomas Nelson, n.d.

Berger, Peter, Brigitte Berger, and Hansfried Kellner. *The Homeless Mind: Modernization and Consciousness.* New York: Random House, 1973.

Berlinerblau, Jacques. "On Faith." http://newsweek.washingtonpost.com/onfaith/georgetown/2008/06/dobson_hears_obamas_footsteps.html (accessed June 26, 2008).

———. *The Secular Bible: Why Nonbelievers Must Take Religion Seriously.* New York: Cambridge University Press, 2005.

———. *Thumpin' It: The Use and Abuse of the Bible in Today's Presidential Politics.* Louisville: Westminster John Knox, 2007.

Blomberg, Craig L., and Sung Wood Chung, eds. *A Case for Historic Premillennialism: An Alternative to "Left Behind" Eschatology.* Ada, MI: Baker, 2009.

Bob Jones University. www.bju.edu.

Boone, Kathleen C. *The Bible Tells Them So: The Discourse of Protestant Fundamentalism.* Albany: State University of New York, 1989.

Borg, Marcus J. *Jesus in Contemporary Scholarship.* Valley Forge, PA: Trinity, 1994.

Bosmajian, Haig A. *Freedom of Religion. The 1st Amendment in the Classroom Series 2.* New York: Neal-Schuman, 1987.

Boyer, Paul. "The Growth of Fundamentalist Apocalyptic in the United States." In *The Continuum History of Apocalypticism,* edited by Bernard McGinn, John J. Collins, and Stephen J. Stein. New York: Continuum, 1998.

Brasher, Brenda E., ed. *Encyclopedia of Fundamentalism.* New York: Routledge, 2001.

Brogaard, Betty. *Dare to Think for Yourself: A Journey from Faith to Reason.* Baltimore, MD: PublishAmerica, 2004.

Brownmiller, Susan. *Against Our Will: Men, Women, and Rape.* New York: Simon & Schuster, 1975.

Bruce, Steve. *Fundamentalism.* Cambridge, England: Polity, 2000.

Burns, David D. *Feeling Good: The New Mood Therapy.* New York: William Morrow, 1986.

Butler, Jennifer S. *Born Again: The Christian Right Globalized.* London: Pluto, 2006.

Campbell, Will. *Forty Acres and a Goat: A Memoir.* Lookout Mountain, TN: Jefferson Press, 2002.

Campolo, Tony. *Letters to a Young Evangelical.* New York: Basic Books, 2008.

Carmody, Denise L. *Women & World Religions.* Nashville: Abingdon, 1979.

Carpenter, Joel A. *Revive Us Again: The Reawakening of American Fundamentalism.* New York: Oxford University, 1997.

Carter, Jimmy. *Our Endangered Values: America's Moral Crisis.* New York: Simon & Schuster, 2005.

Cartwright, Peter. *Autobiography of Peter Cartwright.* Introduction, bibliography, and index by Charles Wallis. Nashville: Abingdon, 1956 (first published: New York: Carlton and Porter, 1856).

Castro, Joy. *The Truth Book: Escaping a Childhood of Abuse Among Jehovah's Witnesses.* New York: Arcade, 2005.

Chancey, Mark A. "The Bible in the Classrooom: Lesson Plans." *Christian Century* 122, no. 17 (August 23, 2005): 18–21.

Christenson, Larry. *The Christian Family.* Minneapolis, MN: Bethany Fellowship, 1970.

Clabaugh, Gary K. *Thunder on the Right: The Protestant Fundamentalists.* Chicago: Nelson-Hall, 1974.

Clark, David M. "Cognitive Therapy for Anxiety." *Behavioural Psychotherapy* 14 (1986): 283–94.

Clark, Elizabeth, and Richardson, Herbert, eds. *Women and Religion: A Feminist Sourcebook of Christian Thought.* New York: Harper & Row, 1977.

Cole, Stewart. *The History of Fundamentalism.* Hamden: Archon, 1963 (1931).

Collins, Francis S. *The Language of God: A Scientist Presents Evidence for Belief.* New York: Free Press, 2006.

Cox, Gary. *Think Again: A Response to Fundamentalism's Claim on Christianity.* Wichita, KS: University Congregational Church, 2006.

Crossan, John Dominic. *The Historical Jesus: The Life of a Mediterranean Jewish Peasant.* San Francisco: Harper, 1991.

Croy, N. Clayton. *The Mutilation of Mark's Gospel.* Nashville: Abingdon, 2003.

Crowley, Sharon. *Toward a Civil Discourse: Rhetoric and Fundamentalism.* New York: University of Pittsburgh Press, 2006.

Daly, Mary. *Beyond God the Father: Toward a Philosophy of Women's Liberation.* Boston: Beacon, 1973.

Dawkins, Richard. *The God Delusion.* Boston: Houghton Mifflin, 2006.

Dayton, Donald, and Robert Johnston, eds. *The Variety of American Evangelicalism.* Knoxville, TN: University of Tennessee, 1991.

Dennett, Daniel. *Breaking the Spell: Religion as a Natural Phenomenon.* New York: Viking, 2006.

Diagnostic and Statistical Manual of Mental Disorders, 4th ed. Washington: American Psychiatric Association, 1994.

Diamond, Sara. *Spiritual Warfare: The Politics of the Christian Right.* Boston: South End, 1989.

Dionne, E. J., Jr. "Message from a Megachurch." *Washington Post,* December 5, 2006.

Dixon, A. C., ed. *The Fundamentals: A Testimony to the Truth.* 12 vols. Chicago: Testimony, 1910–1915.

Dolbeare, Kenneth M., and Phillip E. Hammond. *The School Prayer Decisions: From Court Policy to Local Practice.* Chicago: University of Chicago Press, 1971.

Dollar, George W. *A History of Fundamentalism in America.* Greenville, SC: Bob Jones University, 1973.

Dombrowski, Daniel A. *Christian Pacifism.* Philadelphia: Temple University, 1991.

Dowd, E. Thomas, and Stevan Lars Nielsen, eds. *The Psychologies in Religion: Working with the Religious Client.* New York: Springer, 2006.

Ehrman, Bart. *The New Testament: A Historical Introduction to the Early Christian Writings,* 4th ed. New York: Oxford University Press, 2008.

Eines, Eric. *The Phoenix Affirmations: A New Vision for the Future of Christianity.* San Francisco: Jossey-Bass, 2006.

Eisenstein, Hester. *Contemporary Feminist Thought.* Boston: G. K. Hall, 1983.

Ellens, J. Harold, ed. *The Destructive Power of Religion: Violence in Judaism, Christianity, and Islam.* 4 vols. Vol. 1: *Sacred Scriptures, Ideology, and Violence.* Westport, CT: Praeger, 2004.

———, ed. *The Destructive Power of Religion: Violence in Judaism, Christianity, and Islam.* 4 vols. Vol. 2: *Religion, Psychology, and Violence.* Westport: Praeger, 2004.

———, ed. *The Destructive Power of Religion: Violence in Judaism, Christianity, and Islam.* 4 vols. Vol. 3: *Models and Cases of Violence in Religion.* Westport, CT: Praeger, 2004.

———, ed. *The Destructive Power of Religion: Violence in Judaism, Christianity, and Islam.* 4 vols. Vol. 4: *Contemporary Views on Spirituality and Violence.* Westport, CT: Praeger, 2004.

———. *Understanding Religious Experiences: What the Bible Says about Spirituality. Psychology, Religion, and Spirituality* series. J. Harold Ellens, series editor. Westport, CT: Praeger, 2008.

Elliott, James K. "The Apocalypse of Peter." In *The Apocryphal New Testament.* New York: Oxford University Press, 1993.

Elliott, Kamilla. "The Deconstruction of Fundamental Christianity." *Texual Practice* 20, no. 4 (2006): 713–38.

Ellis, Albert. "A Sadly Neglected Cognitive Element in Depression." *Cognitive Therapy and Research* 11 (1987): 121–46.

———. *Humanistic Psychotherapy: The Rational-Emotive Approach.* New York: Julian, 1973.

———. *Reason and Emotion in Psychotherapy.* New York: Lyle Stewart, 1962.

Ellis, Albert, and Michael E. Bernard, eds. *Clinical Applications of Rational-Emotive Therapy.* New York: Plenum, 1985.

Ellis, Albert, and Robert A. Harper. *A New Guide to Rational Living.* Englewood Cliffs, NJ: Prentice-Hall, 1975.

Ess, Charles. "Reading Adam and Eve: Re-Visions of the Myth of Woman's Subordination to Man." In *Violence against Women and Children: A Christian Theological Sourcebook,* edited by Carol J. Adams and Marie M. Fortune. New York: Continuum, 1995.

Falwell, Jerry. *Listen, America!* New York: Doubleday, 1980.

Finkelhor, David, and Kersti Yllo. *License to Rape: Sexual Abuse of Wives.* New York: Free Press, 1985.

Fiorenza, Elizabeth Schussler. *Bread Not Stone: The Challenge of Feminist Biblical Interpretation.* Boston: Beacon, 1984.

Forrest, Barbara, and Paul R. Gross. *Creationism's Trojan Horse: The Wedge of Intelligent Design.* Oxford: Oxford University Press, 2004.

Fowler, James W. *Stages of Faith: The Psychology of Human Development and the Quest for Meaning.* San Francisco: Harper & Row, 1981.

Fowler, Robert Booth, Allen D. Hertzke, Laura R. Olson, and Kevin R. Den Dulk. *Religion and Politics in America,* 3rd ed. Boulder, CO: Westview Press, 2004.

Friedman, Mike, and W. Steven Rholes. "Successfully Challenging Fundamentalist Beliefs Results in Increased Death Awareness." *Journal of Experimental Social Psychology* 43 (2007): 794–801.

Frykholm, Amy Johnson. *Rapture Culture: Left Behind in Evangelical America.* New York: Oxford University Press, 2004.

Fuller, Robert C. *Naming the Antichrist: The History of an American Obsession.* New York: Oxford University, 1995.

Garrison, Becky. *Red and Blue God, Black and Blue Church: Eyewitness Accounts of How American Churches Are Hijacking Jesus, Bagging the Beatitudes, and Worshipping the Almighty Dollar.* San Francisco: Jossey-Bass, 2006.

Gasper, Louis. *The Fundamentalist Movement.* The Hague, Netherlands: Mouton, 1963.

Geertz, Clifford. "Religion as a Cultural System." In *Reader in Comparative Religion,* 2nd ed., edited by William Lessa and Evon Vogt. New York: Harper & Row, 1966.

Gibbs, Nancy. "Apocalypse Now." *Time* (July 1, 2002): 43.

Goldberg, Michele. *Kingdom Coming: The Rise of Christian Nationalism.* New York: W. W. Norton, 2006.

Goldenberg, Naomi. *Changing of the Gods: Feminism and the End of Traditional Religions.* Boston: Beacon, 1979.

Greeley, Andrew, and Michael Hout. *The Truth About Conservative Christians: What They Think and What They Believe.* Chicago: University of Chicago Press, 2006.

Grenz, Stanley J. *Welcoming But Not Affirming: An Evangelical Response to Homosexuality.* Louisville: Westminster John Knox, 1998.

Griffin, Susan. *Rape: The All-American Crime.* San Francisco: Ramparts, 1971.

———. *Rape: The Power of Consciousness.* New York: Harper & Row, 1979.

Groth, Nicholas. *Men Who Rape: The Psychology of the Offender.* New York: Plenum, 1979.

Groth, A. Nicholas, and William A. Hobson. "The Dynamics of Sexual Assault." In *Sexual Dynamics of Anti-social Behavior,* edited by Louis B. Schlesinger and Eugene Revitch. Springfield, IL: Charles C. Thomas, 1983.

Gundry, Robert. *Matthew: A Commentary on His Literary and Theological Art.* Grand Rapids, MI: Eerdmans, 1982.

Halsell, Grace. *Prophecy and Politics: Militant Evangelists on the Road to Nuclear War.* Westport, CT: Lawrence Hill Books, 1986.

Harding, Susan. *The Book of Jerry Falwell: Fundamentalist Language and Politics.* Princeton, NJ: Princeton University Press, 2000.

Harris, Harriet A. *Fundamentalism and Evangelicals. Oxford Theological Monographs.* Oxford: Clarendon, 1998.

Harris, Sam. *The End of Faith: Religion, Terror, and the End of Reason.* New York: Norton, 2004.

———. *Letter to a Christian Nation.* New York: Alfred A. Knopf, 2006.

Hassan, Farzana. *Prophecy and the Fundamentalist Quest: An Integrative Study of Christian and Muslim Apocalyptic Religion.* London: McFarland, 2008.

Hayes, Judith. *The Happy Heretic.* Amherst, NY: Prometheus Books, 2000.

Hedges, Chris. *American Fascists: The Christian Right and the War on America.* New York: Free Press, 2006.

Heim, David. "Voters and Values: The Divided Mind of the Religious Left." *Christian Century* 123, no. 16 (August 8, 2006): 26–29.

Hill, Charles E., and Frank A. James III, eds. *The Glory of the Atonement: Biblical, Historical & Practical Perspectives: Essays in Honor of Roger Nicole.* Downers Grove, IL: InterVarsity, 2004.

Hill, Samuel S., ed. *Encyclopedia of Religion in the South.* Macon, GA: Mercer University Press, 1984.

Hodge, Charles. *What Is Darwinism?* Princeton, NJ: Scribner, Armstrong, 1874.

Hofstadter, Richard. *Anti-Intellectualism in American Life.* New York: Knopf, 1962.

Hood, Ralph, Jr. "Social Psychology and Religious Fundamentalism." In *Rural Psychology,* edited by A. W. Childs and G. B. Melton. New York: Plenum, 1983.

Hood, Ralph, Jr., Peter C. Hill, and W. Paul Williamson. *The Psychology of Religious Fundamentalism.* New York: Guilford, 2005.

Hood, Ralph, Jr., R. J. Morris, and P. J. Watson. "Maintenance of Religious Fundamentalism." *Psychological Reports* 59 (1986): 547–59.

Hood, Ralph, Jr., and W. Paul Williamson. *Them That Believe: The Power and Meaning of the Christian Serpent-Handling Tradition.* Berkeley and Los Angeles: University of California Press, 2008.

Hudson, Winthrop S. *Religion in America.* New York: Charles Scribner's Sons, 1965.

Hunsberger, Alisat, S. M. Pancer, and M. Pratt. "Religious Fundamentalism and Religious Doubts: Content, Connections, and Complexity of Thinking." *International Journal for the Psychology of Religion* 6 (1966): 210–20.

Hunter, George. *Christian, Evangelical, and . . . Democrat?* Nashville: Abingdon, 2006.

Hunter, James. *American Evangelicalism: Conservative Religion and the Quandary of Modernity.* New Brunswick: Rutgers University Press, 1983.

———. *Evangelicalism: The Coming Generation.* Chicago: University of Chicago Press, 1987.

Inglehart, Ronald. *Culture Shift in Advanced Industrial Society.* Princeton, NJ: Princeton University Press, 1990.

Isherwood, Lisa. *The Good News of the Body: Sexual Theology and Feminism.* New York: New York University Press, 2000.

Jones, Hywel R. "Exodus." In *The New Bible Commentary,* revised. Edited by Donald Guthrie and J. A. Motyer. Grand Rapids, MI: Eerdmans, 1970.

Kaplan, Esther. *With God on Their Side: How Christian Fundamentalists Trampled Science, Policy, and Democracy in George W. Bush's White House.* New York: New Press, 2004. Also issued in 2005 as *With God on Their Side: George W. Bush and the Christian Right.*

Kaplan, Lawrence. *Fundamentalism in Comparative Perspective.* Amherst: University of Massachusetts Press, 1992.

Keylock, Leslie R. "Evangelical Scholars Remove Gundry for His Views on Matthew." *Christianity Today* 3 (February 1984): 36–38.

Kilpatrick, Joel. *A Field Guide to Evangelicals and Their Habitat.* New York: HarperSanFrancisco, 2006.

Kimball, Charles. *When Religion Becomes Evil.* New York: HarperCollins, 2002.

Knitter, Paul F. *Introducing Theologies of Religions.* Maryknoll, NY: Orbis Books, 2002.

Kohlberg, Lawrence. *Essays on Moral Development.* Vol. 1: *The Philosophy of Moral Development: Moral Stages and the Idea of Justice.* San Francisco: Harper & Row, 1981.

———. *Essays on Moral Development.* Vol. 2: *The Psychology of Moral Development: The Nature and Validity of Moral Stages.* San Francisco: Harper & Row, 1984.

Kruglanski, Arie W. *The Psychology of Closed Mindedness.* New York: Psychology Press, 2004.

Kuo, David. *Tempting Faith: An Inside Story of Political Seduction.* New York: Free Press, 2006.

Laarman, Peter, ed. *Getting on Message: Challenging the Christian Right from the Heart of the Gospel.* Boston: Beacon, 2006.

Lawrence, Bruce B. *Defenders of God: The Fundamentalist Revolt against the Modern Age.* San Francisco: Harper & Row, 1989.

Leaves, Nigel. *The God Problem: Alternatives to Fundamentalism.* Santa Rosa, CA: Polebridge Press, 2006.

Lechner, Frank. "Fundamentalism Revisited." *Society* 26 (1989): 51–59.

Lerner, Michael. *The Left Hand of God: Taking Back Our Country from the Religious Right.* San Francisco: HarperSanFrancisco, 2006.

Lincoln, Bruce. *Holy Terrors: Thinking About Religion after September 11.* Chicago: University of Chicago Press, 2003.

Lindsay, D. Michael. *Faith in the Halls of Power: How Evangelicals Joined the American Elite.* New York: Oxford University Press, 2007.

Lindsey, Hal, with C. C. Carlson. *The Late Great Planet Earth.* New York: Harper, 1992 (1970).

Linker, Damon. *The Theocons: Secular America Under Siege.* New York: Doubleday, 2006.

MacNamara, Donal E. J., and Edward Sagarin. *Sex, Crime, and the Law.* New York: Free Press, 1977.

Maher, Derek, and Calvin Mercer, eds. *Religion and the Implications of Radical Life Extension.* New York: Palgrave Macmillan, 2009.

Marsden, George M., ed. *Evangelicalism and Modern America.* Grand Rapids, MI: Eerdmans, 1984.

———. *Fundamentalism and American Culture: The Shaping of Twentieth-century Evangelicalism, 1879–1925.* New York: Oxford University, 1980.

———, ed. *The Fundamentals: A Testimony to Truth.* 4 Vols. New York: Garland, 1988.

———. *Reforming Fundamentalism: Fuller Seminary and the New Evangelicalism.* Grand Rapids, MI: Eerdmans, 1987.

———. *Understanding Fundamentalism and Evangelicalism.* Grand Rapids, MI: Eerdmans, 1991.

Marshall, Peter, and David Manuel, with Anna Wilson Fishel. *From Sea to Shining Sea for Children.* Grand Rapids, MI: Fleming H. Revell, 1993.

———. *The Light and the Glory for Children.* Tarrytown, NY: Fleming H. Revell, 1992.

Marty, Martin E., and R. Scott Appleby, eds. *The Fundamentalism Project.* 5 vols. Vol. 1: *Fundamentalisms Observed.* Chicago: University of Chicago Press, 1991.

———. *The Fundamentalism Project.* 5 vols. Vol. 2: *Fundamentalisms and Society: Reclaiming the Sciences, the Family, and Education.* Chicago: University of Chicago Press, 1993.

———, eds. *The Fundamentalism Project.* 5 vols. Vol. 3: *Fundamentalisms and the State: Remaking Polities, Economies, and Militance.* Chicago: University of Chicago Press, 1993.

———, eds. *The Fundamentalism Project.* 5 vols. Vol. 4: *Accounting for Fundamentalisms: The Dynamic Character of Movements.* Chicago: University of Chicago Press, 1994.

———, eds. *The Fundamentalism Project.* 5 vols. Vol. 5: *Fundamentalisms Comprehended.* Chicago: University of Chicago Press, 1995.

Marty, Martin, and R. Scott Appleby. *The Glory and the Power: The Fundamentalist Challenge to the Modern World.* Boston: Beacon, 1992.

McGinn, Bernard. *Antichrist: Two Thousand Years of the Human Fascination with Evil.* New York: HarperCollins, 1994.

———. *Apocalypticism in the Western Tradition.* Brookfield, VT: Ashgate,1994.

———. *Visions of the End: Apocalyptic Traditions in the Middle Ages.* New York: Columbia University, 1979.

McGinn, Bernard, John J. Collins, and Stephen J. Stein, eds. *The Continuum History of Apocalypticism.* New York: Continuum, 1998.

McGrath, Alister. *Dawkins' God: Genes, Memes, and the Meaning of Life.* Malden, MA: Blackwell, 2005.

McIntosh, Daniel N. "Religion-as-Schema, with Implications for the Relation Between Religion and Coping." *International Journal for the Psychology of Religion* 5, no. 1 (2006): 1–16.

McLoughlin, William G. *Revivals, Awakenings, and Reform: An Essay on Religion and Social Change in America, 1607–1977.* Chicago: University of Chicago Press, 1978.

McNamara, Patrick, ed. *Where God and Science Meet: How Brain and Evolutionary Studies Alter Our Understanding of Religion,* 3 vols. Vol. 1: *Evolution, Genes, and the Religious Brain.* Praeger Perspectives: *Psychology, Religion and Spirituality.* J. Harold Ellens, series editor. Westport, CT: Praeger, 2006.

———, ed. *Where God and Science Meet: How Brain and Evolutionary Studies Alter Our Understanding of Religion,* 3 vols. Vol. 2: *The Neurology of Religious Experience.* Praeger Perspectives: *Psychology, Religion and Spirituality.* J. Harold Ellens, series editor. Westport, CT: Praeger, 2006.

———, ed. *Where God and Science Meet: How Brain and Evolutionary Studies Alter Our Understanding of Religion,* 3 vols. Vol. 3: *The Psychology of Religious Experience.* Praeger Perspectives: *Psychology, Religion and Spirituality.* J. Harold Ellens, series editor. Westport, CT: Praeger, 2006.

Meichenbaum, Donald. *Cognitive-Behavior Modification.* New York: Plenum, 1977.

Mercer, Calvin. "Albert Schweitzer (1875–1965)." In *Dictionary of Major Biblical Interpreters,* 2nd ed., edited by Donald K. McKim. Downers Grove, IL: IVP Academic, 2007 (1998).

———. "Contemporary Language and New Translations of the Bible: The Impact of Feminism." *Religion & Public Education* 17 (Winter 1990): 89–98.

———. *Norman Perrin's Interpretation of the New Testament: From "Exegetical Method" to "Hermeneutical Process." Studies in American Biblical Hermeneutics 2.* Macon, GA: Mercer University Press, 1986.

———. "Sexual Violence and the Male Warrior God." *Lexington Theological Quarterly* 41 (Spring 2006): 23–37.

Meredith, Don. *The Total Man.* Wheaton, IL: Tyndale, 1981.

Meyers, Robin. *Why the Christian Right Is Wrong: A Minister's Manifesto for Taking Back Your Faith, Your Flag, Your Future.* San Francisco: Jossey-Bass, 2006.

Miller, Lisa. "Is Obama the Antichrist?" *Newsweek* 152, no. 21 (November 24, 2008). http://www.newsweek.com/id/169192 (accessed December 11, 2008).

Misztal, Bronislaw, and Anson Shupe, eds. *Religion and Politics in Comparative Perspective: Revival of Religious Fundamentalism in East and West.* Westport, CT: Praeger, 1992.

Mora, George. "The Scrupulosity Syndrome." In *Clinical Psychiatry and Religion,* edited by E. M. Pattison. Boston: Little Brown, 1969.

Moyers, Bill. *Welcome to Doomsday.* New York: New York Review of Books, 2006.

Muller-Fahrenholz, Geiko. *America's Battle for God: A European Christian Looks at Civil Religion.* Grand Rapids, MI: Eerdmans, 2007.

Murray, William J. *Let Us Pray.* New York: William Morrow, 1995.

National Council on Bible Curriculum in Public Schools. www.bibleinschools.net.

Nelkin, Dorothy. *The Creation Controversy: Science or Scripture in the Schools.* New York: Norton, 1982.

Neuhaus, Richard J., and Michael Cromartie. *Piety and Politics.* Washington, DC: Ethics and Public Policy Center, 1987.

New Revised Standard Version.

Nolan, W. M. "Scrupulosity." In *Dictionary of Pastoral Care and Counseling,* edited by Rodney J. Hunter, H. Newton Malony, Liston O. Mills, and John Paton. Nashville: Abingdon, 1990.

Noll, Mark A. *American Evangelical Christianity: An Introduction.* Oxford: Blackwell, 2001.

———. *The Scandal of the Evangelical Mind.* Grand Rapids, MI: Eerdmans, 1994.

Notes of Debates in the Federal Convention of 1787 Reported by James Madison, Bicentennial Edition. New York: Norton, 1987 (1966).

Numbers, Ronald L. *The Creationists: The Evolution of Scientific Creationism* New York: Knopf, 1992.

———. *Darwinism Comes to America.* Cambridge, MA: Harvard University Press, 1998.

Pape, Dorothy. *In Search of God's Ideal Woman.* Downers Grove, IL: Inter-Varsity Press, 1976.

Patterson, Stephen J. *Beyond the Passion: Rethinking the Death and Life of Jesus.* Minneapolis, MN: Fortress, 2004.

Pelikan, Jaroslav. "Fundamentalism and/or Orthodoxy? Toward an Understanding of the Fundamentalist Phenomenon." In *The Fundamentalist Phenomenon: A View from Within; A Response from Without,* edited by N. J. Cohen. Grand Rapids, MI: Eerdmans, 1990.

Pellauer, Mary D., Barbara Chester, and Jane A. Boyajian. *Sexual Assault and Abuse: A Handbook for Clergy and Religious Professionals.* San Francisco: Harper & Row, 1987.

Pelosi, Alexandra. "Friends of God: A Road Trip with Alexandra Pelosi." HBO television documentary, 2007.

Pennock, Robert. *Tower of Babel: The Evidence Against the New Creationism.* Cambridge, MA: MIT Press, 1999.

———, ed. *Intelligent Design Creationism and Its Critics: Philosophical, Theological, and Scientific Perspectives.* Cambridge, MA: MIT Press, 2001.

Percy, Martyn, and Ian Jones, eds. *Fundamentalism, Church, and Society.* London: SPCK, 2002.

Persons, Jacqueline B. *Cognitive Therapy in Practice: A Case Formulation Approach.* New York: W. W. Norton, 1989.

Peters, Ted, ed. *Science and Theology: The New Consonance.* Boulder, CO: Westview, 1998.

Peters, Ted, and Gaymon Bennett. *Bridging Science and Religion.* Minneapolis, MN: Fortress, 2003 (2002).

Peters, Ted, and Martinez Hewlett. *Can You Believe in God AND Evolution? A Guide for the Perplexed.* Nashville: Abingdon, 2006.

———. *Evolution from Creation to New Creation: Conflict, Conversation, and Convergence.* Nashville: Abingdon, 2003.

Peterson, Kurt W. "American Idol: David Barton's Dream of a Christian Nation." *Christian Century* 123, no. 22 (October 31, 2006): 20–23.

Phan, Peter. "Might or Mystery: The Fundamentalist Concept of God." In *The Struggle Over the Past: Fundamentalism in the Modern World,* edited by William Shea. College Theology Society annual publication, vol. 35. Lanham, MD: University Press of America, 1993.

Phillips, Kevin. *American Theocracy: The Peril and Politics of Radical Religion, Oil, and Borrowed Money in the 21st Century.* New York: Viking, 2006.

Piore, Adam. "A Higher Frequency." *Mother Jones* 30, no. 7 (December 2005): 47–51, 80–81.

Powell, James, Jerry Gladstone, and Roger Meyer. "Psychotherapy with the Fundamentalist Client." *Journal of Psychology and Theology* 19, no. 4 (1991): 344–53.

Pruyser, Paul W. "The Seamy Side of Current Religious Beliefs." *Bulletin of the Menninger Clinic* 41 (1977): 329–48.

Ramm, Bernard. *The Christian View of Science and Scripture.* Grand Rapids, MI: Eerdmans, 1955.

Ramsey, Paul. *War and the Christian Conscience.* Durham, NC: Duke University Press, 1961.

———. *The Just War.* New York: Charles Scribner's Sons, 1968.

Rose, Susan D. *Keeping Them Out of the Hands of Satan: Evangelical Schooling in America.* New York: Routledge, 1988.

Rosen, Christine. *My Fundamentalist Education: A Memoir of a Divine Girlhood.* New York: Public Affairs, 2006.

Rossing, Barbara R. *The Rapture Exposed: The Message of Hope in the Book of Revelation.* Boulder, CO: Westview, 2004.

Ruether, Rosemary Radford, ed. *Religion and Sexism: Images of Woman in the Jewish and Christian Traditions.* New York: Simon & Schuster, 1974.

Ruthven, Malise. *Fundamentalism: The Search for Meaning.* New York: Oxford University Press, 2005.

Safran, Jeremy D., Michael Vallis, Zindel V. Segal, and Brian F. Shaw. "Assessment of Core Cognitive Processes in Cognitive Therapy." *Cognitive Therapy and Research* 10 (October 1986): 509–26.

Salkovskis, Paul M., ed. *Frontiers of Cognitive Therapy.* New York: Guilford, 1996.

Sandeen, Ernest R. *The Roots of Fundamentalism: British and American Millenarianism, 1800–1930.* Chicago: University of Chicago Press, 1970.

Sandler, Lauren. *Righteous: Dispatches from the Evangelical Youth Movement.* New York: Viking, 2006.

Savage, Sara. "A Psychology of Fundamentalism: The Search for Inner Failings." In *Fundamentalism, Church, and Society,* edited by Martyn Percy and Ian Jones. London: SPCK, 2002.

———. "Fundamentalism." In *The Psychologies in Religion: Working with the Religious Client,* edited by E. Thomas Dowd and Stevan Lars Nielsen. New York: Springer, 2006.

Schaeffer, Frank. *How I Grew Up as One of the Elect, Helped Found the Religious Right, and Lived to Take All (or Almost All) of It Back.* New York: Carroll and Graf, 2007.

Schultze, Quentin. "The Two Faces of Fundamentalist Higher Education." In *The Fundamentalism Project,* 5 vols. Vol. 2: *Reclaiming the Sciences, the Family, and Education,* edited by Martin E. Marty and R. Scott Appleby. Chicago: University of Chicago Press, 1993.

Schweitzer, Albert. *Von Reimarus zu Wrede: Eine Geschichte der Leben-Jesu Forschung.* Tubingen: J. C. B. Mohr, 1906. English translation: *The Quest of the Historical Jesus: A Critical Study of Its Progress from Reimarus to Wrede.* New York: Macmillan, 1968.

The Scofield Reference Bible. New York: Oxford University Press, 2002 (1909).

Sethi, Sheena, and Martin E. P. Seligman. "Optimism and Fundamentalism." *Psychological Science* 4 (July 1993): 256–59.

Shaffer, Barbara A., and Brad M. Hastings. "Authoritarianism and Religious Identification: Response to Threats on Religious Beliefs." *Mental Health, Religion & Culture* 10, no. 2 (2007): 151–58.

Sharpe, Roger. *Ceremony of Innocence.* Macon, GA: Mercer University Press, 2005.

Sheler, Jeffrey. *Believers: A Journey into Evangelical America.* New York: Viking, 2006.

Shoemaker, H. Stephen. *Being Christian in an Almost Chosen Nation: Thinking About Faith and Politics.* Nashville: Abingdon, 2006.

Smith, Christian. *American Evangelicalism: Embattled and Thriving.* Chicago: University of Chicago Press, 1998.

———. *Soul Searching: The Religious and Spiritual Lives of American Teenagers.* New York: Oxford University, 2005.

Soper, J. Christopher. *Evangelical Christianity in the United States and Great Britain: Religious Beliefs, Political Choices.* New York: New York University Press, 1994.

Spilka, Bernard, Ralph W. Hood, Jr., Bruce Hunsberger, and Richard Gorsuch. *The Psychology of Religion: An Empirical Approach,* 3rd ed. New York: Guilford, 2003.

Spong, John Shelby. *Rescuing the Bible from Fundamentalism: A Bishop Rethinks the Meaning of Scripture.* New York: HarrperCollins, 1991.

Stern, Julian. *Schools and Religion: Imagining the Real.* London: Continuum, 2007.

Straub, Gerald Thomas. *Salvation for Sale: An Insider's View of Pat Robertson's Ministry.* Amherst, NY: Prometheus Books, 1986.

Strozier, Charles B. *Apocalypse: On the Psychology of Fundamentalism in America.* Boston: Beacon, 1994.

Sugg, John. "A Nation Under God." *Mother Jones* 30, no. 7 (December 2005): 33–35.

Sweeney, Douglas A. *The American Evangelical Story: A History of the Movement.* Grand Rapids, MI: Baker Academic, 2005.

Sweeney, Jon. *Born Again and Again: Surprising Gifts of a Fundamentalist Childhood.* Brewster, MA: Paraclete Press, 2005.

Sweet, Leonard, ed. *The Evangelical Tradition in America.* Macon, GA: Mercer University Press, 1984.

Taylor, Iain, ed. *Not Evangelical Enough! The Gospel at the Center.* Cumbria, England: Paternoster Press, 2003.

Terrell, JoAnne Marie. *Power in the Blood? The Cross in the African American Experience.* Maryknoll, NY: Orbis Books, 1998.

Thistlethwaite, Susan Brooks. "Every Two Minutes: Battered Women and Feminist Interpretation." In *Weaving the Visions: New Patterns in Feminist Spirituality,* edited by Judith Plaskow and Carol P. Christ. San Francisco: Harper & Row, 1989.

Tidball, Derek. *Who Are the Evangelicals: Tracing the Roots of Today's Movement.* London: Marshall Pickering, 1994.

Wakefield, Dan. *The Hijacking of Jesus: How the Religious Right Distorts Christianity and Promotes Prejudice and Hate.* New York: Nation Books, 2006.

Wallis, Jim. "An Evangelical Manifesto." *Sojourners* (July 2008): 5–6.

———. *God's Politics: Why the Right Gets It Wrong and the Left Doesn't Get It.* New York: HarperCollins, 2005.

———. *The Great Awakening: Reviving Faith and Politics in a Post-Religious Right America.* San Francisco: HarperOne, 2008.

Walter, John L., and Jane E. Peller. *Becoming Solution-Focused in Brief Therapy.* New York: Brunner/Mazel, 1992.

Warfield, Benjamin B. *The Inspiration and Authority of the Bible.* Philadelphia: Presbyterian and Reformed Publishing, 1948.

Weaver, Denny J. *The Nonviolent Atonement.* Grand Rapids, MI: Eerdmans, 2001.

Welford, Alan T. *Christianity: A Psychologist's Interpretation.* London: Hodder & Stoughton, 1971.

White, Mel. *Religion Gone Bad: The Hidden Dangers of the Christian Right.* New York: Penguin, 2006.

Wilcox, Clyde, and Carin Larson. *Onward Christian Soldiers? The Religious Right in American Politics,* 3rd ed. Boulder, CO: Westview Press, 2006.

Wilcox, W. Bradford. *Soft Patriarchs, New Men: How Christianity Shapes Fathers and Husbands.* Chicago: University of Chicago Press, 2004.

Wilson-Kastner, Patricia. *Faith, Feminism and the Christ.* Philadelphia: Fortress, 1983.

———. "Theological Perspectives on Sexual Violence." In *Sexual Assault and Abuse: A Handbook for Clergy and Religious Professionals,* edited by Mary D. Pellauer, Barbara Chester, and Jane A. Boyajian. San Francisco: Harper & Row, 1987.

Winell, Marlene. *Leaving the Fold: A Guide for Former Fundamentalists and Others Leaving Their Religion.* Oakland, CA: New Harbinger, 1993.

Wink, Walter, ed. *Homosexuality and Christian Faith: Questions of Conscience for the Churches.* Minneapolis, MN: Fortress, 1999.

Wulff, D. *The Psychology of Religion: Classic and Contemporary,* 2nd ed. New York: Wiley, 1997.

Wuthnow, Robert. *The Struggle for America's Soul: Evangelicals, Liberals, and Secularism.* Grand Rapids, MI: Eerdmans, 1989.

Yao, R. *Fundamentalists Anonymous: There Is a Way Out*, 4th ed. New York: Luce, 1987.

Yarhouse, Mark A., and Stephen R. Russell. "Evangelicalism." In *The Psychologies in Religion: Working with the Religious Client*, edited by E. Thomas Dowd and Stevan Lars Nielsen. New York: Springer, 2006.

Index

About the Author

Calvin Mercer teaches religious studies at East Carolina University, where Dr. Mercer recently received a "Scholar-Teacher Award." His three books and 25 scholarly articles are in biblical studies and religion and culture. He is also trained in clinical psychology and practiced professionally part-time for about a decade. He was known as the "go-to" therapist for clients where religion was a factor in their mental distress and/or behavioral dysfunction. In both his teaching and clinical practice, he worked extensively with fundamentalist Christians. Dr. Mercer is the originator of The Monastic Project, a comprehensive program that speaks to a deep yearning many people have for substantive religious experience that goes deeper, offers more, and requires more than either fundamentalism or what Dr. Mercer calls the "easy, quick, sensual froth" offered up by much contemporary religion. He is one of the few scholars considering the religious implications of radical life extension science and other human enhancement technology developments and has a co-edited book on the subject. He frequently gives public lectures on topics of his research. Dr. Mercer can be reached at the following email address: mercerc@ecu.edu.